COUNTRY LIVING

A Source Book
of Projects
and Friendly Advice

by
Lewis & Nancy Hill

Rodale Press, Emmaus, Pa.

Printed in the United States of America on recycled paper containing a high percentage of de-inked fiber.

Designed by Anita G. Patterson

Illustrations by Gene Mater & Margot J. Weissman

Library of Congress Cataloging-in-Publication Data

Hill, Lewis, 1924–
    Country living.

    Includes index.
    1. Agriculture—United States—Handbooks,
manuals, etc. 2. Country life—United States.
3. Self-employed—United States. 4. Small
business—United States. I. Hill, Nancy.
II. Title.
S501.2.H55   1987   630   86–31424
ISBN   0-87857-687-8   hardcover

2 4 6 8 10 9 7 5 3 1   hardcover

CONTENTS

INTRODUCTION

This is a "whether to" book. Our intent is to give you a feel for what it is like to live in the country, to keep a goat, or pig, or cultivate your own orchard or vineyard. We want to heighten your understanding of the alternatives. Should you move to a rural area or stay put? Keep sheep or nurture a plot of Christmas trees in your old pasture? Buy a tractor or rent out the hayfield? Start a bed-and-breakfast place or a riding stable?

Both of us grew up in the Northeast Kingdom, the most rural area of Vermont (Lewis on a dairy farm and Nancy in a village). When we began to tell about the rural projects you might take on, we found that one or the other of us had experience with most of them. The few that we hadn't, we were very familiar with because our friends and neighbors have done them. Based on our collective experiences, we estimate here the amount of time, discipline, and skill each project will demand of you. Most important, we suggest the temperament you'd need to deal with the project.

The Hills' home.

We continue to live in the rural area where we were born, which tells you that we have a bias for country life. It's in our blood. We enjoy living and working close to the land, and the spiritual renewal that we get from nature. The slower rhythms of rural life—social, political, and personal—appeal to us.

Our income is lower than that of our city friends, but for us the advantages transcend dollar value. We enjoy relatively unspoiled air, food, and water. We love living in a small community where we know nearly everyone, and are touched by them—rejoicing at the births, and being saddened at the deaths.

If you are dreaming of a new life in a rural setting, or simply of undertaking a new outdoor project, we hope to help you transform that dream. Dreams precede the great experiments and experiences of life.

> Whatever you can do, or dream you can, begin it.
> Boldness has genius, power, and magic in it.
>
> *Goethe*

N.H. *and* L.H.

Chapter 1

SHOULD YOU MOVE TO THE COUNTRY?

"Aren't you lonely way out here, miles from nowhere?" a visitor to our nursery asked one day. "I live in Brooklyn and I'm often lonely. I can't imagine living here, so far away from other people."

It was the end of an exhausting day in May, the busiest time of year for our nursery, and scores of people had driven to our remote farm that day. We felt anything but lonesome.

True, we can't see any other homes from our place. But we know our neighbors well, and they know all about us. Our neighborhood extends for many miles in every direction, and we rely on each other for everything from a borrowed cup of milk to a medical emergency. Within the last year we have seen our community rally to help a woman who lost her home by fire, to help a young couple whose child needed an operation, and most recently, to find a five-year-old boy who was lost in the woods. Within a half hour after the alarm spread, hundreds of people joined the search. Farmers left their barn chores and joined firefighters, business people, carpenters, and retirees, to comb the region. Coffee and sandwiches were brought in to sustain those who missed their supper in order to find young Stanley (who, it turned out, had innocently crawled under a tractor tarp and fallen asleep).

Periodically, the community gathers to celebrate a couple's 50th wedding anniversary, a homemade Fourth of July circus, or one of life's rituals—a graduation, a wedding, a funeral. In these ways, rural people keep in touch with each other.

Life is different here than that known by the three quarters of the American people who live in metropolitan areas. Though generalizations are unreliable, and you're sure to encounter many exceptions, we'll venture a few of our observations.

For one, certain values are different in the country. People are measured not so much by the size of their bank accounts, what they wear, or what they do for work, as by their personal qualities. How does this affect the way a rural person lives? We'd say it's easier to be yourself and slow down the pace of your life. There is relatively little pressure to compete, conform, or keep up with the Joneses—or to pursue whatever trends are currently about.

We also live more closely in touch with the earth—wildflowers and animals, sunrises and sunsets, and meteorites and galaxies undulled by civilization's lights. Not far from our doorstep we can

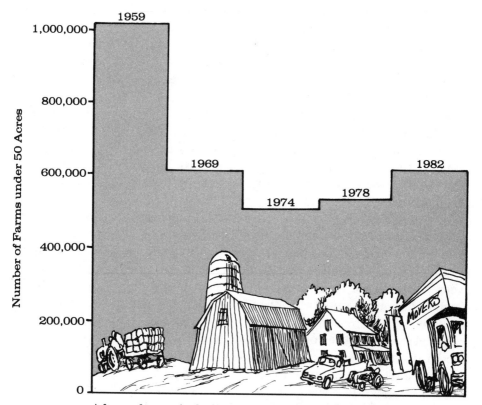

After a dramatic decline, the number of small U.S. farms is rebounding.

picnic, hike, swim, ski, fish, boat, and ride horseback. We don't mean to suggest that the problems of the world disappear, but they do seem to fall into perspective.

Those who live in the country like the sense of having "roots." If they don't already have a country ancestry, they probably are in the process of putting roots down. They are more apt to become emotionally tied to a piece of land because establishing and maintaining a "homeplace" usually demands more work. Along with this responsibility comes a feeling of security and permanence.

Move to the country, and you are likely to become personally involved with government. Because we can see our tax dollars at work in a very immediate way—on our back road, the local school, or public library—we make sure our voice is heard when it comes to spending. We know personally the people who represent us in town affairs and state legislature, and let them know how we feel. Small towns and villages are a good example of democracy at work. People do not feel as lost and powerless as they might in the great structure of urban society.

Is Country Life Less Expensive?

The answer has to be a yes and no. It hinges both on your lifestyle and on where you choose to settle. Rural areas typically offer more options for saving money on food and fuel bills, and there are fewer pressures to spend extravagantly. It is likely that you'll find few occasions that require a fancy wardrobe, and clothing remains in style longer. The longstanding country rule is "use it up, wear it out, make it do, or go without."

You may find it profitable and fun to barter with neighbors and friends, do your own repairing, cut firewood, and patronize garage sales and auctions—all of which will help you cut expenses. Most gardeners agree that homegrown food is a bargain only when they don't count the time involved. But for many people, the most important reason for moving to the country is the ability to produce plentiful vegetables, fruit, eggs, milk, and meat—all unpolluted by sprays and preservatives. To them, earning a good return on their labor is irrelevant.

On the other hand, the items you must buy—clothing, gasoline, the food you don't grow—are likely to cost more than in the city, since

❖

additional transportation must be added to the price. Also, smaller country stores must buy in smaller quantities, and this increases your cost.

Income and sales taxes vary from state to state, and you will find wide differences in property taxes from town to town. In some rural communities, the tax rate soars as citizens struggle to pay for a new school, road equipment, or other large capital investments. If you plan to retire in your new state, check out its inheritance tax laws, since certain states make it expensive to pass on property.

Insurance is likely to cost more if you live far from fire and police departments. Fire insurance may be more costly if you burn wood, but less if you have a farm pond nearby.

Your heating and air conditioning costs will also vary widely, depending on your home's location. Both high, windy, exposed sites and deep frost pockets mean more dollars spent on fuel. And if nature doesn't provide cooling shade and breezes in summer, this may be an extra expense. Country dwellers learned long ago to position their houses to catch the winter sun, avoid the summer sun, and duck out of gales behind windbreaks.

Newcomers to country living are often stunned by the amount of equipment they need. Buying land and outbuildings may also mean buying a heavy-duty lawn mower, several sizes of ladders, a garden cart, a rotary tiller, a chain saw, and a large assortment of gardening and workshop tools. Many also find they need a snowblower or snowplow as well as a small tractor and trailer. And skis, snowshoes, trail bikes, bicycles, and ATVs (all-terrain vehicles) may be valuable transportation as well as merely toys.

Entertainment is likely to be simpler and less expensive. Small towns expect their citizens to be tired at night, so in most there is little commercial entertainment and few, if any, restaurants. Natives socialize among themselves, and often look to community organizations for social outlets: card parties, picnics, cookouts, potlucks, discussion groups, and lectures. In our town, there is no shortage of organized recreation: softball leagues, bowling league (30 miles away), square dance club (10 miles away), and volleyball and basketball at the school gym. The country club has a nine-hole golf course and tennis courts—but for the most part only the summer residents have time (and money) to use them.

❖

Country Neighbors

A city man looking for a rural town to settle in asked an old citizen what he liked about his community. After he'd thought awhile the native replied, "I guess it's the people. They are all so friendly, helpful, and interested in everything about you."

Delighted, the city man pressed on. "What is it that you don't like about the place?" he asked. Once again the native thought a long time. At last he answered, "Same thing, I guess."

The point of this classic anecdote is that the country is not a good place to try to live anonymously. A friend who deserted the country for a city apartment told us, "Even though there are people everywhere, it is the first time in my life that I ever felt completely private and as if no one is watching my every move!" Today, rural communities aren't as tight as they once were, since many inhabitants now work away from the farms; and the telephone, TV, and automobile have expanded local horizons. Nevertheless, the chances are excellent that the folks in your new neighborhood will learn a great deal more about you during your first weeks there than you suspect, and will share the information generously with each other. "What's the news?" is often the way rural people greet each other, and quite unintentionally you will probably figure in some of the answers.

But most people will leave you alone if you make it known that you do not wish to socialize. In the city or suburbs, people tend to socialize with those of the same class; in the country, however, you are likely to encounter all types at public meetings, the general store, and in any business you transact.

Country Occupations

We are continually amazed at the diversity of occupations that now flourish in our rural area. When we were growing up, nearly everyone had a small dairy farm, and although no farmer was wealthy, everyone had enough to live securely. These days it is much more difficult to make an adequate living with a small farm operation, although recent census records suggest the number of small farms is increasing each year. Most are operated by part-time farmers who have other incomes. And full-time farmers of smaller places have diversified their operations rather than risk all their turnips in one barrel. Jack Lyons of Norwich, Vermont, is typical. He raises turkeys, three acres of raspberries, a half acre of asparagus, an acre of blueberries, plus Christmas trees and pumpkins. Like many New England growers, he has solved the labor shortage at harvesttime by letting the public harvest their own.

The country now supports dozens of ways to earn a living that were undreamt of even a decade ago. But these jobs may bring in a great deal less money than the equivalent in a metropolitan area. Some jobs obviously transplant more easily than others. Professionals such as doctors, dentists, lawyers, teachers, nurses, and social workers are in demand almost everywhere, as are electricians, plumbers, mechanics, hairdressers, and others who offer special services. Salespeople, real estate and insurance agents, accountants, and secretaries also can find work in any area.

Rural regions are less likely to provide opportunities for those in the performing arts, publishing, and high finance, although we know many who still successfully manage even those professions. One nearby friend of ours produces TV plays, another works with a large international bank, and still another is a book editor. A teacher at the Julliard School of Music in New York City lives in the village north of us, and the village south of us is home to a professional soprano who sings in Boston. All commute hundreds of miles in order to maintain both their careers and their rural homes. The Burlington Airport has had to enlarge its parking lot several times, in part due to the many urban commuters. Most alternate several days in the city with several at their country home, and in many cases their families live here full time. Thanks to the availability of computers, satellite communications, and fast, dependable delivery services, other folks in our area do commercial art, photography, investment management, and TV writing from offices in their country homes.

A move to the country may give you a nudge to take up a career you've long been considering. As examples, two country inns in our area are operated successfully by urban ex-lawyers and their families, and a former college professor runs a tennis camp. Some people offer services in fields that were their former hobbies, such as repairing computers, videotaping weddings, and reupholstering furniture. Others offer daycare for children, provide taxi service, and bake cakes for special occasions. Retirees have become part-time consultants in their fields. Doctors may continue a part-time practice, or fill in at local clinics. A retired accountant can take on limited income tax work.

One of our favorite newspapers was started by a young man who had driven a school bus when he first arrived in a nearby village. Then, noticing that his new community was pretty much ignored by the county daily newspaper, and that his neighbors were offended by the slight, he and his wife started an 8-page tabloid in his home. Within 10 years his endeavor has grown to a 52-page weekly with a large circulation.

Moonlighting is very common in the country. In our area, one man does landscaping, rents boats, patrols vacant camps, paints buildings, repairs roofs, and serves as a night watchman. In the winter he also plows driveways and shovels snow off roofs. His wife cleans cottages, weeds flower beds, and does laundry for the summer residents. The children mow lawns, act as babysitters, and help a nearby farmer during his busiest times. Busy dairy farmers may also raise vegetables, cut firewood and lumber, and make maple syrup to supplement their income. A weaver in our community doubles as a ski instructor; a computer sales-and-service man produces specialty T-shirts; and a local contractor is also the school janitor, cemetery sexton, and substitute mail carrier. We could go on and on with the list of examples of people we know who moonlight year round. They feel it's worth the effort, for the chance to live in the country.

Recreation Income

You may be able to make money by opening your home or your land to people who flock to the country for recreation and a change of pace. Many look for alternatives to traditional motels and golf courses, seeking out bed-and-breakfasts. Several farms offer city dwellers an opportunity to share a farm life for several weeks each summer. Country inns, though they demand a large investment, are popular too.

Some of the hostelries near us supply little except rooms and meals, while others provide nature hikes, bird walks, picnics, fishing and hunting expeditions, bicycle tours, boat rides, and trails for cross-country skiing and horseback riding.

This type of business is not for everyone, of course. One retired couple longed for more activity after their children left home, and so they started a bed-and-breakfast. Soon they had an abundance of new friends and plenty to keep themselves busy. A neighbor, after listening to their enthusiasm, had a neat sign painted, remodeled several rooms, and eagerly awaited her first customers. It didn't work. Her family, unlike their gregarious neighbors, loathed the new business. They disliked being on call all the time and adjusting their life to guests, who, they complained, were very demanding. They finally took down their sign, and now have a new appreciation of the privacy and independence they had once found boring. For more on bed-and-breakfasts, see page 88.

We are always surprised at how quickly new money-making opportunities catch on. Recreational dirt bikes and all-terrain vehicles had scarcely been on the market before commercial riding places were opened in northern Vermont. Since the machines are best suited to use on larger tracts of rugged terrain than most people own, these trails became very popular. Watching the fad develop, one man in a nearby town decided that a riding and racing course might be the most profitable use for his isolated rocky farm. It became an instant, year-round success. As soon as the snow became too deep for the wheeled vehicles, he converted it to a snowmobile course. Though a racetrack may be far from your notion of an ideal country business, careful observation of current trends may turn up other innovative uses for your land.

Chapter 2
THE SEARCH FOR THE PERFECT PLACE

Some of those who have moved here to northern New England tell us it was the smartest move they ever made. Others have confided it was their worst mistake, and they are looking at homesites in the

❖

Poconos, West Virginia, and the South. We wonder if perhaps a computerized service could match the right location with the right family, just as computers are used to match people seeking mates.

Places Rated Almanac (Random House, 1985) does away with some of the guesswork. It ranks metropolitan areas according to their desirability as places to live, in terms of nine factors that greatly influence the quality of our lives: climate, housing, health care, crime, transportation, education, the arts, recreation, and economics.

As you're looking for a new homeplace, a strong hunch and instant affinity may be the surest sign that you're on the right track. Often a person will respond to something about a place that seems insignificant. It may be a place for a swing in a backyard pine, just like the one you used at Grandma's as a child. Or the barn may be reminiscent of your favorite Wyeth painting. Or a feature may correspond to your dreams—the fireplace would be cozy with the family gathered around it on a winter's evening, or the pond would be an ideal swimming hole for your grandchildren.

When you fall in love with a property, for whatever reason, it is difficult to judge it with an eye to anything that might give you trouble in the future. A beautiful waterfall or lovely mountaintop view has blinded many a buyer to poor soil or a crumbling foundation. As when buying your first car, excitement may cloud judgment, and you may end up with a flimsy convertible of a home when you really need a practical sedan.

If you have plenty of money, you may be able to afford to overlook many bad points of a property. Repairs can be made, additions built, and mountains moved. But we have met newcomers who underestimated their abilities and resources and the cost of fixing up a place was high in terms of labor, money, and discouragement.

A young couple from Boston moved into the woods a few miles from us during the 1960s and started to remodel an old hilltop farm with a beautiful view. They saw the low-priced property as a challenge to their ingenuity, and plunged into fixing it up. They bought goats, sheep, chickens, and a horse, and built a fish pond. They cleared land, and planted a garden and fruit trees among the tree stumps. As the months went on they found more and more problems with the buildings, the water supply, and the septic systems. They worked long days, and spent nearly everything they had, and still there were few signs that the home was getting much closer to their vision. Finally, completely exhausted, they gave up and moved back to "civilization," as they put it.

You can buy property either through a broker or directly from the seller. There are advantages to both methods, but unless you have good connections or are lucky enough to stumble upon a dream house, you'll do best with an agent who represents a local real estate firm. You'll have a choice of a wide listing of properties, and by looking at several at one time you'll find it easier to compare. A broker can also spare you the trouble of looking at homes that wouldn't be suitable. Finally, he or she will handle paperwork and arrange for title searches and guarantees.

The average value per acre of farmland and buildings (1985) varies dramatically from state to state.

The price of real estate, like everything else, is determined by demand, and if you locate an area that is desirable, but not considered "in," the property may be priced surprisingly low. In our region, property on a lake or commanding spectacular views will sell at an extremely high price, while land only a few miles away may be priced (and taxed) at less than a third of the cost. Prime agriculture land, excellent woodlands, attractive brooks, and neighborhoods with many expensive houses will also send prices up. One friend of ours recently got an excellent buy on property on the outskirts of a run-down village. Few people cruising the area would consider living there, even though it's only a five-minute drive to acres of beautiful country.

If you can afford it, seriously consider buying initially all the real estate you expect to need in the future. Of course, you can start with a small amount of land and buy more as your farming enterprise or business expands, but you'll pay far less if you buy the land in one parcel rather than piecemeal. In fact, the land you need may not be available later at any price.

No matter how good the place looks and how attractive the price, try to find out why the present owner wants to sell. Make sure that the reason is not tied to a problem that you have overlooked—underground radon or an unusual number of pests such as mosquitos or rattlesnakes. Seasonal activities such as an annual rock concert, circus, or motorcycle race make some places unattractive, too. A town near us had a fiddlers' concert each summer for years and, though it started as a small event, it eventually attracted a large audience from all over the United States. Finally, nearby residents, fearful that it was lowering their property values (and tired of the noise, fights, traffic accidents, and thefts), forced its closing.

Chapter 3
SIZING UP A PLACE

Once you think you've found the spot where you want to live, look carefully before you leap. If you don't know the area well, try to live there for at least a few days before committing yourself. You may be able to spend weekends or vacations visiting local friends, staying at a bed-and-breakfast spot or motel, or even camping in a tent nearby. A trial run won't tell you everything, but it will help you absorb a bit of the flavor of the area and its people.

Ideally, visit your chosen site at different times of the year so you'll have an idea of what each season has in store for you. Real estate salespeople know that rural property sells more readily in certain seasons. (In an earlier era, New England hill farms were traditionally sold when late winter snows made rocky fields and pastures look clear and open.)

You cannot avoid all surprises, nor would you want to, but in the North you would do well to check out whether windblown snow will block your driveway, if there is likely to be several miles of deep mud between you and town when the snow melts in the spring, and if floods and hailstorms are more than occasional occurrences. Even autumn may bring its troubles: newcomers to the North Woods have told us they never fully enjoy the beautiful fall foliage because the roads and woods nearby their homes fill with hunters, making them hesitant to go outdoors.

Community

Understanding the true essence of a rural community may take years. But you can get important clues before you move in. Consult a reliable real estate agent, the postmaster, clergy, librarian, storekeeper, or town manager. The more people you talk with, the more accurate your picture of the community will become.

Local papers are an excellent introduction to a community. Our new neighbors, before they decided to move in, subscribed to our area's weekly newspaper and read it carefully for months. They were so informed that they not only became conversant with people's names, but they knew who was on the school board, who had just given birth to twins, and who had vacationed in Switzerland last summer. It was invaluable background, and they quickly have become an integral part of the community.

Just as cities or suburbs are considered sophisticated, arty, blue collar, or dangerous, each rural community has a character of its own. Neighborhoods within a single township may be distinct from one another, as are parts of a city. A certain area may have a reputation as the "wrong side of the tracks," as being all newcomers, or as unfriendly to newcomers. Investigate such labels you hear, but don't take them too seriously. The personality of the neighborhood may have changed faster than its reputation. A century ago the large mills in a town near ours gave the area a rough and rowdy reputation that still lingers, despite the fact that the mills are long gone and the town is now a scenic retirement community!

Is your chosen area predominantly artistic, cultural, intellectual, agricultural, homesteady, ultra-liberal, conservative, redneck, business-oriented, professional, filled with retirees, religious, sports-oriented, cultist, or a nicely balanced combination of the above? The clubs and organizations that thrive can give you clues to the sort of community you're choosing.

Try to sense if the town is so tightly knit that you will feel ostracized if you do not join the Grange, Catholic church, local NRA chapter, peace coalition, or the country club as soon as you arrive. On the other hand, you'll want to know if it is the kind of area where everybody does his or her own thing to such a degree that no one is willing to work with others. Such places may have little civic interest in good roads, libraries, recreational facilities, or schools.

If you have children, they will need companions of their own ages, and you'll want to carefully check out the quality of the public schools. Talk with parents and members of the Parent-Teacher Association as well as school officials. One school superintendent, who oversees a union school and a half dozen elementary schools in a county near us, says he was surprised that in his ten years only three prospective newcomers have asked to examine the schools. Don't hesitate to visit classes, look at textbooks, and examine the curriculum. Ask about the ratio of students to teachers, the courses offered, the number of secondary school graduates who go on to college, the school's budget per student, and teachers' salaries. If the teachers and school officials are competent and proud of their work, they should be glad to cooperate.

County and town government policies will affect you in many ways, including your taxes, zoning laws, and roads. Try to determine what kind of people hold office. Are local policies set by an old guard that is hostile to change? Or has control been taken over by a group of newcomers who are intent on changing everything? Within the past decade the population balance in several tiny towns near us has shifted so drastically that the voting newcomers outnumber the natives, and the administration has changed considerably. The result? Although some of the valuable tradition and the political stability of the local government has been lost, the vigor and enthusiasm of the new guard have made the communities more interesting places to live.

Investigate the tax system. It may be structured to encourage new building, industry, and agriculture; or the town may have decided that further growth is unwise. Newcomers may be singled out for especially high appraisals, or there may be an influential group in town that likes to experiment with expensive and impractical schemes that make exorbitant demands for tax dollars. One group in a town near us worked hard and successfully to have several tennis courts added to the local school grounds, even though there was little interest in the sport.

Utilities

If electric and telephone wires don't run to your proposed home site, you may face a big expense. Only a few years ago most electric and phone companies were willing to build lines at no cost to the consumer, to increase their business. Because of high construction costs today, however, most utilities expect you to defray most of the expense. In our town and many others, this factor has greatly discouraged building in the backcountry.

Even if you don't need to bring in a power line, you may want to check out the monthly electric rates. Prices charged by utility companies vary widely from area to area. In rural areas where lines must be maintained to widely separated homes, the higher costs are passed on to the consumer. Some companies charge a higher rate during the winter months, when usage is heavier.

A few rural families enjoy being independent of utility companies. Particularly during the 1960s and 1970s, they severed their ties with civilization, and lived without electricity, gas, or a telephone. After a few years, however, some changed their minds. They missed refrigeration and running water. They worried about not having a phone in case of a fire or accident (and neighbors tired of delivering phone messages). Many, as they aged, became intensely aware of the time and energy invested in sawing boards manually, carrying water, and grinding wheat. Children felt deprived of TV and other electric-powered entertainment enjoyed by their friends. In our region, most who first chose to rough it have either moved closer to town or brought in utility lines.

If you decide to forego dependency on commercially produced electricity and the telephone system, there are alternatives. A CB radio can substitute for the telephone. At high elevations in some areas, wind power can supply enough electricity to operate radios and a few motors. There may be sufficient water power to furnish a home with electricity and even produce a surplus that can be sold to the utilities. Some friends of ours generate most of the power they need with solar cells installed on their roof, and several neighbors have been so impressed with the results that they are installing similar systems.

Zoning and Environmental Laws

If your prospective town or county has a plan for future development, give it a careful reading to find just how the local government sees its past, assesses the area's resources, and plans for the future. Zoning regulations and maps, usually available through local government offices, may label your acres as flood plain, conservation, recreation, industrial, or rural; they may also indicate whether or not your property can be subdivided. Regulations may limit building to one home site per lot of 5 acres, 10 acres, or as large as 25 acres—a factor that could affect your future plans. Zoning may not allow you to keep animals or poultry, start a home business, or even construct outbuildings unless you get a variance (an exemption from the town's zoning regulations).

Although our state has statewide environmental regulations to control large developments, each township is permitted to further regulate building. Some small towns have very restrictive rules regarding growth; others have no local zoning ordinances at all. In our opinion, an area that is well zoned is preferable to one with uncontrolled growth. Although certain zoning laws may appear to work against some of your plans, the ordinances should protect you from a next-door junkyard, gravel pit, landfill, motorcycle racetrack, or large pig farm—ventures that not only would make your life unpleasant, but could also ruin the value of your real estate.

Besides reading the current regulations, check with the residents on how well they're working, whether or not they are being enforced, and whether important changes are planned.

Health

In most areas, the old country doctor has gone the way of his faithful horse and buggy. Luckily, however, people in the medical profession are included in those who prefer to live in the country. In rural regions, doctors often share a practice with several others in a health center. Although this may mean that you must travel some distance for your medical and dental needs, health care is often as good as that found in urban areas.

Because regional hospitals are likely to be some distance away, many rural communities band together to sponsor an ambulance service, sometimes in connection with their fire department. Well-trained volunteer rescue squads are vital contributors to health and safety in many rural areas.

You may also want to investigate available nursing home and home health care facilities, should you or a member of your family need them in the future. Although the latest medical equipment is not always found in rural nursing homes and health centers, the care is likely to be more personal.

Land

When you look over prospective property, keep the sun in mind and note the "lay of the land"—which areas slope to the south, north, east, and west. This is especially important if you plan to garden where the growing season is short, or if you want to raise heat-loving crops such as grapes or tomatoes. Land that slopes toward the south or southeast collects many more hours of sunlight than land sloping west

Trees should be situated at top of slopes to avoid frost pockets (shaded areas).

or north. It warms up faster in the spring, stays warm later in the fall, and is heated more intensely during the summer. On the other hand, a northerly slope may be better where summers are hot and dry, or if you will be growing cool-weather crops such as peas, greens, asparagus, hay, or Christmas trees.

Certain plants blossom early in spring and are sensitive to spring frosts, including most tree fruits, blueberries, strawberries, and nuts. The plants of melons, beans, squash, pumpkins, eggplants, tomatoes, and peppers can also be ruined by late spring frosts. A gentle slope is usually the best frost-free site, as long as no hedgerows or trees hinder the passage of cold night air down into a valley below.

The micro-climate at the precise spot you are considering may be quite different from the weather just a few miles away. For example, the United States planting zone map may show that your land is in Zone 5, where a wide range of plants grow well, but a lake, river, mountain, or localized prevailing air current may, in fact, create the conditions of Zone 3, 4, or 6. Temperatures may even fluctuate widely from one part of your property to another. We put thermometers in various locations about our place, and discovered several spots that were more likely to escape the frost on nights when the temperature hovered around 32 degrees F. Our local radio lists daily temperatures contributed by a volunteer CB radio network, and the reports often vary as much as 15 degrees within a 30-mile radius.

The county agent or a knowledgeable local gardener can tell you if the degree days, length of the growing season, rainfall, and minimum temperatures will permit you to grow the crops you have in mind.

Soil

If you plan to raise crops or animals, the soil on your prospective property should be of great interest to you. An ideal location is unnecessary if you intend only to grow small amounts of food for yourself, because most places can be improved enough to carry on small-scale projects. If you plan to raise produce for market, however, you need as many factors as possible in your favor.

Worn-out land demands much money and time to rebuild. And wooded brushland may be hard to clear. You might think it romantic to emulate the early settlers, hacking out a homestead from the heart of a forest. But the romance soon wears thin for most modern pioneers. Trees are likely growing in the abandoned fields of worn-out farmland, so a newly cleared plot will probably offer poor soil filled with tree roots. Much nitrogen in the soil will be used up by the bacteria that decompose the roots, which means you must go to the work and expense of heavy fertilization—and it is difficult to add enough nitrogen without overdosing your crop.

An extension service soil map can give you an idea of the soil type and general condition of the land. The map can be puzzling at first, but by studying the legend and the various soil types, the different markings will soon make sense. Since the map may have been made several decades ago, keep in mind that conditions may have changed over the years. Also, soils often vary considerably within the same field in fertility, alkalinity, and trace elements. All of these aspects can be improved more easily than soil *structure*, however, which is difficult to change and even to determine.

Usually you can't be sure of soil structure without digging a lot of holes. But you can get a good idea by inspecting plant growth and rock outcroppings, and examining the soil near the surface. Eroded ditches and gullies give you a peek at what lies beneath the thin top layer of soil.

The best fields for most crops contain a thick layer of topsoil, well drained and well supplied with organic matter. It should be reasonably free from rocks and roots. Soil will be much more difficult to work if there is a rock ledge or layer of clay hardpan only a few inches down. And soil composed mostly of gravel, sand, rock, or heavy, wet, mucky loam will also start you out at a disadvantage. Still, even these inferior soils may be used for growing firewood, Christmas trees, or timber.

Even though the acidity-alkalinity factor (pH) of the soil is not considered as vitally important as it once was, it still deserves investigation, especially if you plan to grow certain crops. A soil that tests between 5.5 and 6.5 is suitable for growing most crops; but alfalfa, apples, clover, and pears are some of the plants that thrive in less-acid soils of 6.5 to 7. Blueberries and bog cranberries, on the other hand, do well only when the soil is very acid, below 5.5. Unless a plant needs a pH much higher or lower than what you have, it will usually thrive as long as the soil is well supplied with nutrients, humus, and trace elements such as iron.

A small soil test kit is a good investment, or you can send samples to the state extension service for testing. (Ask your county agent for

❖

details about how to collect the samples.) You can get an idea of the pH by looking at the vegetation growing naturally. Wild blueberries and acid-loving plants such as sorrel indicate an acid soil, at least in the top layer; natural stands of hemlock, oak, and pine trees signify a deep acid soil. A large number of native white cedar (American arborvitae) or heavy growths of clover and goldenrod are a sign that the soil is alkaline. Hard water in local springs and wells also indicates general soil alkalinity.

Signs of fertile soil include an abundance of tall grasses, clovers, dandelions, and a heavy stand of healthy maple trees growing naturally. Weeds, mosses, and scrubby, brushy plants warn that the soil is depleted of nutrients. Larch, alders, and willows indicate that it is likely to be wet for most of the year.

Although you can tell a great deal about your prospective land by careful observation and by studying booklets and soil maps, ask an agronomist or soil expert to examine it if you are seriously considering purchase of the land for a specific crop. Unless your farm is very small, it probably contains several types of soil, and locating these will permit you to grow a variety of crops successfully.

Woods

A forest may turn out to be your most interesting possession. Some of our happiest hours are spent in our maple woods, hemlock grove, and coniferous forest, in every season of the year. In the summer twilight the hermit thrush sings in the tall trees, and an autumn sunrise glowing through red and golden falling leaves is breathtaking. We follow deer and wolf tracks on our snowshoes in winter, and anticipate the spring beauties and violets that carpet the forest floor in May.

Our woodlot is also productive, yielding a constant supply of firewood, fence posts, and other homestead necessities. And over the years we have sold its pulpwood, sawlogs, firewood, Christmas trees, and maple syrup.

When you look over a woodlot on your prospective property, notice how it has been used and cared for in the past. Unfortunately, mismanagement of forests is common, and many of the mistakes of the past are still clearly visible over the countryside. Even the best farmers have regarded their woods as less consequential than their field crops or herds. They carefully selected their best animals for breeding stock, but in the forest they cut the best trees and left the junky ones to reproduce. It is even likely that the previous owner of your place may have found it more convenient to clear-cut entire areas rather than to harvest selectively—a treatment that leaves a forest unproductive for a generation or two.

If you are inexperienced in evaluating woodlands, ask a professional forester for help. Recently, county foresters have become so involved in environmental projects that they are often not as readily available for free consultations as they once were, but if you are in no hurry, they will get to you eventually. If you need a quick opinion they will recommend a private forester in your area who will work with you for a fee.

An expert forester can help you determine the woods' current value and future potential, and will also tell you which trees to encourage and which to weed out. A good stand of maple, spruce, oak, or pine is typically more valuable than one of beech, cedar, fir, or larch; but a nearby fence factory, shingle mill, or wood chipping plant may increase the value of even these trees.

With luck you may find you can say, along with Emerson, "I too have a new plaything, the best I ever had—a woodlot."

Country Buildings

If you are inexperienced in examining a house, it's best to hunt up an expert to help you. Some areas have professionals, often semi-retired contractors, who will go with you and point out any important faults with the place. If such a service is not available, you may want to employ a contractor to take on the evaluation.

After you've checked out all the usual things you'd look for when buying a house—sound sills and roofs, a basement that doesn't become flooded each spring, and proper wiring and plumbing—take a good look at the outbuildings. Sheds and barns that you don't need around a country place may be a liability rather than an asset. It may be tempting to acquire and preserve a large old barn for its rustic appearance, but the expense may not be justifiable if you have no real use for it. Unused buildings deteriorate quickly, encourage rodents, and are a fire hazard. They require painting and repairs, and they may be dangerous to children. They will probably also increase your taxes and insurance rates, whether you use them or not. If they are built with hand-hewn timbers or covered with weathered barn boards, you may be able to make good use of them or sell them at a good price. It should be possible to salvage lumber, doors, and windows for use in constructing other buildings, too.

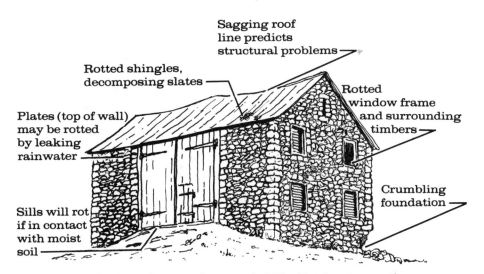

An aging barn is apt to have an Achilles' heel or two or three. Repairs to post-and-beam structures are surprisingly expensive.

On the other hand, a beautiful old barn is a link with the past you may not want to lose. If you can afford the upkeep, it can be useful for animals, storage, or a playground for the children on rainy days. We've also seen old barns converted into a guest house, a studio for art, music, or writing, and areas for meditation and entertainment. Don't be too hasty to demolish old sheds. You may need them to store firewood, as a tool or garden house, or to dry beans, flowers, herbs, and other produce. Often they can be redesigned as a house for boiling maple sap, a cider-making shop, or a roadside stand for marketing produce. Our neighbors use an old milkhouse as shelter for their children while waiting for the schoolbus in bad weather.

If your prospective property comes with no storage building or garage, be sure there is a spot to conveniently build one of a practical size. By the time you have lived in the country a few years you will have collected considerable equipment that should be sheltered. Although some country dwellers park all their worldly equipment in the front yard, weather greatly shortens the life of cars, tractors, tillers, mowers, and chain saws.

Water and Sewage

A reliable water supply and trouble-free sewage disposal are taken for granted by city dwellers. An endless supply of water flows in (although it may not taste like a mountain spring), and disappears into pipes leading to unknown destinations. But in the country water is never taken for granted. Although drilled wells and electric pumps now assure that good water is available nearly everywhere, most of us in the country know exactly where it comes from and where it goes, and we appreciate that sooner or later we will be involved in repairing both systems.

Find out everything you can about the water system. If a spring provides fresh, pure water the year round, you are lucky, especially if it is at an elevation high enough to ensure good water pressure without a pump.

You will probably want to have the water analyzed, not only to see that it is free from harmful bacteria, radon, and minerals that will affect the taste and plumbing, but also to be sure that no harmful chemicals have leached in over the years. Local health officers can tell you where to send it for testing.

Poor sewage systems and animal wastes have always been a potential source of pollution to water in rural areas, but now there are additional hazards. Huge amounts of herbicides and insecticides have been spread on agricultural crops for the past quarter century and much of this is now leaching into our water supplies. Also, chemicals migrate from small rural industries and landfills. (One small New England town recently had its entire water supply polluted by the chemicals used by a large nursery, and another by the chemicals from a dry cleaning plant.) Since chemical pollution moves through the soil so slowly, it may take years before it finally reaches your spring or well. Try to find out if heavy doses of herbicides have ever been used on orchards, corn, nursery stock, Christmas trees, or similar crops in your locality, and if there have been farm dumps or landfills nearby where toxic chemicals may have been buried in recent years.

❖

Search for restrictions on the water rights of your prospective home. The deed may show agreements made years ago, allowing your neighbors certain rights to your water source, or allowing their water pipes or drainage pipes to cross your land. These rights may be legal even if not supported by a recorded document. If people have been using water that originates on your property for many years, it may be difficult to stop them.

Also, check out local laws concerning water. You may be forbidden to dig a well, or to dam up or use water from a stream. Very old deeds sometimes give adjoining landowners control over water on other people's property.

Septic System

Track down the septic tank and drainage field. Ask the owners if the system has given them trouble in the past, and for a second opinion, you might ask a local plumber. If the lawn seems to have been dug up recently by something other than moles, check out the reason.

Many early rural septic systems were primitive, allowing wastes to flow into a ditch or nearby stream. Slightly more advanced are simple septic tanks made of logs or timbers buried in the ground. In time, the wood in them rots and the earth covering them caves in.

The most satisfactory system is a steel or concrete tank buried in the ground. Pipes from the tank lead to a leach field where a series of

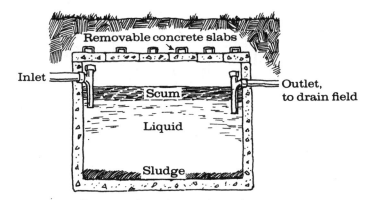

Cross section of a septic tank.

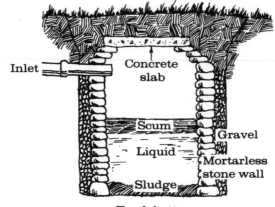

Inlet | Concrete slab

Scum | Gravel

Liquid

Mortarless stone wall

Sludge

Earth bottom

Cross section of a cesspool.

perforated pipes enable the wastes to drain into the land and be neutralized by the soil before they reach a stream or an underground water supply. In order to work well, or "perk," the leach field must be of sandy or gravelly soil. If the soil is heavy, the pipes must be buried in sand or crushed rock that has been trucked in. Even the best system does not break down all the wastes, so eventually the tank must be pumped out.

Chapter 4
THE TRANSITION

We have talked with many friends and acquaintances who have moved to the country, and their stories describe a great deal of planning, difficult decisions, and hard work—whether they have acquired simply a plot of land, a delapidated farmhouse, or even a relatively new home.

Our new neighbors, long before they moved in, deliberated over whether to build a new, energy-saving underground home, or to renovate the existing 1840 farmhouse. They eventually moved the old house to a better location and made a great many renovations and additions to it, incorporating the lumber from an old barn. The family did a lot of the work themselves, and they are happy with their beautiful old/new, well-insulated country home.

If you face a similar decision—whether to remodel an aging house or to start from scratch—one of your best resources is a good local contractor. Ask your contractor to examine the buildings carefully, and tally up an estimate of the work to be done and the price tag. Although it may end up costing more to remodel than to build a new home, it could be well worth the cost to you. Many people are drawn to the country because of the beauty of a vintage home, and feel that any shortcomings can be corrected without destroying its charm. Numerous old homes in our area, including our own, have been made brighter and more comfortable with the addition of a solar room, den, living room, or modern kitchen.

To bring a vintage house up to current standards of comfort may take a complete dismantling of either the outside or inside walls. Windows, doors, water pipes, and electric outlets should be carefully caulked, insulated, or weather stripped because they are chinks in the home's insulating armor. Windows, especially, let in a lot of cold air.

Your contractor and perhaps an energy expert from the extension service can help you decide what is the best approach for your climate. Double-glazed windows are not frost-free in our subzero winters, so triple glazing is recommended here. We not only put storm windows on our old house each fall, but also cover them inside with sheets of clear plastic. A friend who built a house with a lot of glass, on a windy hill near here inserts tight-fitting, 2-inch-thick Styrofoam panels into the inside frames of the windows on the coldest nights. Others use shades of insulated quilt material, and we see some North Country homes with their entire north side covered with plastic film each winter.

The high and low temperatures in your area will determine how careful you must be to make your home energy efficient. Every time the wind from Hudson Bay sweeps across our farmstead, we are very grateful that we tightened up our old house. (Rumor has it that only several barbed wire fences separate our county from the polar

❖

Recordkeeping

As you carry out your plans, remember to keep good records of your spending, and retain receipts and other proofs to back them up. Not only will they be invaluable for tax purposes, but eventually the day will come when you either sell your property or transfer it to your heirs. Under present tax laws, when you figure capital gains on property you are selling, you deduct the cost of all the improvements you have made since you bought it, provided you have not already deducted them as running business expenses. Save receipts for building additions, major repairs, landscaping, and other projects so that you can submit the proof necessary to receive such credits.

When we're adding to our property or remodeling, we locate on charts such things as the underground water and sewage pipes, buried electric lines, field drainage tiles, and the electrical wiring of the buildings. Our collection of maps has saved endless hunting and trial runs, and enabled us to make repairs quickly.

regions!) A few years ago, many newcomers to these mountains built large ski chalets with high cathedral ceilings and lots of glass so they could enjoy the lovely view. Even with elaborate heating systems, they found they were never comfortable, and now some of those homeowners travel south for the winter.

The location of the present house may also affect your decision. The early settlers, a practical lot, usually built their homes in a sheltered spot, close to the road, and near a spring that could supply water by gravity. A great view, or privacy, was not as important to them as it may be to you, so if you acquire an old house that you are fond of, but it is in the wrong location, talk with a skilled contractor. He or she can build a new foundation in your choice spot, and move the house for you so carefully that not a brick on the chimney is disturbed, although before the remodeling is complete, it will probably cost much more than building a new house from scratch.

Inside the Country Home

Whether you decide to build a new dream house or to remake an existing one, your country home may benefit from features unlike those in a town house.

The mud room. Rather than a formal entrance foyer, a well-planned rural home has a mud room where family and visitors can shed their wet (and sometimes animal scented) clothes and muddy boots before tracking into the house. If anyone in the family gardens or works with animals, a sink in or near the mud room eliminates a lot of dirt in the house. It's a handy place for washing garden vegetables on the way to the kitchen, too. Some homes even have a shower there.

The country kitchen. Like its old-fashioned farmhouse ancestor, a country kitchen today is the heart of the home, where family, friends, cats, and dogs gather. Not only a place to cook and preserve food, it's also where we eat, talk over a cup of tea, read the newspaper, and in the winter, warm our toes, dry our mittens and nest in the rocking chair by the woodstove. The larger the living space, the better; but the work area itself should be compact and efficient. If you have the luxury of designing a new kitchen, plan lots of continuous work space for rolling out pastry, kneading bread, and processing food, and making butter, cheese, or other dairy products. If you don't have a pantry, make room for a freezer and plenty of storage space for appliances and processing equipment such as pressure canners, juicers, and grinders. Good access to the garden, pantry, and root cellar is helpful, and a vinyl-backed nylon mat near the door will collect mud, grass, pebbles, and other miscellany before it reaches your floor.

The root cellar and canned goods storage area. If you intend to harvest and store some of your own food, as most rural folks do, you'll want a cool basement area for jars of jellies, juices, pickles, wines, and canned goods, and a root cellar for storing such things as apples, carrots, potatoes, turnips, and beets.

We dig our root crops after the weather becomes cool in the fall, and store them in large plastic laundry baskets. After packing them in sand, peat, and sawdust over the years, we finally discovered that layering them in dry maple leaves kept them fresh looking until spring, and without rotting.

Our cellar has a dirt floor, so our root cellar is a simple area shut off from the rest of the basement. It has an outside window that we

❖

open on cool nights and close on warm days after the vegetables and apples are in. We close it completely after the weather gets a bit below freezing. Our friends with more modern homes keep an air-conditioning unit in their root cellar, so they have even better control over the temperature and humidity.

The pantry. Farmsteads were originally built with a pantry or buttery, but in modernizing they were usually removed or, like ours, converted to a bathroom. Because we live four miles from the village and our trips to the store are infrequent, we converted part of our large woodshed to a new, old-fashioned pantry. A child visiting us recently commented, "It's like a store!" In addition to food packages and cans, the pantry is the place for a freezer, flour bin, and infrequently used appliances. During cold weather it becomes a walk-in refrigerator, and throughout the holidays the shelves are filled with pies, cookies, turkey leftovers, and other items which were once found in a proper pantry.

The woodshed. We have noticed that few plans for country homes mention a woodshed. If a wood-burning furnace is your primary source of heat, the wood should be stored near it in the basement, of course. But if stoves are used in the living space, it is a nuisance to carry logs and kindling wood upstairs, and a shed attached to the house is a real convenience. If possible, the shed should have windows that can be opened to dry wood that has been stored before it is completely dry.

Heating

This brings up the question of whether or not to use wood heat. Like many others in rural areas, we burn wood because it is a renewable resource, close at hand, and less expensive for us than electricity, oil, or gas. With careful cutting, our woodlot should go on producing indefinitely, just as it has for nearly two centuries. But we are quick to admit that wood has many disadvantages as a primary heat source. It is dirty and creates dust throughout the house, and some people are allergic to the smoke or to the mold spores on the wood. Wood stoves and furnaces cannot be left unattended for more than a few hours.

Heating with wood provides lots of vigorous exercise. We calculate that a piece of wood is handled at least nine times between the

❖

Felling

Bucking
and splitting

Loading
truck

whirr

Unloading
truck

Stacking

Loading
cart

Stacking
by stove

Loading
stove

Dumping
ashes

For some people, the nine steps involved in heating with wood
only increase the fuel's charm.

time the tree is sawed down to finally taking out the ashes. You can
buy wood all cut and split, of course, but the higher cost may put the
expense of wood heat beyond that of more convenient fuels.

THE TRANSITION

❖

For all of these reasons an automatic heating system is a better choice for people who are elderly, handicapped, or away from home a good deal and cannot tend a wood fire. An alternative is a wood-fired system that kicks in with oil or gas when the fire goes out or is too much trouble.

Because we have wood available and are able to cope with its demands at this stage of our lives, we feel it would be silly to waste it. We enjoy the heat of a wood stove, even when the electric power is cut off, and also enjoy the feeling of being less dependent on the moods of a foreign cartel. Of course, we aren't completely independent. We use gasoline to cut the wood and haul it to the house, and we have an oil furnace that triggers on when we're away for long periods and can't stoke the fire.

We're using wood more efficiently now, too. A century ago, it took 12 cords of wood and three roaring stoves to heat our house each winter. By caulking, insulating, and using our new solar room, we are able to heat a larger space with just 6 cords of wood and one small stove. To distribute heat throughout the house we have installed small fans in doorways, the type used to cool electronic equipment.

Our old house had no fireplace, and we have resisted installing one, opting instead for a Vermont Castings stove that can be used as an open fire with a screen in front. Since we live on top of a hill where downdrafts often push smoke *down* the chimney, we seldom use it open. We don't miss it much, because fireplaces are an inefficient heat source, and unless you install tight glass doors, a lot of room heat goes up the chimney along with the smoke. Nevertheless, a fireplace is undeniably charming, and many country dwellers would not be without one.

On a large lot, you also have plentiful access to free energy—the sun. Although solar energy is inadequate for a primary year-round heat source in most of the United States, it can be a useful supplement for heating both air and water nearly everywhere. For years we discussed adding a solar room to our 150-year-old farmhouse. We had doubts about its practicality, because here in the North, winter days are extremely short and often cloudy and stormy. But now that we have completed the room, we realize that we should have built it long ago. The front faces southeast and the large triple glazed windows catch the first rays of the winter sun, which continue to pour into the room all morning. The southwest end collects all the afternoon sun.

Since the sun is at a low angle from November until March, it floods the room with heat whenever it shines. From April until October, the higher path of the sun keeps the room from getting too hot.

We were delighted to find that, with the use of the small doorway fans to circulate the heat, sunny days provide enough heat to warm the entire house. Even on hazy days a surprising amount is collected. The additional light from our large windows makes winters far less depressing, and we find ourselves less apt to succumb to cabin fever.

Solar systems are classified as "active" or "passive." Active solar heating uses the sun to heat water or some other liquid which is then pumped throughout the building. During the heat of the day, unneeded hot liquid is stored in insulated tanks and then is distributed at night.

In passive designs such as ours, the sun passes through the windows of a room or add-on greenhouse and directly heats the living space. The day's heat is stored in walls or beds of rock, sand, or concrete; at night, fans or blowers can be used to circulate the stored heat throughout the house.

The sun may also be used to heat water. In one method, water in a solar chamber is heated directly by the sun and piped into an insulated storage tank in the house. This system is easy to build, but can be used only when the temperature is above freezing. Year-round solar water heating requires a heat exchanger. A solution of antifreeze is heated by the sun, pumped through the exchanger's coils so that it releases its heat to the domestic water supply, and is then returned to the sun chamber. The antifreeze must be nontoxic, in case it accidentally leaks into the water supply. A solar water heater can be used in conjunction with a conventional unit; heat sensor switches automatically shift from one heat source to another, ensuring a continuous supply of hot water without having to fiddle with controls and valves.

Wind, Water, and Solar Energy

Home-scale windmills and water-powered generating systems are more efficient than ever, and the technology for both continues to improve. Still, relatively few people live where these sources can be used practically. We had always felt that our mountainous location provided more than enough wind to supply a good-sized town with power, but when a neighbor installed a nearby test windmill a few years ago, he discovered that our erratic gales averaged only 5 mph throughout the year, far less than the 8 mph minimum required for effective use of a generator.

In the country, you have more ways of generating your own heat and electricity.

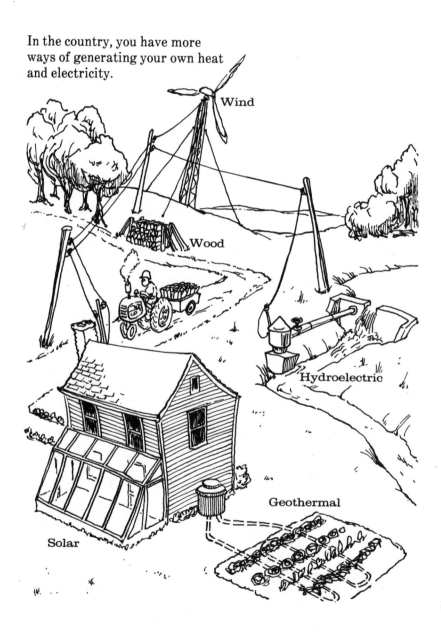

Wind

Wood

Hydroelectric

Geothermal

Solar

Traditional water mill wheels required enormous amounts of moving water to produce electricity, but new miniature turbines can easily operate lights, TVs, small appliances, and motors with relatively little water. Larger units are necessary to furnish enough power to operate water heaters, ranges, and heavy motors. To be practical, the flow must be year-round, and the supply pipe and turbine must be protected from freezing. We know of a man who built his house directly on the bank of a fast-running mountain stream so he could install the turbine in his basement.

Even if your location is ideal, a windmill or water turbine may not be practical unless the going price for electricity is unusually high. Installation of these units and the associated batteries is expensive, and we've heard of a few disappointed buyers who have found that neither system produces as much power as they had been led to expect. Both require maintenance, and this can mean that you or someone else has to work in cold water or at the top of a swaying 80-foot tower. You may find it more practical to heat your house and water with an inexpensive fuel and solar energy, and make the most of insulation and weatherproofing.

Solar photovoltaic cells are another possible source of energy if you want or need to be energy independent. These generate electricity with no moving parts, just as they do in home calculators, so little maintenance is required. Photovoltaic cells can furnish power not only for home and farm use, but also in out-of-the-way spots where building a power line would be impractical—for example, to furnish power to pump water from a distant well, or to supply an electric fence in the back forty. Acquaintances of ours who live off the beaten path on a nearby mountain are delighted with the results their home system provides, despite the fact that our area gets less sun than much of the country. Several of their neighbors are considering an installation, even though they are served by a reliable utility. The technology of solar cells continues to advance, so before you make any plans, be sure you have the latest information.

Chapter 5
COUNTRY MOBILITY

Country living tends to demand more of motorized equipment and vehicles. You may need a heavy-duty lawn mower to cope with rougher ground and a larger lawn. Many of us even use a second mower to cut tall weeds and grasses once or twice a season. Trimmers, electric hedge clippers, rotary tillers, and snowblowers must be more rugged.

Before you invest in costly equipment that may be idle much of the time, be sure you have a barn or shed to protect it from weather and theft. Machinery not only deteriorates rapidly in appearance and value if left outside, but it also needs a great deal of tinkering and repairing each season to keep it running well. We have friends who value their small tractor so much that they enlarged an outside door in their farmhouse and park it in its own room. We were astonished when, on being shown around, we entered what we thought was a bedroom and found their prized tractor sitting there, gleaming like new.

Primary Vehicles

Cars and trucks are likely to be short-lived in the country, especially if their owners live on back roads and contend with road salt, flying stones, potholes, and occasional washouts. Long ago we gave up trying to keep our car clean. Some of our neighbors say that they never wash their cars, except for weddings and funerals, and claim dirt is the only thing that holds their rusted vehicles together.

Many people who contend with back roads and bad weather own a four-wheel-drive car, van, or pickup truck. We chose a front-wheel-drive car for its superior handling in snow and mud. Since we work at home and choose the times we go out, we don't need four-wheel drive.

Many people we know spare their cars by using small motorcycles or mopeds for short trips in mud season. The new all-terrain mountain bikes, with stronger frames and fat balloon tires, are practical for traveling hilly dirt roads. They have many advantages for rural riders. Although they don't move quite as fast as a racing bike, their low gearing enables you to go off the road, into the woods, and even up mountains over rough terrain. They are more expensive than an ordinary bicycle, currently running between $300 to $500 for a good model.

Trucks

Many rural folks use a small pickup as a substitute for a car, but most of us choose pickups as second vehicles. They're nearly indispensable for moving lumber, insulation, manure, firewood, rubbish, trees, produce from the orchard and garden, small animals, and auction purchases.

So many sizes and models are available now that a choice can be difficult. A two-wheel-drive model may be adequate if your work is mostly on dry, moderately level fields and ordinary roads in good weather. But if you plan to get out wood, move supplies over difficult terrain, and get to town when the roads are too bad for the car, you'll want a four-wheel-drive truck. If you operate a market garden, nursery, or greenhouse, a pickup with a detachable cover may be most practical. Many of our friends use these both for business and for camping. The little minitrucks are economical and easy to handle, but they may be too light for certain farm and construction chores. Check to see if they are sturdy enough to move the fertilizer, plywood, or sheep you plan to truck around.

Some pickups are luxurious, and if yours is to be used in lieu of a car you may prefer one with all the extras. But if you use it mostly for work, choose a model that provides the least opportunity for things to go wrong. Layers of chrome or a row of lights across the top aren't necessary to move crates of chickens or bales of hay. Before you invest, you might notice what your neighbors with similar needs are driving.

Tractors

Sooner or later most people with a country place consider buying a tractor for those jobs that a truck can't handle. Tractors can till land, move timber, clear brush, pull stumps, mow hay and weeds, cultivate crops, and possibly satisfy a childhood dream as well. We don't have one, but probably would if we didn't have a farmer-neighbor who kindly pulls us out of a snowbank now and then, hauls out our Christmas trees, clears away our drive after a heavy snowfall, and moves manure to our garden.

Think of a farm tractor as an enormous horse. Its strength is measured in terms of horsepower (although 1 hp does not accurately

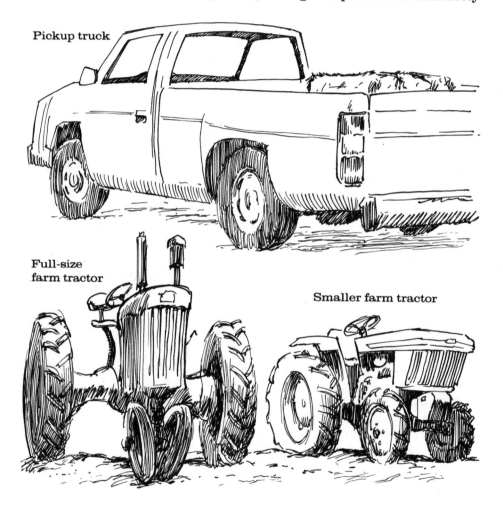

Pickup truck

Full-size farm tractor

Smaller farm tractor

Rural wheels.

compare with the power of one work horse). The size you need will depend on how and where you plan to use it, and the types of implements you'll be attaching. Mowing, for example, requires very little horsepower compared to plowing in heavy clay soil. A tractor over 30 hp is unnecessary in most small farm operations, unless you're planning to do a great deal of heavy cultivation or pull heavy loads, in which case a tractor with between 30 and 60 hp would be more practical. If you like the idea of a big tractor you can usually find

Garden tractor

Two-wheel tractor

Hand cart

All-terrain three-wheeler

enough uses to justify its existence on your farm; but the larger the machine, the more maintenance is required and the greater the repair bills will be.

Attachments are bought separately and changed as you use them: trailers, winches, cultivators, plows, harrows, manure spreaders, or more unusual implements like post-hole diggers, log splitters, water pipe layers, and landscape rakes. They are either mounted on the front of the tractor or attached to the drawbar and pulled. Most models have a three-point hitch on which attachments can be mounted and raised and lowered hydraulically—a handy feature for maneuvering the equipment and for carrying it when it's not in use. Refinements are available to keep the attachment at a constant height relative to the tractor when mowing and such.

Diesel engines have now pretty much replaced gasoline in most larger tractors, and are offered on some of the smaller ones as well. Diesel machines use less fuel and require far less maintenance. You have your choice of transmissions as well. Certain Ford tractors, for instance, provide 24 forward speeds, 11 of which are under 1 mph and useful for such things as controlling the application rate of sprays or fertilizers.

Tractors don't just pull things. They supply power to other machines, so another term you'll hear in tractor discussions is PTO, meaning "power take-off." This device supplies power from the tractor's engine to mowers, tillers, electric generators, sprayers, power pruners, and many other implements. There are three types of PTO: transmission, live, and independent. The transmission type allows you to depress the clutch of the tractor and disconnect power to the PTO shaft. The live PTO continues to work when the tractor is not moving. And the independent PTO can be used separately from the tractor's clutch.

Four-wheel-drive and front-wheel-drive tractors have superior traction in wet, slippery conditions. They are more fuel efficient, too, and tests have shown that they deliver more horsepower. Crawler tractors, which have steel tracks instead of wheels, are still used in the woods and for earthmoving, but on farms most have been replaced by four-wheel-drive tractors with oversized wheels.

Tractor Selection

When we started our nursery business nearly 40 years ago, a small farmer didn't have many tractors to choose from. There were only a few manufacturers, and each had only a few models. An explosion in the number of part-time farmers has changed all that, and you may feel, before your search is completed, that there are almost too many varieties on the market.

After lengthy discussions with your tractor-using neighbors, begin your search by comparison shopping with several dealers in farm machinery. Choose a nearby dealer who appears likely to be in business for the foreseeable future (taking a tractor a long distance for service is a nuisance). Don't be surprised to find a brand-new tractor may cost a great deal more than a new car.

Among the familiar American brands are Ford and John Deere, but Kubota and other imported tractors are catching on. A good dealer will be able to advise you of your options when you provide an accurate list of how you'll be using the tractor. Ask to see the available implements, and find out how difficult they are to use.

If you'd prefer not to invest heavily, but need a good-sized model, you may want to consider a used machine. A well-cared-for tractor depreciates less rapidly than a car. The safest source, if you're a neophyte, is a franchised farm equipment dealer who sells good, second-hand models with a warranty and can get parts you need in the future. Buying from an individual is fine, as long as you know what you're doing; but you probably won't get any kind of guarantee. Farm dispersal auctions and used equipment auctions are even more risky.

Tractor buffs disagree about the wisdom of buying models that are more than 20 years old. Parts may not be readily available, and if they are, only expensively. The old-time Ford and Ferguson models manufactured in the late 1940s and early 1950s have a reputation as uncomplicated, solid machines that continue to be easy to operate and maintain.

You'll probably want to get one with a three-point hitch, since all implements made over the past 20 years will require it. Consider getting a live PTO. And although they won't be features of an older tractor, seat belts and a rollover-bar will protect you from the unthinkable.

Many part-time farmers enjoy their tractors more than any other part of farm life. It gives them an excuse to play with a powerful toy and get some work done at the same time. Tractors aren't difficult to learn to drive, and young people take to them quickly. However, practice and caution are in order to safely manipulate a tractor on

❖

hills and rough terrain. And it's a challenge to back a tractor into a barn with a four-wheel trailer attached.

Your dealer will explain about maintenance and provide you with the necessary greases and oils. Full-time farmers often have an underground gasoline or diesel fuel tank, but small operators usually either bring fuel home in cans or store larger amounts in a 55-gallon barrel in a shed. If you buy fuel for agricultural purposes in large quantities, you may not have to pay the tax, and you will have a sales slip that you can use for income tax purposes.

Small Tractors

Unless your acreage is large, or you work in the woods, you probably won't need one of the large tractors your farming neighbors use to cut corn, bale hay, and skid logs. You will probably get along nicely with one of the new suburban models that come in nearly every size and horsepower. Many attachments are available to fit them, ranging from corn planters to fruit tree sprayers and corn shellers. You have a choice of two- and four-wheel-drive models, and of gas or diesel engines. Some come equipped with such extras as automatic shifting, power steering, electric start, and hydraulic lifts. Before making a final purchase, you might ask the dealer for names of local people who have bought a model so that you can watch the machine at work.

Walk-Behind Tractors

These two-wheel tractors look a bit like garden rotary tillers, but are much more versatile. They may be more practical than a sit-down tractor if you have a small farm (five to seven acres) and if you don't mind walking. Their engines—from 8 to 15 hp—provide power for tillers, mowers, plows, wood splitters, electric generators, pumps, rakes, snowblowers, and many other things. They can pull a small cart, in which you can put a seat. Two-wheelers are more maneuverable than tractors—they turn easily, fit between 2-foot rows, and can get into corners and close to trees, shrubs, and fences.

Two-wheelers are easy to transport in a small truck, take up little storage space and maintenance, and are much less expensive than other tractors, with current prices starting at around $3,000. Although farm implement dealers may carry them, they are more likely to be found in large garden centers and in stores that sell chain saws, motorcycles, and lawn mowers.

Good domestic models include the Intec and the Gravely. Popular Italian makes are the Ferrari and the Mainline.

All-Terrain Vehicles

These rugged, speedy, two-wheel trail bikes and three- and four-wheeled recreational machines have large, soft tires that enable them to go over deep mud, rocks, and even through snow. They are promoted mostly for sport, but they can also be used for many small farm chores—inspecting your property or checking fences quickly, herding animals, skidding out small logs, and running errands. With a trailer, the three- and four-wheelers can move firewood, fertilizers, plants, soil, animal feed, and other light loads. Most of them have a minimum number of parts to go wrong, and start well even in cold weather.

Some ATVs can be registered for road use and are handy for quick trips to town or to visit a neighbor. We enjoy riding our little Honda two-wheelers on abandoned public roads in the backcountry.

Chapter 6
JOINING
THE COMMUNITY

At a party we attended recently, a man looked out the window at a group of grazing cattle and asked, "Are those Holsteins out there?" He made the breed rhyme with vines, and the hostess later said, "Can you imagine living in dairy country for ten years as he has and not knowing what a Holstein is?

"And he doesn't even know the name of the farmer who owns them," she continued. "He only meets other retired city people like himself."

It is possible to live an isolated life in a rural area, or to associate only with people with interests just like your own, but that would be to miss the unique flavor of country life. The post office, local store, and church coffee hour are gathering places in our community where news gets exchanged, newcomers meet their neighbors, and we discuss questions such as whether or not to build a new school or buy a snowplow.

With luck you will move to a friendly community where you'll be welcomed with open arms. But some people who move into certain areas of the country complain that they don't feel completely accepted by the natives, even after living there for years. There's a story of a family that moved from a small town in New Hampshire, on one side of the Connecticut River, to a town on the Vermont side, just six miles away. Their baby girl was six months old at the time. Although she lived the rest of her 93 years in the Vermont home, the minister said at her funeral, "We loved her, even though she wasn't one of us."

Whether this story is myth or fact, it is conceivable you may feel that your homegrown neighbors are not overjoyed to have you there. It's not true, however, that country folks dislike, sight unseen, the city people who buy their farms. Rather, they likely are acutely aware of your unfamiliar ways. You eat dinner at night, they eat their main meal at noon and have supper in the evening. You may choose to work late at night and sleep late; they're in bed soon after 9 P.M. and up at the crack of dawn.

The differences may go deeper. Historically, urbanites have considered native rural people as hayseeds, and the bumpkin has long been a stock character in plays and movies. You may not feel that way at all about the natives, but if they think you do, they may find it difficult to relax in your presence, and some may try to avoid you altogether. Sometimes their sensitivity may show up as arrogance.

These sensitive rural dwellers are likely to take their cues from you, the "folks from away," and leave the relationship in your hands. If you are friendly and seem interested in their lives and work, most will be eager to share them with you and will eventually let down their guard and become real friends. But if you remain aloof, the natives will probably let you go your own way. Small communities aren't likely to be well-enough organized to send out a welcome wagon to greet newcomers. To meet the natives, you may need to take the first steps yourself—invite someone for a cup of coffee, share a loaf of bread, or ask the neighbor's children in to play with yours.

In our community many newcomers hire the local folks to work for them—cleaning, washing, gardening, and such. Even though they are happy to provide goods and services, most of the long-time citizens are proud and do not like to be "beholden" to their employers. They prefer to think of their relationship as "helping out" rather than as hired hands.

One of the oft quoted examples in our town is of a retired doctor who rented a summer cottage here many years ago. He needed some wood for his fireplace and, hearing that a neighboring farmer had some, drove over one day and knocked on his door. The farmer opened the door with a curt, "Yes?"

"I'd like to order a load of firewood," the doctor began, "and I would like it delivered to my home on Thursday morning about ten o'clock."

The farmer looked over the well-dressed man for awhile, then took the pipe out of his mouth and said slowly, "I don't take no orders from nobody," and he shut the door.

The moral, of course, is to feel your way carefully into each new situation, and be careful not to offend by "ordering" anyone to do anything. The doctor would have fared beautifully if he had chatted a bit, admired the man's garden, and then said matter of factly, "By the way, do you ever sell any of that beautiful wood over there? I sure could use some." The farmer would allow that he might consider parting with a load, never letting on that he had spent the entire winter cutting it for exactly that purpose.

Community Organizations

Much of the activity in small towns is sparked by civic organizations. Healthy communities seem to be blessed with a small group of dedicated, public-spirited citizens who serve on town government and school boards, keep the fire department and rescue squad active, and organize fairs, bazaars, talent shows, and suppers to earn money for worthwhile causes. They beautify the park, paint the library, save historic sites, and sponsor lecture series, library teas, and concerts. And they support the churches and serve as youth club leaders.

As soon as you show any interest in an organization, you will probably be invited to join. Before long, you may find yourself an officer or part of a committee. Getting involved in community activities has its benefits (you will meet people and quickly become an integral part of your community), and its drawbacks (newcomers have been known to become so involved in community service that they considered returning to their regular jobs to avoid collapsing of exhaustion).

If you decide to get involved, be discriminating. We've noticed that the newcomers who turn out to be the happiest in our community join organizations only after they have become very familiar with them. People who join hastily in an effort to become acquainted may soon decide to resign, either because they have become too busy or because they've found the organization is not to their liking. In an urban area you can easily pull out of a group and join a new one. But in the country the people who belong to the literary club or Secret Knights are likely to resent—and may not forgive—your leaving or becoming inactive. And, unfortunately, you can't get away from your former co-members as you might in a more populated area.

Although you'll undoubtedly be welcomed in organizations and community activities, the locals, as you might expect, are likely to be disturbed and resentful if you try to change old traditions before you've spent some time there. They've been getting along just fine without you. More than once we've heard, "They came here because they liked our town, and now they can't wait to change it!"

Small towners like to deliberate things carefully, and not "fix things unless they are broke." We recall one capable retired city executive who riled up the town by trying to speed up the action of the town improvement committee by running it as if he were directing the board of his company.

Slower is better. One friend in rural Massachusetts tells us of a couple from Boston moving into their neighborhood. Within a few months the man was attending all meetings of the school board, selectmen, and zoning committee, offering input to such a degree that everyone was becoming weary at the length of the meetings. Meanwhile his wife was doing the same at meetings of the library and historical society. Both were certain that this was the way to be accepted and useful to their new town. Our friend compared them with another family who had moved in, listened carefully and quietly at

❖

meetings, and finally realized that there was usually a good reason for doing things the way they did, even though they didn't always agree.

Although their communities may not be as tightly knit as they used to be, small-town people continue to support each other in ways that might surprise a newcomer. They mobilize to help out when a family loses its possessions by flood, fire, or other disaster. Community dinners or dances are given to raise money for people who have had large medical expenses. When someone is ill or dies, neighbors and acquaintances invariably take food to the family, and help out in any way they can. It can be a heartwarming experience to participate in the life of a small town, where each person plays an important part in making the community work. It won't be all that long before you'll be considered an old-timer, and you'll find yourself worrying about all those newcomers coming in.

Security and Safety

City visitors are surprised that we glance out the window to identify each car that comes along our road. We keep an eye on our neighbors, and they on us. In some rural communities, people rarely lock their doors when they are away because they have a good neighborhood watch.

One day last winter a moving van stopped at the vacant home of summer residents a half-mile away from us. A farmer who lives within sight of the home saw the van, called us, and within five minutes both of us were on the spot. The driver turned out to be a relative of the summer residents, and simply was dropping off a note. But this was a good example of cooperative neighborhooding at work.

Thefts are most likely to occur when isolated rural homeowners are absent, but a few simple precautions can reduce your chances of being chosen. Ask the local newspaper reporter not to print news about your vacation until after you return. If your location is vulnerable you may not want to advertise your overnight trips either, because news travels fast in a small town, and a robber might be listening at the post office or local store. Keep clothes hanging on an outside clothesline, park a car in the driveway, install an outdoor security light that comes on at dusk, and arrange indoor lights and radios to go on and off in different rooms at random times. All these may help create an impression that someone is home, or will be soon. If you will be away for a prolonged period, consider a housesitter.

On the theory that what thieves don't know won't help them, some people decline to open their homes for charity house and garden tours. The visitors have been known to include people plotting a future job. People who work away from home, or those who are otherwise away a great deal, can use opaque curtains to keep crooks from examining the interior of their homes.

If you operate a home business, try to deal in checks and credit cards rather than cash. Large amounts of money in a cash register or drawer are sure to be noticed and probably discussed, so keep it out of sight. Make trips to the bank often (and at varied hours).

Vandalism can be an even more frightening threat than robbery because it seems to strike without reason. Strong locks are often effective for discouraging vandals and amateur crooks, but if anyone truly wants to get into your home, a lock seldom proves to be much of a barrier. You may decide to invest in a sophisticated system that will detect a break-in and then call you at another number, a designated neighbor, or the police station. The device can be programmed to call three or four numbers in sequence, if calls go unanswered. Many vacation homes in our area have these devices, and more than once surprised crooks have been caught red-handed because of them.

If you buy such a system, be sure your outside telephone wires are protected or concealed so they cannot be cut easily. To discourage crooks some people post signs warning that an alarm system is in place, but other homeowners feel that such signs merely advertise that there is something inside worth stealing.

Dogs have long been used as country sentinels. Some folks have found that geese are light sleepers and have better hearing than dogs; the birds quickly alert their owners whenever strangers are about, or when wild animals or the neighbor's cattle are invading their garden.

Fire Protection

In the city people barely look up when a fire siren howls and trucks race down the street. But when the fire whistle blasts in our town, not a single individual over the age of five is unconcerned. We check to see if smoke is billowing up anywhere in the neighborhood, and call friends to ask where the fire is and if our help is needed. No matter what's burning, it's likely that someone we know is in trouble.

Because of the isolation of country homes, fires are often more frightening than in the city, and the number of old cellar holes scattered all over rural areas attest to this fact. The fire department is probably far away and the roads may not be good, especially in wintry weather. Rural fire departments are staffed by volunteers, and although they are generally competent, most of the crew may be at work when a call comes in.

Fire is a real threat, one that we keep in mind year-round. Homes heated with wood are at risk from poorly maintained stove pipes and chimneys. Barns can be torched by lightning and the spontaneous combustion of hay. Sparks from burning rubbish may ignite cut-over woodlands and dry unmown hay.

Just as country dwellers must be more aware of their water supply and sewage disposal than people on town systems, they also take much more responsibility for their own fire control. We place extinguishers in the kitchen, near the furnace, and in the workshop, and we check them frequently to see that the pressure is still up. Many rural folks permanently attach a garden hose to a basement faucet, making sure it is long enough to reach every part of the house.

Since there will be no hydrants around, a small pond close to the house is good fire insurance—and, in fact, it may lower your insurance rates. Ideally, a pond should be near enough to the road for the fire truck to reach it quickly. In winter, you may want to put a thick float of Styrofoam on the pond so the water won't freeze deeply in that spot and you can break through the ice easily. If a pond is too expensive or impractical, a small above-ground swimming pool works well. We have one in our backyard—15 feet in diameter and 4 feet high—and it holds over 2,500 gallons of water.

Because fuses are likely to blow in a fire, make sure your water pump is on an electric circuit by itself so it will be less likely to blow if a short occurs elsewhere. You might also consider buying a small gasoline-powered pump to draw water from a swimming pool or pond.

Have a ladder accessible that is high enough to reach your upstairs windows in case that is the only way into and out of the house. Keep your chimneys in good repair, and don't let the creosote build up. If fire starts in the stovepipe or chimney, treat it with a fire extinguisher. Water can easily crack hot bricks, tile, or concrete, and such breaks are difficult to repair. Fire extinguishers also do far less damage to your home than water.

❖

From experience we have learned not to place a smoke detector too close to the wood stove, because the alarm goes off whenever we stoke the stove. Instead we have installed a heat sensor near our stovepipe, and now a loud bell lets us know if it is getting too hot. If you have sheds and barns, equip them with smoke or heat detectors that will ring a bell in the house.

You'll want to plan alternate exits from your home in case some doors are blocked by fire. Keep a chain fire ladder available by a second-floor window. Store flashlights in a handy place, and make sure everyone knows where they are. You can install emergency lights that come on when the regular lights go off; they will help you find your way out of a smoky room even if you are partly asleep. You may even want to hold occasional family drills so everyone is familiar with the escape routes and knows how to call the fire department.

Many times we've read of rural families escaping with only their night clothes and traveling miles to a neighbor's in bitter winter weather. Because of this possibility, foresighted people in frigid climates sometimes keep a few warm clothes in an outbuilding.

Coping with a Cooler Climate

If you are making a move to a cooler climate you'll soon learn that the best way to adjust to subzero winters, damp springs, and changeable fall seasons is to dress for the weather rather than by the calendar. When in doubt, layer.

When we visited suburban friends last winter, we were mildly shocked to find them driving off to a concert on snowy roads wearing dress shoes and lightweight jackets. Unlike us they had never been conditioned to rural driving. We've been thrown into snowbanks by unexpected black ice, and marooned with a flat tire late at night. And, we occasionally stop to help fellow travelers out of the ditch. With these emergencies in mind, we always carry insulated overalls and boots when driving in winter. We also keep in the car a flashlight, jumper cables, flares, snow shovel, nylon tow rope, blanket, and several candles for emergency heat.

Since ice storms, blizzards, and winds occasionally isolate those who live on rural roads, we keep on hand such foodstuffs as powdered milk and canned foods, as well as a nonelectric can opener. People who depend on electricity to pump their water can keep a supply of bottled water. You'll get by nicely if you have firewood and a wood stove, and a few kerosene lamps, lanterns, and candles. We've used Sterno in the summer when the wood stove would be too hot. We even keep a battery radio on hand, too, to keep in touch with the rest of the world. Each of us has special necessities. One friend says she keeps a jar of ground coffee on hand, after having a caffeine fit for two days when her electric grinder had no power.

You can buy an alarm system that tells you when your power is off, so you can take appropriate action: solar water heaters must be covered because if the pump can't circulate the water, they will get too hot; and greenhouse plants that depend on automatic watering must be watered by hand.

A voltmeter is another handy gadget that tells you if your power is dangerously low and apt to burn out motors. We once lost a freezer because we didn't realize we were in a brownout.

Emergency Generators

You may not find an electric generator to be a necessity, as it is for dairy farmers who depend heavily on milking and refrigeration equipment. But one makes sense if you are absolutely dependent on a furnace, water pump, or freezer, if you need water for animals, or if you own an automated greenhouse.

Living in a remote spot brings with it the chance that a flood, hurricane, or tornado may knock out the power for days. If your electric lines run through woods, you should expect an occasional outage whether or not a natural disaster happens, since trees and limbs can fall at any time. And there are other unpredictable causes. We once lost our electricity when a drunk driver hit a pole; another time, lightning burned out a substation; and one winter the 45-below temperatures contracted the wires so tight that some of them snapped.

Generators come in many sizes, so figure out your needs before buying one and be prepared to have the necessary fuel on hand to operate it. Whatever model you choose, start the engine periodically to make sure it is in running condition. You may want to consider models that run on bottled gas instead of gasoline, because they are easier to start and keep running after long periods of disuse.

Chapter 7

HOLDING ON TO TIME AND PRIVACY

Robert Frost's time-worn line, "Good fences make good neighbors," holds more than a kernel of truth. We need boundaries of respect, not only for each other's property but also for each other's time and privacy.

In the days before telephones, rural neighbors dropped in on each other without warning. The visited party was usually glad for a breather from the hard farm work, and welcomed an excuse to stop and talk. Often the company pitched in and helped.

Times have changed. You may have a problem managing your time in the country, because both rural and urban visitors often categorize those who operate home businesses or part-time farms as not having real jobs (perhaps because the work takes place in a setting that appears idyllic). So it is that friends who wouldn't think of dropping in unannounced on a banker, teacher, or shop supervisor nevertheless make unannounced visits on those who work at home. When these visits jeopardize a critical work deadline or planting schedule, they may jeopardize a friendship as well.

We've spoken with home-based artisans whose work is interrupted by an exceptional number of visitors. Glass blowers, potters, sculptors, weavers, furniture makers—all need customers for their products, of course, but giving people tours and advice can drain much time from the workday. One home-based printer tells us that retired printers and newspaper men for miles around drop by frequently to reminisce about the days of lead type and stone makeup. It is difficult for him, and it may be for you, to handle such people without hurting their feelings, and still get your work done.

House guests can be another problem, particularly if you move to a region noted for its superb skiing, hunting, fishing, mountain climbing, or other leisure attractions, because your city friends may regard your home as a vacation resort. One autumn Sunday in our church, a neighbor of ours noted that the sermon was going to be about the feeding of the five thousand, and whispered that it sounded a great deal like her summer at home.

Some guests may not even be friends of yours. A farm family in our neighborhood was surprised on a summer hay day when a couple they didn't know appeared in their front yard with dog, children, and sachels, cheerfully announcing, "Our mutual friends, the Walkers, said to be sure to look you up and say hello. We'll pitch in and help, so don't worry about us!" Our neighbors rearranged their life and became hosts. The friends' friends stayed four days and had a wonderful time. But the hosts lost many hours of work in the garden and hayfield, and the woman was exhausted physically and emotionally from arranging meals and extra laundry.

As far as we know, there is no sure-fire solution to the problem of controlling your working time if people drop by when you work where you live. Each ameliorating tactic seems unfriendly and even callous. Popular authors Scott and Helen Nearing, best known for *Living the Good Life*, finally posted a sign at their gate which read, Visiting Hours, Afternoons 2-5 P.M. They also developed a well-organized system for encouraging their visitors to paint buildings, construct stone walls, and help with the garden.

Depending on your occupation, you may be able to come up with jobs you can do while chatting with visitors, but this will be difficult if you are running a noisy lathe or composing music. By summoning up plenty of self discipline, you can escape the demands and temptations of the social world by scheduling unconventional working hours. A friend of ours begins writing every day at 4:30 A.M., and is assured of being undisturbed until 9. Another writer had his wife fend off phone calls and visitors until noon; gradually everyone learned his self-imposed schedule, and those who didn't were politely asked to wait until later in the day.

Some people with home businesses have found privacy by building a hide-away studio or workshop in the woods; others rent office space in town. A workplace located away from the home creates a psychological boundary, and it becomes obvious to people that you actually are

❖

working. You also may find that you are more likely to keep normal work hours.

If all else fails, you might try the old "suitcase at the door" ruse. This is reputed to have been created by Florida retirees whose homes were frequented by winter vacationers from the North. If unexpected guests appeared the host would say, "Sorry we can't invite you to stay, but we're expecting friends who will be arriving anytime." At the first chance one of the family slips out, phones a neighbor, and within minutes a group of "guests" arrive shouting fond hellos as they unload a car full of suitcases!

Summertime

We chuckle when we hear the lyrics, "Summertime, when the livin' is easy. . . ." Gershwin, born in Brooklyn, probably only dreamt of what it was like to live in the country year-round.

People who visit the country to relax on vacations may find that they become workaholics when they move in permanently—tied to the chores of home, garden, shelter, animals, and visitors. Weekends are only an opportunity to get another job done. On hikes, we prefer to walk in *neighbors'* woods, to observe all the work *they* should be doing.

Sometimes it's easy to forget why we are living in the country. Our nursery business kept us going spring and summer from dawn till late at night, and one day we posted a sign for ourselves: Don't Forget to Smell the Flowers.

Armed with this thought, we manage, occasionally, not to feel guilty when we take time to actually look at the daylilies we sell, enjoy a picnic lunch beside the brook, inspect a robin's nest filled with perfect aquamarine eggs, or walk into the meadow at dawn to see the dew-covered spider webs sparkling like diamonds in the morning sunlight. We make homemade ice cream, and invite family and friends for ice cream socials, paddle the canoe on a nearby pond, or go to the county fair. Our nighttime walks to the brook put the world in perspective—the constellations, Milky Way, Northern Lights, and the more earthly glowworms, fireflies, and hoots of a bear. When we look back on each year, on New Year's Day, with journal in hand, these are the times we talk about; forgotten are the new roof or the remodeled septic system.

Posting Land

"Posting" means putting up signs that forbid others to hunt, fish, trap, or trespass on your land. Anyone can tack up a sign that says Posted or Keep Out, of course, but to legally post your land you must do it according to the laws of your state. The signs must be of a certain size and material and include your name and the date. They must be placed in specified locations, and in many states, the fact that you are doing so is recorded annually in the proper town or county office.

Why do people post their land? One winter we were concerned that our new Christmas tree plantation was being devastated by snowmobiles and cross-country skiers, and up went the signs. You may want to prevent people from entering an old building that's in dangerous condition; stop fisherpersons from trampling fields of grain; keep hunters from shooting farm animals and pets; or shoo away trespassers who build campfires and litter your property.

Posting gives other messages, however. It may be interpreted to mean that you do not want to share the fish and game on your property with outsiders, and long-time hunters in the area may consider it an unfriendly gesture. To avoid possible ill will, talk with other landowners about local attitudes toward posting. If public feeling is against it, the signs may keep out only the thoughtful people who would do no damage anyway—while having no effect on the less considerate. And by allowing hikers, hunters, and fisherpersons access to parts of your property that you don't see often, they may help keep an eye on it for you. If shooting near your home worries you, see if your state allows you to post a small "safety zone" in the area around your buildings. Our neighbors who used this method say it worked better than large-scale posting of hundreds of acres. Hunters thoughtfully kept their distance, and our friends didn't have to worry about their children and golden retriever.

Chapter 8

WHERE THE WILD THINGS ARE

One newcomer to New England frets every time we meet her because her husband has lured her up to this wilderness, away from the galleries and museums of New York. She doesn't seem to be aware of the wonderful paintings that nature provides for her daily, in the landscape just outside her windows—snow sculptures whipped up by the wind, fuchsia sunrises, luminous golden autumn leaves. She misses a great deal in the endlessly changing woods and wild pastures by not taking an interest in what's happening there.

We are always amazed at how differently individuals react to something so straightforward as a walk in the country. Some, like our acquaintance, seem oblivious to the beauty and activity of the natural world surrounding them, and are intent only on getting from place to place. Others sense danger in every insect, weed, and animal. Still others are thoroughly absorbed in the animal life, geology, and weather phenomena. They read the landscape like a giant chart, identifying birds, animal tracks and noises, wildflowers, grasses, shrubs and trees. They spot glacial markings, arrowheads, and fossils the rest of us usually miss, and it is these people who get the most out of country life.

But nature is not completely wholesome, and a certain caution is necessary. There are wild plants in every area that are unsafe to eat, and animals that can be dangerous, and it is important to know where it is safe and legal to walk and collect "wild things." Trips with knowledgeable companions, and reading books and field guides about the nature of your region are good ways to begin your education and enjoyment of birds, fish, stars, plants, animals, geology, or whatever

interests you. You may also want to take advantage of the organized hikes and naturalist lectures of the Audubon Society or Sierra Club.

Experts can also help you identify plants that are endangered by people. Even if you only pick flowers of certain plants, they may not be able to seed and produce offspring the following years. Don't be tempted to transplant them to your garden, either; most wild plants have a favorite place to grow, and do not do well in spots not of their own choosing.

The Edibles

Few of us would consider foraging for our entire food supply unless testing our abilities on a survival hike. But on our place, we look forward to such seasonal wild treats as strawberries and raspberries, and try to beat the bears to the low-bush blueberries that ripen on nearby hillsides. We are among the country dwellers who watch for edible fiddlehead ferns to peep up along wooded roadsides in the spring, and guard unashamedly the secret location of prolific wild butternut trees. We gather wild peppermint for tea, dandelion greens and watercress for salads, and pick caraway seeds along unsprayed roadsides. Although we are not confident enough of our own knowledge to select wild mushrooms for dinner, we envy the fungus hunters who troop over the fields and woodlands each summer in search of their favorite delicacy.

Before you take your basket on an expedition, remind yourself that poisonous plants and berries abound in every area, and many resemble their edible companions. Inedible blue cohosh has often been mistaken for the blueberry, for example, and both deadly nightshade and baneberry look good enough to be a tasty treat. Each year we hear horror stories about people who have mistakenly consumed the wrong variety of mushroom, or have stewed rhubarb leaves for greens. One of our friends nearly died from eating hellebore on a spring scavenging trip. She thought it was some sort of wild corn.

Some plants are dangerous to touch as well. Poison oak and ivy abound in many places, as do stinging nettles, and it is prudent to learn to recognize them before you walk around the countryside in shorts and sandals.

The potential dangers should not stop you from enjoying wild foods and hikes in the woods, but if you are not knowledgeable, take your first nature hikes with someone who is experienced. And be certain young children have learned to recognize poisonous plants, as well.

Whose Woods These Are
We Ought to Know

Because country roads are usually not bordered by No Trespassing signs and high walls, it is tempting to think that everything not cordoned off or secured is public property. Perfectly honest people have been known to cut Christmas trees, dig shrubs, pick apples, and collect rocks from stone walls as if they were in the public domain, simply because the area seemed uninhabited and wild.

Although years ago, when rural farmlands covered hundreds of acres, no one might have cared, these days people who own country acreage are likely to be possessive about it. A large lumber company would probably not mind a bit if you were to gather berries on their large tracts of land, nor would most other large landowners. Nevertheless, it is best to ask for permission before you pick or picnic on any land that is not your own, even if you find no Keep Out signs.

Coping with Our Fellow Creatures

Most of us are thrilled to encounter an unexpected wild fox, deer, or bobcat. We remember how excited we were the spring morning a black bear staggered sleepily across our road, and we remember our moment of fright when a partridge flew out of a snowbank at the toes of our snowshoes. We love the bird songs, the spiraling howl of wolves at sunrise, and the otter slides on the brook.

Occasionally newcomers to the country are startled to find that everything about the wild world is not gentle and loving. We were walking with a friend one evening when we heard the piercing scream of a rabbit that apparently was seized by a fox or wolf. Our friend was upset, and later told us that the sound lingered in her memory for days. Her Thornton Burgess image of happy woodland creatures was replaced by something closer to reality.

The unknown in nature can be worrisome. Our five-year-old nephew, born and bred in suburbia, was obviously uncomfortable on a winter picnic to our maple woods. In spite of his mother's reassurances, he was insistent that dangerous "wild things" were not far away. Chris was very happy when we reached home safely, and didn't guess that the creatures in the forest were probably more frightened of him than he of them.

We would not belittle the potential danger of meeting a poisonous snake, rabid animal, startled moose, mother bear, or cornered bobcat, but ordinarily a wild animal tries to avoid any close encounter with humans. In some areas an abundance of hikers and campers, combined with an absence of hunters, have led to animals losing their fear of humans and becoming aggressive and dangerous. Coyotes, mountain lions, and bears that live near human habitats occasionally threaten people, but such encounters are rare. To avoid danger, simply use discretion. Never feed friendly looking deer, or get close to a strange acting fox, and don't wander between a mother bear and her cubs. Common sense is as important in the woodlands as in the subway.

After living on the edge of the North Woods for many years, the only encounters from which we have emerged hurting were those times we stumbled into a nest of black hornets, or their equally vicious cousins, the yellow jackets. We have also learned not to walk across a lawn of blossoming clover in sandals that scoop up bees, or to venture into unfamiliar snake country without being on guard.

Newcomers to our area are often surprised by the armies of insects that co-exist with the humans. Black flies often make it impossible to enjoy the outdoors on warm June nights, and clouds of cluster flies invade all the buildings in early fall. We have learned to place ant traps about in the spring, so the creatures won't take over the kitchen and pantry; to keep door and window screens tight to keep out the hordes of moths that gather around our lights in summer; and to fight off the earwigs that multiply by astronomical numbers.

When Wild Creatures Become Too Domestic

Last spring, as the scent of roasting turkey wafted out through a kitchen window, there was scratching at the door. Thinking it was the cat, we opened it and found a skunk with a hopeful look on his face. Later, our uneducated cat tackled it in our back shed, and the smell quickly spread throughout the house. We aired it out, but realized we were still carriers the next morning in church when we saw the puzzled glances of the people sitting near us.

Many rural gardeners find their benevolent attitude toward animals fades when their choice plantings are devastated by the creatures they admire. When we were selling fruit trees, over and over we heard sad tales from people who had set them out and were shocked to find several years of growth wiped out by deer in only a few hours. More than once those herds of beautiful brown-eyed deer have devastated our berry patch, Christmas tree plantation, and orchard. Some years the rabbits, woodchucks, porcupines, mice, and raccoons consume more vegetables and berries than we do.

Similarly, our baby chickens and geese have nourished skunks, weasels, and foxes. Our neighbors have lost bee colonies to bears, and young calves and sheep to wolves. Nearby ponds have been drained by water-loving muskrats, and communities of beavers have chewed down every pondside tree. We even find reason to complain about the wonderful birds, despite their beauty, songs, and insect control. They grab our strawberries, raspberries, and blueberries mere minutes after they ripen, it seems. Squirrels not only harvest every nut they can carry, but appear to delight in nipping the buds off roses and lilies, and in taking one and only one bite from every apple they can reach. One year an invasion of garter snakes made some of our customers flee to their cars with threats of never returning.

We find ourselves arguing with those who defend bats by quoting how many millions of insects they consume on a summer night. The furry creatures have collected in our barn lofts and attics to the point that we have considered marketing guano. We have found that the mail-order electronic sonar repellents keep out squirrels, mice, and rats, but they haven't worked for bats. The only solution we've found is to keep their nesting places well lit and cool; then, after they have left for the winter, we carefully seal up any openings they might squeeze through next spring.

After years of trying to outwit the deer with noisemakers, foul smells, and other repellents, we finally built a 9-foot-high, sheep-tight fence all around our gardens, orchard, and nursery.

The fence keeps the deer out, but doesn't discourage mice, rabbits, woodchucks, or porcupines. These smaller animals can be controlled by electric fences and mothballs, and our more determined neighbors prefer woodchuck bombs, guns, and traps. We spread orchard bait just before winter each year to control field mice. A barking dog often proves to be good protection, but it must be trained to drive away the invaders and not tangle with skunks or porcupines.

Your local game warden can advise you on how to cope with beavers and other protected species by trapping and moving them to another location.

Hunting, Fishing, and Trapping

Although hunting, fishing, and trapping are denounced by animal rights groups, those on the other side of the argument maintain that their activities keep animal herds in balance, prevent mass starvation from overpopulation, and keep animals from becoming a menace to humans and agriculture. People who have grown up in the country are more likely to find hunting acceptable than city dwellers, since it has always been part of their lives. Transplants from the city often find the question of killing wild animals something that must be sorted out in their minds, and they wrestle with the question: Exactly how much dominion should humans take over the fish and animals? Whatever stance you take, you will find kindred spirits among your neighbors.

If animals are a problem but you don't want to hurt them, a box trap (the Have-a-Heart is one brand) will capture them alive. If you move the captured animal to a new neighborhood, pick a place that is not inhabited, if possible. And make sure the animal's new home is some distance away from yours. One of our neighbors caught six weasels in his barn over the course of last winter, and he transported each of them three miles away. Then he got suspicious, and colored the seventh with green dye before releasing it. A few days later he caught a green weasel—apparently for the eighth time.

Rural people often supplement their food supply with wild meat, but many of our neighbors who fish and hunt regard these activities primarily as a sport and care little if they don't catch or shoot anything. Like golfing to a businessman, it provides an acceptable excuse for a rural workaholic to get away for a day. In many states, the opening weekend of deer, moose, or elk season comes close to being an official holiday.

Hunting and fishing are regulated by state fish and game departments. They issue licenses, usually through local municipal offices,

❖

and use the fees collected to hire law enforcement wardens, establish wildlife preserves, stock brooks with fish, and run conservation camps for children. They attempt to keep game populations stable by adjusting the length of hunting or fishing seasons in accordance with the supply of fish and game. The timing of the legal seasons, consequently, may vary from year to year, so keep up to date on the current regulations if you are a hunter or fisherperson. It could be embarrassing (and expensive) to drive proudly through town with a deer on your car, and suddenly discover that the season had been delayed a week that year.

In most states, landowners and their families (but not guests) can hunt and fish legally on their own property without a license, but they must still obey fish and game laws. A game warden may give you permission to shoot animals out of season if they are devastating your crops.

Chapter 9
IMPROVING YOUR LOT

In giving a talk to a gardening group, we once used the word "dirt." A club member interrupted. " 'Dirt,' " she said, disgustedly, "is something to sweep off the floor. 'Soil' is what you mean." We have tried since to use the proper terminology, but we grew up hearing the expression "poor dirt farmer." Though we were never sure whether "poor" referred to "dirt" or to "farmer," it is obvious that if the first is poor, the second is likely to be also.

The condition of your soil is very important, no matter what you call it. Orchards, berries, vegetables, nursery plants, grains, and even hay, all need deep, fertile soil to grow well.

Although you may be one of the few lucky buyers whose farm was previously owned by someone who kept the soil in peak condition, it is far more likely that it needs attention before it can successfully grow the crops you want. In most rural areas, even soil that was once fertile and lavishly productive has been impoverished by years of poor farm practices.

If you own more than a few acres of land, it is unlikely that the soil types are identical throughout your property; the most recent glacier to cover the northern United States left deposits of various soils in different pockets as it receded. Our hillside is quite alkaline, but the soil on neighboring hills only a few miles away is so acidic that it supports an entirely different type of plant life.

If you are growing a variety of crops, even in small amounts, you are most likely to be more successful if you take care to choose the best spot for each one. Most crops need a rich soil that will hold moisture without getting soggy. Potatoes need a deep, moderately acid soil; clover and alfalfa need one that is more alkaline; strawberries need a rich acid soil, but it doesn't need to be as deep as for some other crops; and blueberries do best in a very acid soil. The poorer areas of your land, even if unimproved, may be suitable for growing timber and firewood, and if kept fertilized, pasture grasses or Christmas trees.

The USDA Soil Conservation Service has classified the various soil types, and most areas have been surveyed and mapped. Your county agent will either be able to advise you or put you in touch with a specialist who can determine your soil's structure and help you manage it properly.

The original quality of the soil—before the land was cleared—is important, but the way the land has been used over the years has also influenced its present condition. Cultivation leaches out lime and fertilizer, and destroys humus. Both cultivation and over-grazing can cause erosion. The soil's history can have baffling consequences. New landowners we know were puzzled when they traced the poor growth and scab on their potatoes to an extremely alkaline patch of soil. When they questioned the previous owners they found that large amounts of wood ashes had been dumped in that spot for many years.

Nutrients and Humus

Humus, the material produced by decomposition of organic matter, is a basic part of healthy soil. It is rich in nutrients, retains moisture, and provides a loose medium in which roots can grow easily.

❖

Before soil conservation and fertilization were well understood, farmers tried to restore a field's fertility by letting it lie fallow and uncropped for a year or more, then plowing under grass and weeds to add humus and nutrients to the soil. This method was only partially successful, and unless the fertility was restored with fertilizer of some sort, the farmland usually had to be abandoned after a generation or two.

Worn-out soil not only lacks the major nutrients—nitrogen, phosphorus, and potassium—but also such trace elements as boron, iron, and zinc. These minerals must be present in the soil to enable plants to grow well, and to provide better nourishment in the food grown for us and our animals. These necessary elements can be added to the soil, but unless a sufficient amount of humus is also present, the soil is not alive and cannot produce healthy plants. Humus has the ability to absorb nutrients and hold them for release as they are needed.

Animal and poultry farms usually have an abundance of one of the richest sources of humus—manure. Farmers once gave it away freely in our area, but these days you're lucky if you live near a farm that will *sell* it to you. Most of us have to find other ways of adding organic matter, and it can be a challenge to one's ingenuity. Peat moss works well for small areas, but is very expensive if your project is a large one. Nurseries and market gardens often convert other materials to humus by composting them. They collect truckloads of leaves from city streets and parks, and wastes from slaughterhouses, sawmills, and food-processing plants.

Most of us who garden in the country wouldn't dream of being without a compost heap. It not only produces excellent fertilizer, but it's also an ecologically sound way to dispose of garbage, farm refuse, manure, old hay or ensilage, weeds, leaves, and garden wastes. We put compost on our fruit trees and berry plants, till it into our vegetable and flower gardens, and use a great deal in potting soil mixtures and in the holes we dig for newly transplanted trees and shrubs.

The term "compost pile" is used to describe anything from a pile of rotting wood shavings in a back corner of the yard to a scientifically layered pile of various organic materials placed in an elaborate container made from wood, fiberglass, or cement blocks. Entire books have been written on how to build a proper compost pile and how to encourage the materials in them to decompose quickly, without odor.

The Hills simply pile alternate layers of manure, soil, and green matter between walls of cement block.

Our method is simple. Next to our vegetable garden we have constructed two side-by-side bins of cement blocks, piled on three sides. They measure 6 feet square and 3 feet high. In one space we alternate layers of organic material (vegetable garbage, garden wastes, weeds, maple leaves, grass clippings) with layers of soil and layers of manure; and we keep it moist so the fermenting materials won't heat up too much and destroy the nitrogen. The heap soon fills with earthworms, which help it settle and decompose rapidly into a rich, black humus. When one enclosure is filled we let it rest until the composting process is completed; and then we use it as the other bin is being filled. It takes about a year for a pile to decompose; if a pile isn't completely composted, we use it from the bottom first. One of our friends has only one compost pile, but it is very high. She keeps adding new material to the top, and digs out the finished compost from the bottom.

Although compost supplies humus, moderate amounts of the most important nutrients, and many trace elements, you may need to provide additional amounts of nitrogen, phosphorus, and potash for good growth. These elements can be provided by adding farm manure, dried manure, or a commercial dry or liquid natural fertilizer. Organic gardeners in the country have a wide choice of materials which add nutrients to the soil. Some, such as fallen leaves, lawn clippings, and mill wastes will probably be available to you for only the cost of collecting them and bringing them home.

Manure

Fresh animal manure can be spread directly on hayfields, orchards, berries, and other perennial crops in late fall or very early spring. It can also be used for sheet composting (see below). All manure, except rabbit and guano, which can be used fresh, should be at least partly rotted when applied to gardens in the later spring. Fresh manure can cause an off-taste in vegetables.

Manure adds humus as well as nutrients to the soil. Its value depends on how it has been handled and stored. If not stored under cover, it looses nitrogen quickly to rain and sunlight. Poultry and horse manures are considered "hot." They should either be composted as soon as they are produced, or mixed with cold manures (such as cattle and pig) or other organic matter to prevent them from "burning out" their nutrients as they ferment. Farmers used to throw their horse manure into the pig pen each day, where the pigs would keep it aerated and mix it with their own.

Protect the nutrients in manure after spreading by tilling it into the soil as soon as possible after application; or, if you are spreading it on fields, plan to apply it just before heavy rain so that the rainwater can wash it in. As we mentioned, fresh poultry manure is one of the richest and strongest, but because it can ferment and kill young plants, it should be used sparingly or in composted form near plants. Cow, goat, and sheep manure are fairly rich in nutrients, and horse and pig are less so, but all are good sources of humus. Guano, the dried bat manure that has been collected in large caves, is a rich source of nitrogen and other elements.

Because most dry organic fertilizers work slowly, many people use the liquid variety to speed up the growth of plants. Liquid seaweed (kelp) and fish emulsion are especially rich in nutrients. Like many gardeners we are firm believers in using manure tea. It can give plants a quick shot of nutrients, and stimulates them to grow quickly at the right time—an important factor if your growing season is short.

To concoct it, we throw a couple of shovels full of fresh or dried manure into a burlap bag, tie it up, and drop it into a large plastic garbage can full of water. The resulting "tea" is a fast-working tonic for our flower and vegetable garden.

Apply liquid fertilizer once every week or two on flowering plants and vegetables as long as they seem to benefit from it. For trees and shrubs, however, use it only until mid-summer, like any other fertilizer, in order not to encourage any late season growth that might be damaged by fall frosts.

Sheet Composting

An excellent way to create superior soil for a vegetable garden, berry patch, or nursery is sheet composting, or field composting as it is sometimes called. Some of the most beautiful gardens we have ever seen were testimonials to this method.

The sheet composting method creates humus right where you plant rather than in a separate pile. Manure can simply be spread over a hayfield, but to improve the soil for a cultivated crop, several layers of organic materials are spread over the entire plot. Leaves, shredded bark, other mill wastes, spoiled hay, silage (hay or corn stored in a silo), peat, garbage, and garden wastes are some of the materials that are layered alternately with manure. Each layer should be at least 3 to 5 inches thick before settling, and the total thickness can vary from inches to nearly a foot after settling. Any moist material such as fresh farm manure should be covered immediately with a layer of green matter such as hay, shredded bark, or waste from wood-working mills to preserve its nutrient value. Cover dry leaves and hay with a heavier material (or apply them during a rainstorm) so that they won't blow away. As a final layer, cover the area with newly cut, unwilted hay or straw to keep the other layers moist and to speed decomposition. If the soil is heavy and needs to be lightened, a layer of moderately coarse sand can be used as a final cover.

Complete decomposition may take two to three years, depending on the materials used and the amount and frequency of rainfall. When the process is complete the layers will have turned into rich, loose, black soil, perfect for planting.

Although sheet composting is laborious and time consuming,

when done properly, the results are impressive. Because it takes time for sheet compost to decompose, you will need two garden plots—one to use while the other is composting.

Green Manure

We divide our garden plot into two, and plant millet on one half each year as a soil builder. We plow it under and allow it to rot in the soil. This is known as green manuring. Whenever you want to improve the soil over a large area, and sheet composting would be impractical, this process can be a realistic alternative. Although green manuring bypasses the animal, it nevertheless builds the soil and provides a cover that prevents erosion.

Prior to planting, the field should be plowed, cultivated, and fertilized with a complete fertilizer. Your county extension service or farm store can recommend the best variety of grain for your region, the proper amount, and how much lime and fertilizer will be needed for your soil. If you plant only an acre or two, you can probably do the job yourself by using a two-wheeled tiller and then fertilizing and seeding by hand. But for larger plots, it's best to hire a neighboring farmer or contractor to do the complete job. It makes little sense to buy thousands of dollars worth of machinery you will rarely use.

For *spring* planting, the green manure crop is usually oats, millet, buckwheat, or rye. In late summer, it is plowed under rather than harvested, and the lush tops and extensive root system decompose to add a wealth of humus and fertility to the soil.

For planting in *late summer* or *early fall,* use winter rye and plow it under the following spring. The soil will be ready for planting vegetables and other crops as soon as the rye has partially decomposed, probably within a few weeks.

If the soil is in moderately good condition, one well-fertilized cover crop will probably be enough to prepare the soil for use. If your soil is badly worn out, however, you may want to plant a second crop—winter rye—directly after tilling in your spring crop of oats or millet.

Another common method to improve poor soil is mixing clover seed with the oats or millet. Don't harvest the grain or plow it under, but allow it to freeze and die naturally, making a nice straw mulch for the clover, which will live over. Grow the clover an additional year, and then plow it under. Since it is a legume, it will add valuable nitrogen to the soil.

Acidity-Alkalinity

In addition to the nutrient level of the soil, you must also be concerned with the pH, a measure used to indicate the degree of acidity or alkalinity. If your soil is rich in humus, you don't usually have to be as concerned about it, but even under the best conditions some crops are unable to make use of the fertilizer in the soil unless the pH is right for them. A pH of 7 is neutral, 6 acid, and 5 very acid; 8 is considered too alkaline for most crops (see chart on page 68). Most crops grow best at a pH between 5.5 and 7.

To determine the pH of your soil, buy a simple, inexpensive soil test kit, or have your extension service test it for you. Soil can vary widely within a small area, so make several tests, and test your soil each time you plant a new crop. We live in an area that is rich in limestone, but you may very likely find that your soil isn't. Add 10 pounds of lime per 100 square feet to raise the pH one point. Like us, you will probably find it is difficult to spread lime by hand, especially finely ground limestone, so you might add a spreader to your list of equipment investments. Small push spreaders are good enough for small lawns and gardens, but you will need a large, tractor-drawn one for fields and pastures. Fertilizer and lawn companies may be able to spread the lime for you, saving you both the cost of the equipment and also a lot of heavy lifting.

You may have a soil that is too alkaline for acid-loving crops such as blueberries, potatoes, strawberries, beets, ginseng, blackberries, and certain nursery crops. It can be made more acid by adding peat moss or cottonseed meal. Because several months must pass before these materials are effective, we acidify the soil by digging large holes for each bush and filling them with acid soil from a peat bog or pine woods. After planting, and each year thereafter, we apply a mulch of pine needles. These plants nearly always thrive in their new environment.

Commercial growers often use sulfur to acidify their land. Your fertilizer supplier can tell you how much to use for your crop. Aluminum sulfate is commonly sold for that purpose, too, but even in small amounts it can poison the soil and impart an unpleasant taste to berries. We advise against using it, although it is a product that occurs naturally in the environment.

Whether you raise or lower the pH of your soil, the first treatment should not be the last. Additional applications will probably be needed every two or three years. Rains and melting snow leach away lime in soils that are naturally acid, and at the same time

pH Recommendations

Neutral or Alkaline (pH 7 or more)

Alfalfa	Cabbage	Celery	Hydrangea	Parsley
Arborvitae	Calendula	Clematis	Lettuce	Petunia
Asparagus	Carrot	Clover	Lilac	Sweet pea
Barberry	Cauliflower	Geranium	Nasturtium	Wheat

Near Neutral to Neutral (pH 6.5 to 7)

Apple	Chrysanthemum	Endive	Onion	Raspberry
Aster	Corn	Fir, balsam	Pansy	Rhubarb
Beet	Cosmos	Gladiolus	Pea	Rose
Broccoli	Cucumber	Hollyhock	Peony	Soybean
Buckwheat	Dahlia	Iris	Poinsettia	Spinach
Carnation	Delphinium	Marigold	Poppy	
Chives	Eggplant	Melon	Radish	

Acid (pH 5.5 to 6)

Bean	Franklinia	Oats	Potato	Strawberry
Begonia	Gooseberry	Parsnip	Pumpkin	Tomato
Blackberry	Grape	Pepper	Rutabaga	Turnip
Bleeding heart	Hemlock	Phlox	Rye	Wild flowers
Currant	Lily	Pine	Spruce, red	(most)
Ferns (most)	Oak	Plum	Squash	

Very Acid (pH below 5.5)

Azalea	Blueberry	Cranberry	Orchid	Rhododendron

percolate aluminum and iron compounds—which acidify—upward from the subsoil. In areas such as ours, however, rain causes lime to percolate from a large vein beneath. Consequently, in order to grow the blueberries we want, we must test the soil annually and treat it when necessary.

Mulch

When you walk through deep woods, you notice a beautiful forest floor covered with a lush layer of organic material. Dead leaves, needles, and ferns slowly decompose and create new, rich soil as they lie protectively around small seedlings. Trees and other plants obviously grow better when mulched, but since gardens, berry patches, and orchards do not naturally provide a protective cover as the forest does, we gardeners must collect and apply the materials if we are to imitate the ideal growing conditions that nature provides.

Mulches do a lot of good things. They protect bare soil from being baked in the sun, and keep it from blowing away in the wind. They prevent erosion by softening the blow of pounding raindrops. They insulate the earth by keeping it cooler on hot days and warmer on cool ones and at night, and they help keep vegetables and strawberries clean. As they decompose, mulches add humus and nutrients to the soil just as they do in the forest. Huge numbers of earthworms work continuously beneath the mulch, keeping the soil loose and thus encouraging tiny roots to grow rapidly.

We use a wide variety of materials. Lawn clippings, leaves, hay, shredded bark, and other farm and mill wastes are all good. Some gardeners use sawdust but we don't like it because it packs too hard and robs nitrogen from the soil as it decomposes.

Gardeners who live in Zone 5 or warmer may want to try Ruth Stout's famous mulch method. She covered her vegetable garden with a thick layer of hay and left it in place year-round, adding a fresh amount each spring. When she planted, she simply pulled the hay aside and planted the seeds, then pushed the hay back around the plants after they came up. The hay helped suppress the weeds, and the soil remained friable and loose, effectively freeing her from hoeing and tilling.

Much as we admire Ms. Stout, her method has never worked well for us in our northern garden, because we need to till our cold soil several times each spring to help it become warm enough for the seeds to start growing. Here in Zone 3, we apply mulch only after the soil has become thoroughly warm and the seedlings are several inches high.

Although we spread fast-rotting mulches such as chopped green hay or lawn clippings around the annual vegetables, we prefer more durable materials around our fruit trees. When the soil is thoroughly wet in the spring or after a hard rain, we spread a layer of compost or manure around each plant, 1 to 2 inches thick, and as far out as the branches spread. Over this layer we place magazines or newspapers about the thickness of one large city daily newspaper. Contrary to what some believe, we have found no appreciable difference between the mulching qualities of *New Republic* and *The National Review*, nor have we had any problem with toxic inks. We completely cover the paper with a third layer of hay, shredded bark, or shavings. This cover is attractive, eliminates weeds, and allows moisture to reach the roots.

Chapter 10
PROJECT PRIORITIES

During the two centuries that Lewis's family has lived on this homestead in northern Vermont, they have derived nearly their entire livelihood from the land. Over the years they adapted by changing crops as marketing conditions demanded. We and our ancestors have produced milk, butter, cream, cheese, and maple syrup; raised poultry, sheep, beef animals, pigs, bees, turkeys, ducks, horses, and geese; and grown nursery stock, fruits, berries, lumber, and firewood. Great-grandfather Hill's account book indicates that his livelihood came from supplying the needs of his family and neighbors from the cradle (he sold one for $2.15) to the grave (a casket brought $2.50).

Fortunately, those of us who live in the country today do not need the varied skills of the early homesteaders. Very few of our country neighbors make their living entirely from their farms. Most use their land only to supplement a retirement income, a home business, or salary from an off-the-farm job. They raise such things as vegetables, fruits, eggs, meat, wood, and honey for their family's needs, and some barter their surplus or sell it at a roadside stand or farmers' market, or to a local store or restaurant.

Whether you take on projects for profit or fun, or hopefully both, don't let them become too big for you to manage without wrecking your sanity. Forty years ago a dairy farmer in our town decided early in his career to keep his operation to the size he and his family could easily manage by themselves. His neighbors, meanwhile, followed the advice of government agents and farm equipment salespeople, adding more cows, installing bigger milk tanks, building larger barns, renting more land, and buying huge tractors and other machinery. In spite of the temptation, he followed his own drummer, and concentrated on a relatively small number of high-producing cows, kept his limited fields fertilized, and serviced his equipment. He paid off his mortgage and was able to retire early, while his colleagues continued to work longer and longer hours to pay for all their labor-saving machinery.

In moving to the country, the great variety of projects may make you feel like a kid with a bunch of quarters surrounded by video games. A good way to begin is to list all the projects your family has in mind. To clarify your ideas, you may want to make three lists: (1) the money-making ventures, if any; (2) those that produce food for home use, such as a vegetable garden or milk goat; (3) those that can be classified as hobbies, such as keeping a riding horse or landscaping the new pond.

Read about each choice in the following chapters to evaluate the time, expertise, and money required. You'll then be in a good position to eliminate certain choices and decide whether it is feasible to grow carrots, keep bees, or start up a bed-and-breakfast hostelry.

Try not to underestimate the amount of time and cash each project will require. Nonfarmers often do not understand that both money and hard work must be expended to raise food, for example. Our friends tell the story of the year they decided to send a fresh homegrown turkey as a Christmas gift to several city friends as a special treat. They bought a dozen small birds at the local farm store at $4 each, fed them many bags of grain at $15 per bag, and spent hours away from their regular chores building the necessary shelters, fences, and other equipment. In the fall they took a whole day off to dress and wrap the turkeys for their trip to the city. After Christmas, three of the well-meaning friends added to their thank-you notes that it was especially nice to know that "because you raised the turkey yourself, it didn't cost you a thing."

We have all seen advertisements that take advantage of this popular misconception. They promise big profits if you will raise mink, chinchillas, ginseng, or blueberries, or do some sort of craft at home in your spare time. No mention is made of expenses or uncertain markets. It is possible, of course, to earn money on such projects, but not quickly, and not without work and careful planning. One farmer we know enjoyed saying that it took at least ten years to master any one single farming enterprise, because that's the time necessary to make every possible mistake once.

A newcomer to our town recently became very excited about raising bees. He ordered a dozen swarms and bought a collection of second-hand hives that were advertised in the local paper. His backyard was soon buzzing with activity, and he was about to order several cases of glass jars for his honey when the state inspector found a fatal bee disease in his swarms. All the bees had to be destroyed. If our friend had researched his project thoroughly, he would have learned that danger always lurks in used bee equipment, and he would have carefully sterilized it.

We occasionally meet people who don't understand that peach and apple trees won't grow into perfect specimens without care, nor will wheat, berry bushes, or a crop of broccoli. Many have learned the hard way that syrup does not run directly from maple trees, and honey cannot be collected by opening a faucet at the bottom of the hive.

We should also point out that not all homegrown foods are cheaper than store-bought, if you count your labor. Raise a steer and you'll have tasty, chemical-free beef, but unless you raise most of its food you might get cheaper meat at the supermarket or from a neighbor who specializes in beef. The argument can also be made that you can't save money by raising pigs, lambs, poultry, or fish on a small scale. But this line of reasoning ignores the satisfaction and pleasure of growing and eating your own organically raised, chemical-free food.

There's no arguing the economic potential of raising your own fruits and vegetables, however. A former customer of ours took up gardening after she had commuted to work each day with a friend.

Twice a week the women shopped at a supermarket on their way home. Though their families were the same size, our friend was stunned to find that her grocery bill was usually twice as large as her co-worker's. Gradually she realized that homegrown food made the difference, and the supermarket subsequently lost some business as she began to garden.

Nontaxable Income

Some of the most satisfying income on a small homestead is nontaxable. The food and forest products that you grow and use yourself are good examples. Although it is difficult to place a dollar figure on this kind of income, a practical neighbor told us recently that he figured his large garden, orchard, berry patch, poultry flock, bees, and woodlot (combined with a freezer, canning equipment, and a root cellar) add at least $2,000 to his family's annual income.

He did not figure in his family's hourly wage, of course, but wrote off this time as exercise and recreation. He also likes the fact that no sales tax is computed on the items he no longer needs to buy, and no federal or state income tax is charged on the $2,000 he no longer has to earn to pay for food and fuel.

Another obvious way to save, and thus earn more nontaxable income, is to repair, build, and remodel your place without calling in outside help. We feel this is an important part of our income and we keep on hand a stock of such items as plastic steel, caulking compounds, tapes, glues, nails, screws, bolts, washers, extra V-belts, spark plugs, and plumbing and electrical parts.

If you are new at home repairing, consider hiring skilled tradespeople and working closely with them. You also can sign up for courses in wiring, carpentry, plumbing, and auto repair, and consult well-illustrated how-to books.

Operating a small farm has certain tax advantages that can save money on the Ides of April. As long as you are operating a bona fide business enterprise rather than a hobby farm or an operation obviously designed to lose money, you are entitled to fill out Schedule F and take advantage of the regulations. If at least two-thirds of your income is from farming or fishing, you can even file your return and pay your taxes before March 2 instead of April 15, and save filing and paying estimated taxes throughout the year.

It is important to know if you qualify as a farmer. Raising animals, poultry, and bees qualifies, but the government doesn't classify raising worms as farming. Orchard, berries, and vegetables also are considered agriculture by the IRS, but raising timber is not. Order a copy of the "Farmer's Tax Guide" from your IRS, and study the fine print carefully, because you may find it difficult to locate local tax consultants who are real experts in filling out farm tax returns.

Depreciation can be a large deduction, so read Publication 534, "Depreciation," also. By buying machinery, fertilizer, and other supplies at the right time, you may be able to take a larger deduction during a year when income has been high.

Small business owners can also find tax advantages. "Tax Guide for Small Business" and "Business Use of Your Home," both from the IRS, should supply the information you need. Recent rulings make it easier than it once was for home craftspeople, writers, and those operating a small business to deduct the expenses of having a shop or office in the home, but you will need to know what qualifies and what does not.

If you are self-employed, you are also allowed to set up an IRA. You can invest a certain percentage of your profits each year, and defer the taxes from both that amount and the interest earned on it until you have retired and are likely to be in a lower tax bracket. Many small businesspeople and farmers have found that this incentive to save taxes also gives them the impetus to save for a secure future.

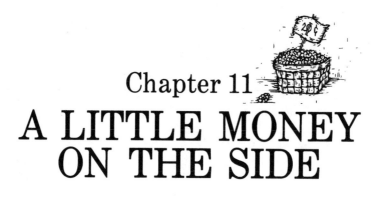

Chapter 11
A LITTLE MONEY ON THE SIDE

People will drive great distances if they like your service, product, or meals, even if you live way out in the country. The year-round population of our township is similar to that of surrounding townships—only 600 to 800 people—but this is enough of a market to support such diverse retail operations and services as a quality blacksmith, several small country inns, bed-and-breakfast hostelries, restaurants, two tearooms, a bakery catering business, a yarn shop, several gift shops (one specializing in homemade lampshades decorated with pressed wild flowers), a clothing shop that features clothing and yard goods imported from Scotland, two cross-country skiing centers, several real estate and insurance agents, and even a small advertising agency. All are thriving small businesses that attract clientele from a wide area.

If you sell directly from your home, your privacy will be affected. Customers are rarely impressed by advertised "open" hours, and are likely to drop in anytime. Friends of ours who have home businesses tell us they must leave the premises in order to get any rest on their days off.

If customers come to your home, some kind of liability insurance is advisable. Businesses open only at certain times of the year may qualify for lower rates.

Perhaps you would prefer that the world did not beat a path to your door at all hours of the day and night. Alternatives that work well in rural areas are mail-order and wholesale businesses. Nestled away in our backcountry area are many such operations, including a large supplier of jewelry-making equipment, a quiltmaker who sells to Bloomingdales and other city outlets, a knitter of chic sweaters that go to boutiques all over the country, several home knitters who use machines to create ski apparel, a weaver of speciality items, an antiquarian book dealer, and several producers of Christmas wreaths and other decorations.

Since the laws regulating home businesses vary from state to state, check those that pertain to your venture. Agricultural home businesses are not regulated as heavily as most, but you may need to get licenses and fulfill certain other requirements. If you have a trade name, you must register it with the state and probably record it in your town or county office. In most states you must register with the state tax department and collect sales tax on certain items. If you sell milk, plants, or processed foods, or if you keep bees, you will need to be certified by your state agricultural department. There may also be environmental and safety regulations with which you must comply.

Regardless of the quality of your products, they will be judged by their appearance. Your fruits and vegetables, for example, may be free

❖

of preservatives and pesticides, but if they lack good color and have blemished exteriors, they won't sell. When we were children, we resented the fact that our families invariably sold our best vegetables, firewood, and maple syrup—while keeping the lesser grades for our own use. Now that we're older and wiser, we know that's often the way it has to be if you sell only top-quality merchandise.

Tips for Increasing Profits

• Sell when prices are optimum. If you grow vegetables and fruits, be among the first to have them ready. The highest profits go to those gardeners who produce fresh asparagus, corn, peas, and spinach *before* they become plentiful and the price drops. To get a jump on the competition, plant varieties that mature early, start plants under plastic or glass, and keep your land fertile and productive.

• Store squash, carrots, turnips, potatoes, dried beans, and apples, and sell them *after* the season, when supplies are lower and the prices higher.

• Process your produce into chutney, jelly, jam, juices, apple butter, maple candy, relishes, and pickles. Package it in attractive containers, and sell year-round.

Promoting Your Business

To help sell your products, give your company a memorable name, and repeat it on your signs, truck, labels, stationery, and any other advertising. Beekeeping friends of ours call their place Sweet Promise Farm, a term they use on all their honey labels. You may be able to use an interesting regional name, such as Granite State Apples, Northeast Kingdom Balsam, or Loon Island Cheese. Local landmarks may suggest names—Moss Glen Falls Jelly or Rocking Rock Baskets.

Choose a logo that makes your product instantly recognizable and distinguishable from others. There are very few children in this

Labels on your products can be as friendly and personal as
mass-produced packaging is not.

country who do not recognize the golden arches of McDonald's from
hundreds of yards away, or the image of Morris on a cat food
advertisement.

A slogan may be helpful, too. When we started our plant nursery
specializing in hardy plants, we came up with the phrase, "If it will
grow in Greensboro, it will grow anywhere." It became well known,
and was an asset to our business.

Most small rural businesses spend relatively little of their total
budget on advertising. If you have no experience, you may want to
enlist the help of an agency in setting up a campaign; but don't
overlook free advertising. If your business is unusual, local newspapers and even national magazines may be willing to cover it. A word of

caution, though: lots of publicity may not be desirable for a small business. After *Woman's Day* wrote up a friend's modest herb business, hundreds of thousands of requests flooded in for catalogs.

By displaying your products at fairs, craft shows, and local businesses, you can keep your name before the public. With this in mind, one grower we know provides flowers for the tables at a nearby restaurant; another donates them occasionally to the local TV station, which gives him credit in exchange.

List your business in the Yellow Pages and other local directories to help potential customers find your business. In backcountry locations, a printed map is useful, too. Because our first-time customers stopped in the local village for directions to our nursery, we photocopied maps for the local general stores, garage, and post office. The clerks were happy to hand out maps instead of lengthy explanations, and the customers reached us in a good mood, after making all the right turns.

Other publicity techniques are available to country businesses. Open houses with refreshments, prizes, and demonstrations always attract the public. Vermont Castings, a prominent stove manufacturer, provides an annual picnic for its large and enthusiastic group of stove owners, and a garden center near us organizes tours of outstanding gardens in the area.

It has been our experience that many clubs in rural areas are on the lookout for speakers. If you make it known that you are available to talk or show slides about your specialty, invitations are likely to pour in from all manner of groups.

Keep a pile of catalogs or price lists handy, so your clients can pick them up for their friends. If you do mailings, provide a pad on which visitors can record their addresses and those of friends they wish to receive catalogs. We increased the volume of our plant business by advertising gift certificates in our catalog and in the local newspaper at Christmas.

Hiring Help

Managing workers has its own set of challenges, and we use all the labor-saving equipment we can to help us do most of our work ourselves.

❖

If you hire people who supply their own equipment and workers, they are classified as contractors and you don't need to worry about liability insurance, workmen's compensation, withholding income tax, or Social Security. You are liable for all of them, however, if you yourself hire a worker for more than a few days at a time.

If you need only part-time help, look for teachers, retirees, and others who may be willing to moonlight to supplement their income. Teenagers are another labor pool, but if you hire a minor, be aware of the strict laws regarding child labor. Also be sure to get from your county extension office or state department of labor a copy of the regulations about juveniles and dangerous equipment. The term "dangerous" includes not only such obvious things as explosives, chemicals, and chain saws, but also tractors, ladders, and large animals.

Keeping Records

One of our farming neighbors was in the habit of writing all his records on the milkhouse wall. One day when he was away, the milk plant sent around a man to whitewash the building, and he lost everything.

Many industrious people fail in business because they don't realize that good recordkeeping is as important as working hard. If you keep animals, record their birthdates, or ages when you acquired them, as well as any medical problems they may have had, and list shots that are due. You'll want accurate breeding data, too, so you will know when to plan on offspring. Keep production records for your dairy animals, also.

Monitor horticultural and forestry projects by carefully recording the varieties you planted and when, and the outcome. Did the plant produce prolifically or sparsely, early or late? By noting the prices and kinds of fertilizers and other supplies used each season and the times they were used, as well as the results, you will be better able to budget your time and finances in future years.

If your bookkeeping is up to par, it should show at a glance how you are doing financially. Home business operators sometimes get so involved in their work that they forget to keep an eye on their profits. Even if you are bored by bookkeeping, records, and deskwork, check frequently to see that the bottom line is in black ink rather than red.

Establish a separate checking account for your business, and pay all your business bills from it rather than intermingling personal and business accounts; and resist paying business bills in cash, with no record of payment. You will save a lot of time and sputtering over your tax returns if you set up your system so the dispersal columns in your account book correspond to the deductions you are allowed on the Federal Income Tax form (Schedule F, if your operation qualifies as agricultural, or Schedule C, if it is a nonagricultural business).

As we said earlier, if two-thirds or more of your income is from farming or commercial fishing (according to present law), you can file your income tax before March and pay the total amount. Otherwise you must file and pay an installment on your estimated tax four times a year, and file your 1040 and other tax returns with any balance due on April 15. If you make a profit on your home business or farm operation, you must also pay a self-employment or social security tax. Since you will have no employer to share this tax with you, it can take a hefty bite from your earnings. Be sure to include this portion of your tax with your regular payments on your estimated income tax, or you will get a sizeable bill for the interest soon after.

If you operate a farm or home business with a spouse or other people, you can form a partnership or incorporate in order to get a tax advantage. Consult a tax specialist before you set up your operation to avoid the hassle of changing your method of reporting after the business is in full swing.

Forming a Corporation

Set up a corporation just to operate a small family business? That may seem ridiculous, but each year more small operators find it to their advantage. Incorporation was once a major undertaking, but new laws have made it simpler in many states, and it can usually be done without an attorney. Requirements about the number of shareholders are less stringent, fewer officers are required, and corporate records are not as complicated as formerly. A corporation still must hold business meetings periodically and keep detailed records of business decisions.

There are both advantages and disadvantages to incorporation. If more than two people are involved, it is easier to divide the corporation's shares than to write a complicated partnership agreement.

There are often tax benefits, as well, and it is easier to sell or pass on the business. Another advantage is that business liabilities are likely to pose less risk to you individually. Finally, that "Inc." on your stationery and advertising gives the impression that you are an established concern, which may help sales and possibly make it easier to borrow money or to establish credit accounts with suppliers.

Among the disadvantages are that corporations require more paperwork and are more complicated to dissolve than individual businesses or partnerships. Unless you are familiar with incorporation procedures, discuss the pros and cons with an accountant or lawyer before you make this move.

Selling from Your Home

When your home is also your retail outlet, try to make it as welcoming as possible—a place people will like to visit. Attractive, easy-to-read signs are important. Post them so that people will be able to find you, and once there, know where to park. One of our pet peeves is businesses that announce themselves with numerous highway signs but fail to mark the entrance so that we drive right by. (States differ in their regulations on signs and billboards, so check out the laws in your state before you hire a sign painter.)

Provide plenty of space for customers to safely drive in, park, load up, and leave—even during your busiest times. Following some crazy law of the universe, customers seldom arrive in predictable numbers. No one may come for hours, then suddenly a crowd appears out of nowhere.

Create a leisurely atmosphere. If people enjoy the setting, they are more likely to linger, buy, and return. In our plant nursery, we provided a play area for young children so their parents could relax and make decisions. All it took was a sand pile with a few shovels, pails, and small plastic trucks. If your customers come long distances, they will welcome a restroom, drinking water, pot of tea, and a picnic table with chairs or benches. With these amenities your shop will provide a happily different atmosphere than a supermarket or shopping center boutique.

You may find other ways to capitalize on a country business. If you sell handcrafted furniture, for instance, show how it can fit into a home setting. A demonstration of how a product is made is always good merchandising. Free samples increase sales, too. At the Cold Hollow Cider Mill in central Vermont, browsers watch a giant cider press at work as they sip a free cup of cold or mulled cider. Another innovative Vermont business, the Morse Farm, demonstrates maple sugar making, to the delight of the busloads of travelers who stop there. If you are a craftsperson, you have the advantage of being able to demonstrate how your pottery, candles, or patchwork quilts are created. One friend of ours carves birds while his customers watch, and another weaves on a large loom in full view of buyers.

Your products should be displayed attractively and as irresistibly as possible, and ideally in such a way that the customers can serve themselves. You may want to provide leaflets that give directions and answer customers' questions about the product. Include anecdotes or any historical information that will make it more interesting or memorable. If you sell food products such as honey, wheat, or fruits, you might include sample recipes and other suggestions for their use—all with your name imprinted on the sheet, of course.

Mark everything accurately, so that customers do not need to ask the cost. If you recite prices upon demand, it creates the impression that you are making them up on the spot, and the buyer is likely to believe that everyone is not being treated equally.

Even if you have liability insurance, you should eliminate potential hazards such as dangling wires, hoses, ladders, farm chemicals, and mudholes. If you have pets that scratch or bite, or become entangled with visiting pets, keep them corralled during business hours. Use fences or hedges to keep curious customers and small children within the sales and display area and out of your home or pond.

A loud outside telephone bell helps us to avoid losing calls when we are working outdoors or with a customer. In the busy spring season, our hundred-meter dashes for the phone slim us down better than aerobic workout sessions. Portable telephones are handy, too, but we find them a nuisance to carry around.

Running a Pick-Your-Own Operation

Pick-your-own (PYO) gardens and orchards are popular with customers who enjoy self-service and lower prices. You'll attract consumers who do not have land to grow their own produce, as well as

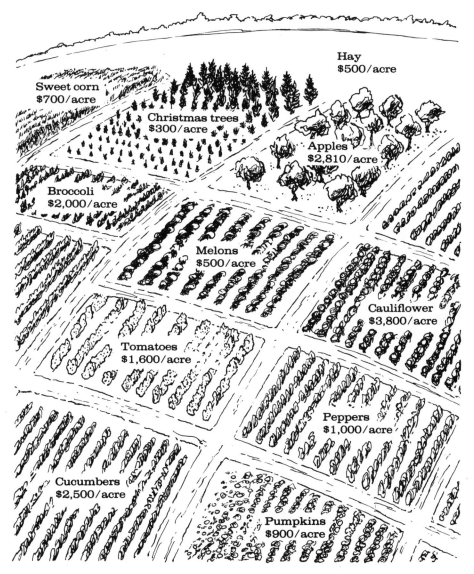

The cash-per-acre yield varies greatly from crop to crop. Note that these figures don't take labor cost into consideration.

A LITTLE MONEY ON THE SIDE

83

❖

those who like the fun of harvesting without spending time and energy in gardening.

The idea appeals to growers, too, since harvesting and selling often take as much time as raising the plants. And a PYO operation eliminates bookkeeping and the expense of hiring additional laborers at harvesttime. Interestingly, too, customers are far less fussy when they pick produce themselves than when they select it at a roadside stand or marketplace.

Among the most popular self-service items are berries, tree fruits, Christmas trees, and such vegetables as pumpkins, squash, tomatoes, peppers, and cabbage. Leafy vegetables, peas, and corn do not lend themselves as readily to PYO. Since harvesting requires a practiced hand and eye, customers frequently have difficulty judging when these vegetables are at their best, and are likely to damage the plants. Root crops, such as potatoes, require more labor to harvest and are seldom marketed in this way, either.

PYO operations are not without problems. Customers may resist staying in a certain row until it is picked, preferring to jump around and select only the finest specimens. Others may trample the produce or just park there and eat. You may have to prohibit dogs and small children from running wildly over your rows.

A PYO operation requires careful advance planning and close supervision. Label the rows by number or letter so you can assign them to customers. You may want to take reservations so that people are assured of finding produce when they arrive. Be prepared to sell containers, also, because only experienced customers are likely to remember to bring their own. Most growers have found that their profits are better when fruits and vegetables are sold by weight rather than by the pint or quart, so invest in reliable scales. Weighing also sidesteps hard feelings because neither you nor your customers feel cheated, and it discourages overloading the containers.

Before you jump into a PYO operation, check out the competition carefully. Currently, Vermont growers say that the market for strawberries is flooded in many parts of the state, and the only farmers making a good profit are those who diversify their crops. The largest operation in Vermont, The Harlow Farm, grows 12 acres of strawberries, 16 of blueberries, 5 of raspberries, and a few of apples and plums. Not all is PYO however.

Operating Other Retail Outlets

You don't have to sell from your home, of course. You can sell farm produce at a stand or out of the back of your truck on a main road or at a farmers' market. Most states have a council on the arts to help craftspeople locate cooperatives, fairs, and other outlets. You might consider joining forces with someone else who sells related but noncompeting products. Each year a weaver, a potter, and a silversmith hold a one-day open house near our town. They have established a reputation, and people look forward to the event as a time to look at samples, buy, and place orders for custom-made pieces.

Making It Wholesale

Your production volume must be much larger in a wholesale operation to make the same profit as in retail, since you will probably be selling at roughly half the price. You save by not having to advertise to the public, hire salespeople, or pay for the upkeep of a sales outlet. And a wholesale operation usually enables you to have better control over your hours than a retail business; still, you may need to deliver items such as produce early in the morning so that your clients will have them on hand when customers arrive. Your location is less important than in a retail enterprise, but a lot of time and money can be lost if you must make frequent long-distance deliveries. To avoid this, you should either be located reasonably near your outlets, arrange for shipment by another carrier, or entice your customers to pick up your merchandise.

The potential market should be your first consideration. Investigate all the possible buyers before you take the plunge into wholesale selling. If you want to sell fresh produce, for example, consider local hotels, restaurants, canneries, health food stores, and roadside stands. Small stores may buy, too, especially if they can advertise that the produce has been raised locally and without pesticides. Large chains, on the other hand, are often reluctant, or forbidden, to buy from anyone except their wholesale suppliers. Market gardeners who live near an urban area can take their fruits and vegetables to large wholesale markets, and for those who live a considerable distance from the city, a cooperative may handle the produce. An organic

❖

growers co-op in our area successfully ships carrots to the Boston wholesale market 200 miles away.

In a wholesale business you must be absolutely sure that you can supply whatever you have promised, since your outlets depend on you to provide for their customers. Since you will doubtless have competition, you must plan very carefully if you are to both maintain quality and also keep your prices low enough to attract business.

One disadvantage to wholesale selling is that, although retail customers expect to pay cash for their purchases, the people who buy from wholesalers usually do not. This practice of delayed payment not only necessitates more complicated billing and bookkeeping, but when you have problems in collecting, it may upset your own financing.

Running a Mail-Order Service

Retail mail-order businesses are popular in rural areas. In our own sparsely populated part of the country, enterprising people ship gift food packages, maple syrup, honey, hams, jams, jellies, and condiments from their homes. Such agricultural items as Christmas wreaths, herbs, nursery plants, and seeds also lend themselves to mail-order merchandising. Whether you produce the items yourself or import them from France, mail order is a practical way to sell. For several years we used our printing press to run a small personal stationery business during the Christmas season by placing ads in the Sunday *New York Times.* The ads brought in several hundred orders on some days, which was all we could handle without hiring extra help.

Mail-order selling appeals not only to those who live off the beaten track, but to anyone who does not have the personality or patience needed to deal face-to-face with the public. You can keep better control over your life and enjoy flexibility in choosing your working hours. Further, you forego the bother of a public sales area.

Buying by mail is on an upswing, in part because so many women have recently entered the labor force and have less time to shop. A lot of people simply enjoy the convenience of buying from their living room and the fun of getting packages in the mail. Some cottage industries have evolved into large corporations by providing superior goods and services to mail-order buyers. The nationally famous L. L. Bean firm started by making a better winter boot in a small Maine town.

You'll need some equipment. An accurate mailing scale is a requirement, as are shipping containers, packing and sealing materials, and files for keeping records. As your business grows you will undoubtedly consider purchasing computerized mailing lists, a postage meter, a copying machine, and a computer to save time.

Building up a mail-order business takes time, and it can be difficult to balance the number of customer orders with your available goods. Unsold merchandise can sometimes be disposed of through special sales, but it is an unhappy experience to return checks for products you do not have, and good will invariably suffers. In order to maintain an adequate inventory, it may be practical to buy from other producers, or to make an arrangement for them to "drop ship" their merchandise directly to your customers.

In a mail-order business, your potential clients are from the entire country, and even the world. To reach this wide market, many people advertise in the mail-order classified columns that are featured in magazines and newspapers. The names of customers who respond to this kind of ad can be the start of a list for future mailings.

You can also buy or rent mailing lists from firms that specialize in them. (See the Yellow Pages or magazines that cater to the mail-order industry.) These lists are sorted into categories according to the type of merchandise that the customers have bought previously, the periodicals they subscribe to, and other interests. You can also obtain lists for a certain region, if you don't care to ship all over the country. Lists are available on computer disks, and on perforated gummed labels that can be photocopied and used over and over. Some companies will mail your advertising directly, or insert it into their related mailings. Prices are usually quoted per 1,000 names, and the cost varies widely. A mailing list consisting only of buyers of expensive merchandise will cost far more than a list of people who have merely made an inquiry about a low-cost item.

We keep our mailing list on the computer because we can add and drop names easily and still keep them in alphabetical order. The computer prints the names on gummed labels that can then be attached to catalogs. If the labels also carry a computer code, a special mailing can be sent to buyers in a single Zip Code region or to those who have shown an interest in a certain product in the past.

Unless you handle only an item or two and sell by inserting advertisements in newspapers and magazines, you will need a catalog or price list. A successful catalog isn't easy to produce, and you may

want help from an advertising agency in designing one. One of the best catalogs we've seen is put out by the White Flower Farm in Litchfield, Connecticut. The descriptions written by the pseudonymous Amos Pettingill are lively and full of humor, while giving more information on the plants and their culture than do many garden books.

A catalog doesn't need to be elaborate or slickly produced to be effective, though. Customers enjoy dealing with a practical firm such as the Country Store in Weston, Vermont. Their homespun-looking black-and-white catalog successfully projects the atmosphere of a small-town store.

Starting a Bed-and-Breakfast

When retired friends of ours were asked by a nearby innkeeper if they would be willing to provide rooms for overflow guests, they agreed. And they enjoyed the sociability so much they added additional guest rooms and opened a year-round bed-and-breakfast (B&B).

They are only one of several families we know who take in paying overnight guests. B&Bs are catching on, after having been popular for many years in Europe.

Assess the potential of your home as a guest house. Guests need privacy, and so do you, so be sure it is large enough to accommodate the number of guests you expect to serve. A private bathroom is desirable, but not essential (many B&B guests share with a family). An adequate septic system *is* necessary, however, as is plenty of hot water for baths, showers, and laundry.

You can control the amount of time you spend on a B&B to a certain extent—by determining your "open" dates, and whether you operate only on weekends or seasonally. But a B&B operation will mean that you cannot take off on a trip of your own on the spur of the moment.

As a proprietor of a commercial establishment, you must keep it immaculately clean and relatively uncluttered. Most hosts offer a Continental breakfast of juice, some type of rolls (muffins, donuts, croissants, coffeecake), and coffee or tea; but others offer a full breakfast for an additional price.

Before you make your final decision, stay in a few B&Bs to test the waters. Imagine yourself in the place of the hosts; it will give you valuable insights when you open your own. We have stayed in places where the host and hostess served afternoon tea as we arrived, and mingled with the guests for after-dinner coffee in their living room, treating us as members of the family. It was an ideal situation for us, but we're not so sure we could be as charming as our hosts on a long-term basis!

You can let the public know of your B&B through guidebooks or via a Reservation Service Organization (RSO). Some guidebooks charge an annual fee for listing, while others choose the spots they list. RSOs not only publicize your business, but handle reservations, deposits, and other fees for you. They sometimes offer you cheaper group rates on insurance policies, and some screen guests in advance.

Before you hang out your shingle, check the regulations covering a B&B operation in your area. Does zoning allow it? Do you need a state or local license, or health department approval? Will your present homeowner's liability insurance cover paying guests? And check out how your operation may affect your income taxes.

Chapter 12
THE COUNTRY VEGETABLE GARDEN

Our meals at home do not feature snails, truffles, or caviar, but we consider the food gourmet fare nevertheless. Fresh asparagus, new peas and potatoes, crunchy young carrots, and juicy corn on the cob, all just minutes from the garden—these are beyond comparing to those that have been trucked for miles and spent days in the market.

A country place provides ample space for a serious garden. Rather than planting in sedate, square-foot, space-conserving rows, you can allow yourself to be just as individual and artistic as with your interior decorating: play with colorful annual flowers among the carrots and beans, design unusual shaped raised beds, and construct attractive paths. You can fit a sundial, birdbath, bench, and small pool stocked with goldfish into a well-planned food garden as easily as in a flower border.

Country homes tend to be better suited to harvesting and storing food, with spacious kitchens, room for freezers, pantry space, and cellars for storing vegetables, apples, vinegar, jams, jellies, pickles, and homemade wines.

In the country you will undoubtedly have a compost pile (see page 62), and find many unexpected sources of material for it and to use as mulch. Nearby farms may have inexpensive manure, spoiled hay, or silage; sawmills and woodworking shops create mountains of sawdust, shredded bark, shavings, and wood chips; and food processing plants have waste products they must dispose of. In our area, utility companies grind up tons of tree prunings and give them away.

How to Carve a Country Garden Out of an Empty Field

1. Choose the site with the best growing conditions, close enough to your home so that it's handy to cultivate, weed, harvest, and chase out wild animals.

2. Stake it out.

3. Use a rotary tiller, or have it plowed if the plot is large or if the soil and sod are so heavy that they would challenge an ordinary garden tiller.

4. Condition the soil: spread manure or compost, and other amendments your soil needs, such as sand (to lighten it) or lime (to raise the pH). (See "Improving Your Lot," Chapter 9.)

5. Fertilize: if the soil appears to be in poor condition, or if a soil test indicates the need, add manure or apply a balanced dry fertilizer according to the directions on the bag, spreading it evenly over the area by hand or with a spreader.

6. Till or harrow the plot thoroughly on a day when the soil is dry enough to break apart easily. Go over it, breaking up the sod clumps until the soil is completely pulverized. Rake out any weed roots and remove the stones.

7. Enclose the space with an animal-tight fence, if one appears necessary. Make the gate large enough for your machinery to get in and out.

8. Plant seeds, set out transplants, and get out your weeding tools.

With the advantages of gardening in a rural setting may come challenges in the form of weeds and wildlife. Weeds, the "thugs of the plant world," as Anthony Huxley has called them, enjoy the freedom to spread in the wide open countryside. Dandelions, thistles, kale, and groundsel are more than generous with their offspring, and the fallow fields that are a part of the landscape we all admire are nurseries for billions of seeds that fly for great distances and parachute down to your garden. Weed seeds also arrive in the farm manure you spread, and drop from hay mulch into your fertile earth. If fields border your garden, you'll also need to declare a constant war against the root spreaders (quack grass, horsetail, and such). Even a tiny piece of root left in the soil will quickly generate a whole new plant.

The solution to the weed dilemma is to nip them before they bud. If weed seeds mature, which they often do within a few weeks, they'll sprout next spring and compete with your vegetables for space, moisture, and nutrients. Not only that, but some seeds can remain viable for decades, waiting far down in the soil to be brought to the surface where they can germinate. If you attack weeds vigorously early in summer, you'll have fewer weeds to cope with in the future. But once they've become well established, your work will never end.

Wildlife visitors in the country may be no worse than those in suburban gardens, but you are likely to see more of them, and they are very knowledgeable. Friends of ours have an electric fence around their garden. The current went off for only a few hours one night last fall, but by the time they went to gather the brussels sprouts the next day, the deer had devoured every stalk. We surround our gardens and orchards with a tall sheep fence, but it doesn't keep out the raccoons that go for the corn, woodchucks aiming for the cabbages, rabbits for the greenery, and birds for newly planted seeds. All around the countryside we see devices intended to outwit these clever gourmets: scarecrows, aluminum plates strung over the rows, plastic snakes, and noise makers.

Each year after we have tilled, fertilized, planted, weeded, and fought off the bugs and wildlife, we forget how much additional time it takes to harvest and preserve crops for winter eating. We spend many hours in late summer and autumn filling freezers, the pantry, and the root cellar. Picking, shelling, and blanching peas is the most time-consuming, and it takes a good half day (or all evening) to cook a crop of corn and scrape it from the cob for canning or freezing. Broccoli and cauliflower take much less time and effort, and the root cellar crops are easy: just dig and store. But having our own vegetables in the middle of winter more than compensates for all the work.

Equipment

Unless your garden is very tiny, you may want a two-wheeled rotary tiller. Get one rugged enough for your job, but if you have only a small garden, a light, narrow model will be easier to maneuver, and it will enable you to place the rows closer together.

You may also want to buy a compost shredder, fertilizer spreader, sprayer or duster, and seeder. If your garden is large, a small suburban-type, four-wheeled tractor may be worth its expense. With attachments, you can use it to till; mow tall grass and weeds; move fertilizer, soil, peat moss, and plants; and bring in the harvest.

A storage shed near the garden is indispensable for storing gardening tools and equipment in one place. It is also a handy place to keep fertilizers, mulch materials, seeds, pots, and that important tool, your gardening record notebook.

Garden Size

"Never plant a garden any larger than your wife can keep hoed" is an old Yankee saying, and it is worth remembering, no matter who does the hoeing. Even after years of gardening, we find it hard not having an enormous plot, and we tend to plant all the seeds in a package, even though we need only a limited number of radishes and zucchini. Consequently, we don't always get all our thinning done early enough, and don't keep the weeds under control very well after mid-summer, when harvesting begins. Bigger is often not better, and although needs vary, a patch 50 by 60 feet should allow a family of two or three to grow the vegetables they need.

If your time schedule limits the size of your garden, it makes sense to plant only your favorite vegetables and buy the remainder from local growers. Pumpkins, squash, cabbage, corn, tomatoes, and potatoes are available at most country roadside stands and farmers' markets. Or, like some of our busy friends, you may decide instead to grow a little of everything in your garden for daily use, and buy large quantities as needed for preserving and storage. This practice also allows you to better choose the time you freeze your winter supply, rather than having to do it the day it ripens in your own garden.

Even though a shortage of land is not often a problem for rural gardeners, many we know are practicing intensive gardening. Raised beds allow you to grow more food in less space; you'll spend less time tilling, hoeing, and weeding. And you won't need as much fertilizer or mulch material.

Seedlings

Most vegetables thrive and produce if you plant the seeds directly in your garden. But certain ones should be started inside, especially if you grow vegetables to sell, or live where growing seasons are short. In late winter, we start tomatoes, peppers, broccoli, brussels sprouts, cabbage, cauliflower, celery, eggplant, herbs, melons, pumpkins, squash, and even a few lettuce plants. These are planted outside when the weather warms. People who want only a few plants aren't likely to fuss with raising seedlings, but instead buy started plants from local greenhouses. A market gardener near us orders his plants by mail from one of the large southern growers listed in farm magazines.

If you choose to start your own seedlings, you can grow them in a sunny window, hot bed, near the kitchen stove, under grow lights, or in a home greenhouse. Our best results have come from starting them under grow lights in the house in late winter, then moving them into our small greenhouse once the spring days begin to lengthen and warm. Our three-shelved grow light unit holds 12 large flats and 9 small ones, making it possible to start thousands of seedlings at each planting. We can do at least three plantings, each about a month apart, if we wish to sell started plants.

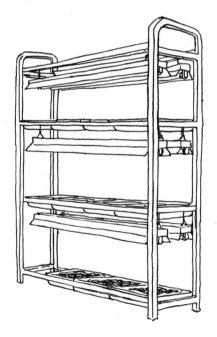

Grow light unit with three shelves for seedling flats.

Although we had trouble growing seedlings at first, success came after we discovered grow lights. We also learned to use nothing but sterile, artificial soil, to water the plants carefully with slightly warmed (never hot) water, and to keep the air temperature between 75 and 85 degrees F. until the plants are well started.

For the first few days the tiny new plants grow well with only the nutrients stored in the seed, but after that they need more food. Liquid seaweed and fish emulsion are both ideal fast-acting fertilizers and safe to use when mixed according to the directions. One year we added dried manure to the mix to help feed the plants, but once was enough. The plants grew beautifully but our house reeked for days from the smell, and the manure provided a breeding place for clouds of small black flies.

As soon as the seedlings sprout their second set of leaves—the first ones that really look like leaves—we transplant them into flats or small pots filled with either commercial potting soil or a mixture we make ourselves of one part (by volume) good loamy soil, one part sand, and one part peat moss.

Planting Basics

The garden is ready to till in the spring when the soil has dried enough to remain loose when you try to form it into a ball in your fist.

Plant on a warm sunny day when the soil is dry, if possible. Walking on wet soil compacts it, and makes it hard for the roots to grow. Overcome the temptation to plant the seeds too close together. As we've said, we have trouble following our own advice, and usually end up having to thin everything heavily later on. We rationalize that we can eat our thinnings—crisp small radishes, tender beet greens, and tiny carrots.

As soon as the soil is ready, plant peas, radishes, greens, broccoli, brussels sprouts, cabbage, turnips, parsnips, carrots, and beets. Most other vegetables are tender to frost, and those seeds shouldn't be planted or the transplants set out until all danger of frost is over, unless they are protected with hotcaps or another frostproof cover.

Summer in the Garden

If you have done everything right, the plants should begin to thrive, and it would seem that all there is left to do is to relax and await an early harvest. Instead, seedlings must be thinned and mulch spread; weeds must be pulled; insects such as cabbage worms and potato bugs must be dealt with; and blights and other diseases, checked. Plants that grow sluggishly need to be side-dressed with liquid seaweed, fish emulsion, or manure tea.

When nature doesn't cooperate and the rains come irregularly during the summer, the plants will need additional water. Sudden, brief summer showers often soak only the top inch of soil, and then quickly dry out in the sun before the roots of the plants can absorb water; a light watering has the same effect. When you water, apply it slowly so it won't run off, and use enough to soak through the mulches and down to the roots. The best time to water is early morning or early evening, when winds are usually light and there is less evaporation than at midday.

"The best fertilizer is the footsteps of the gardener" is a gem of wisdom that should keep us on our toes (and knees) in the garden. Success with plants can't be assured with a secret ritual, miracle fertilizer, or spray, but rather by good soil preparation, timely planting, and frequent attention. Don't be discouraged if things go wrong occasionally. Droughts, hailstorms, and invasions of slugs mean that every crop may not be a big success each year. During a cool summer our pumpkins will get no larger than baseballs, and a hot season will make the spinach go to seed before we can pick it. Still, we always seem to end up with plenty of garden sass, as our Yankee forebears called it, and are able to stock our root cellar, freezers, and pantry each year.

Harvesting may be the most important part of gardening. If you are successful at all else but fail to pick your food when it's at its prime, you might as well buy week-old produce at the supermarket. Root crops such as carrots and beets allow a long season of harvest, and you also have some latitude in picking greens, vine fruits, and cabbage. But asparagus, sweet corn, green beans, cauliflower, broccoli, kohlrabi, summer squash, and peas must be gathered on their own schedules, precisely when they are ready. Those who are not alert at harvesttime must pay the price of gigantic zucchini, tough peas, yellow cauliflower, and overripe corn.

Perennial Pleasures

Our perennial food beds provide lots of good eating while we await the first peas and carrots. Rhubarb, Jerusalem artichokes, horseradish, and perennial herbs are easy to grow and produce reliably each year. Asparagus takes a bit more care, but we feel it is well worth it. A family of four will do well with a perennial patch of 5 or 6 rhubarb plants, 25 asparagus plants, 5 horseradish plants, and a small herb bed.

Perennial foods should not be planted in your regular garden, but at one edge, or in a separate bed where they won't be disturbed. They need a spot in full sun, deep fertile soil, and freedom from the competing roots of trees, shrubs, and berry bushes. Don't overlook regular applications of fertilizer or compost, plus a heavy mulch to discourage weeds.

Winter Gardening

Because we prefer homegrown food to any from unknown sources, we grow much of our greenery throughout the winter: potted herbs such as parsley, rosemary, and bay are grown on the window sills; we sprout alfalfa seeds in glass jars; and we enjoy salads of Belgian endive by lifting chicory roots from the garden in the fall and wintering them in our cool cellar until they sprout heads in the spring. In late fall and early spring, we use an outdoor grow frame to raise cold-hardy Chinese greens such as Kyo Mizuna, Michihili, Pak-Choi, and Siew Choy, as well as Oriental turnips. Grow frames are similar to cold frames, but are more heavily insulated and are angled toward the south to catch as much of the winter sun as possible. Our frame lengthens the greens growing season by several months.

A Market Garden

A market garden is a good way to earn extra dollars. Roadside stands pop up everywhere in rural areas as soon as the spinach and lettuce crops are ready, and do a thriving business until the last pumpkin, winter squash, and bunch of variegated corn is sold in October.

Getting started selling vegetables takes less investment than many other businesses, and some crops are ready to sell only a few weeks after planting. Often children on school vacation manage the family stand, and we know many retired people who make extra money, get outdoor exercise, and meet new friends by selling their garden surplus at a farmers' market.

Some market gardeners keep their enterprises modest, but others go on to grow and sell many acres of produce. A successful organic

(continued on page 100)

Vegetables at a Glance

The amounts given are for planting in rows. If you use raised beds, adjust the recommended amount accordingly, since the plants will be growing closer together.

a = Frost sensitive. Plant outside after danger is over.
b = Best started inside in late winter and transplanted.
c = Hardy to light frosts. Can be planted outside early.
d = Heat-loving plant. Does not like cool temperatures.

	Crop	Feet of Row, Hills (for family of 4)	Days to Germinate	Days to Yield	Spacing in Rows (inches)
a	Beans	30–75	5–9	60–80	3–4
d	Beans, lima	40–80	6–8	75–90	3–4
	Beet	50–75	7–9	60–70	3–4
b	Broccoli	20–40	4–8	70–80	15–18
b	Brussels sprouts	10–20	4–8	70–90	15–18
b	Cabbage	30–40	4–8	60–100	15–18
	Carrot	50–125	10–15	60–75	3–4
b	Cauliflower	30–40	4–8	55–70	15–18
b	Celery	10–30	12–20	120–145	6–8
c	Chard	40–60	7–11	45–55	10–15
a	Corn[1]	50–100	5–9	65–120	9–12
d	Cucumbers	2–6 hills	7–9	55–70	5–7
abd	Eggplant	30–40	7–10	70–100	20–30
	Endive	15–25	10–15	65–75	8–10
	Kale	5–15	6–8	60–75	18–24
	Kohlrabi	25–40	5–8	55–70	7–9

[1]Hybrid corn is hardier and can stand light spring frosts.

	Crop	Feet of Row, Hills (for family of 4)	Days to Germinate	Days to Yield	Spacing in Rows (inches)
c	Lettuce	25–35	5–8	45–50	6–12
b	Lettuce, head	25–40	5–8	45–70	12
ad	Muskmelon	5–10 hills	8–10	80–110	1 per hill
ad	Okra	30–40	8–10	50–65	12–15
b	Onion[2]	25–40	7–10	90–110	3–5
	Parsnip[3]	25–40	10–15	100+	3–4
c	Peas	100+	7–12	60–75	1–2
abd	Peppers	30–45	7–14	70–120	20–25
	Potato[4]	100+	7–14	75–120	10–12
ad	Pumpkin	3+ hills	8–10	85–120	8–12
c	Radish	10+	3–7	21–30	1–2
c	Spinach	30–50	7–10	40–55	5–6
ad	Squash	3+			
abd	Tomato	50–70	7–10	60–100	30–35
	Turnip	30–40	5–9	50–90	5–10
ad	Water-melon	5+ hills	8–10	80–130	12 per hill

[2]Onion seed may also be planted outside in late fall. Started plants or sets should be put out in early spring.

[3]Parsnips are sweeter and better flavored if left in the ground over winter and eaten in early spring as soon as they can be dug.

[4]Potato eyes may be ordered through seed catalogs, or whole potatoes may be cut in pieces with an eye on each one. Buy seed potatoes only, because eating potatoes are often chemically treated to keep them from sprouting.

farm in our village is run by a young couple who sell at a roadside stand and to local stores. Their produce is grown with the help of student apprentices from a nearby agricultural college, and the stand is usually unattended because customers leave their payments on the honor system. Other growers in our area sell their entire crops wholesale through a marketing cooperative.

It is important to adjust the size of your plantings to your abilities and the potential market. A few springs ago, two young men visited our nursery and casually mentioned that they had bought some land in a nearby town and planned to establish an organic market garden. They had spent all their money on seed for their 14-acre patch, but were not yet sure how they were going to till the land or pay for the hay they planned to use for mulch. We were familiar with the property they had purchased and mentioned that the soil was very poor. They agreed, but were certain the hay mulch would quickly improve it. They seemed to be unfamiliar with such problems as weeds, deer, woodchucks, droughts, and wandering cattle.

Nor did they sound concerned about selling the tons of produce their hoped-for garden should produce. "People are clamoring for health foods," they said. Further conversation revealed that they had both grown up in city apartments, and their knowledge of farming had come mostly from a short course at a nearby commune. We admired their enthusiasm, but knowing how much work was involved in keeping our own small garden under control, we wondered if they had any idea of how long it would take just to walk the length of all the rows of their 14-acre garden. We never heard at what stage they gave up, but they were gone by the following year. Sadly, their fate is not uncommon, but it can easily be avoided by starting on a modest scale, then increasing the business gradually as you become experienced in production and marketing.

Even with careful planning, however, market gardening, like any farming, has its "down" moments. Success depends greatly on conditions over which you have little control. Late spring and early fall frosts, hail and wind storms, and flash floods can devastate a planting very suddenly, just as you are beginning to count your profits. So can sudden invasions of insects or animals. Unfortunately, too, during years when growing conditions are good, a surplus of produce may depress the price. But you can hedge your bets by diversifying crops, taking precautions against frost damage, and not counting your cucumbers before the cash register rings up the sale.

Chapter 13
THE BERRY PATCH

Berry growing has a lot to recommend it. The plants are inexpensive and easy to care for. They begin to produce fruit at an early age, and on a home scale require no special equipment for growing or harvesting. The flavor of berries picked fresh cannot possibly be matched by store-bought fruit, and stores rarely give you much of a selection of varieties.

Although we're enthusiastic about all kinds of berries, we hesitate to advise you about which and how many to plant. This depends on your family's tastes and the amount you plan to preserve for winter eating. Here's our idea of a patch for a country place:

25 summer-bearing strawberry
25 everbearing strawberry
15 red summer-bearing raspberry
5 red fall-bearing raspberry
5 yellow raspberry
5 black raspberry

5 purple raspberry
2 red currant
2 white or black currant
2 gooseberry
4 elderberry
4 blueberry

Commercial Potential

Berries are one of the most lucrative crops, calculated on a per-acre basis. Fresh berries can be marketed wholesale to stores, restaurants, canneries, and producers of juice, jam, or jelly, or sold direct on the farm. Because hand picking is time-consuming, and pickers are often hard to find, a pick-your-own operation works well for many small- or medium-size growers.

Strawberries, blueberries, and red raspberries are the crops most often grown commercially. To cover the possibility of something going wrong with any one, many growers raise all three. You may be able to tap a local market for raspberries in the less conventional colors (black, purple, and yellow), blackberries, dewberries, boysenberries, loganberries, or youngberries. Cultivated elderberries, currants, and gooseberries are not as well known, but they are often saleable when processed into preserves and offered at roadside stands and gift shops.

Berry Yields

The amount of berries an acre can produce varies widely according to the climate, variety planted, soil condition, and pest problems, so the figures we give here are only approximate.

Highbush blueberries are planted at about 1,350 plants to the acre. The mature plants should yield about 5,000 pounds over a 30-day season.

Red raspberries are usually planted at about 2,000 plants per acre. Purple and black raspberries should be planted further apart, so fewer plants are needed. Yields should be about 2,000 to 2,500 quarts to the acre for reds, and nearly twice as much for blacks and purples. Much higher yields for all varieties are not uncommon.

Set strawberries from 6,000 to 10,000 plants per acre in the matted row system, depending on the row spacing. In the hill system, from 14,000 to 25,000 are needed. In an experiment conducted at the University of Vermont, yields varied from 5,000 to 16,000 quarts per acre, with 10,000 the average.

Our first attempts at fruit growing were unsuccessful because we succumbed to glowing catalog ads and ordered varieties that were not right for our climate. If you plan to grow berries commercially, be especially sure to order varieties that are right for your planting zone and soil conditions, and choose marketable varieties, too. We think the taste of our yellow and purple raspberries is wonderful, but many buyers still expect a raspberry to be red, so a large-scale commercial operation may not do well with unfamiliar varieties. Experiment with them on a small scale before committing yourself to several acres.

Check with your state extension service for information, and ask if there is a small fruit grower association in the state that you can join. Some states have active groups that work together to help their industry through tours, promotional activities, legislative committees, and research projects.

❖

Strawberries

Strawberry plants are not difficult to grow, and produce berries the year after planting. The plants are inexpensive and produce a large amount of fruit in a small space. (Each plant should, with all its runners, produce one quart of fruit—enough for several strawberry shortcakes.) On the minus side, strawberries require a large amount of hand labor for weed control and harvesting.

Unless there are nurseries nearby, buy your plants by mail. Order only those varieties that are disease-resistant, and make sure they are certified disease-free. Many plants are now propagated by tissue culture, and these may be the best choice because you can be certain they are disease-free. If new, healthy plants are set in a new location each year, diseases such as red steele, wilts, and leaf scorch are not likely to be a problem. Newer varieties may be more disease-resistant, better flavored, and more productive than older kinds. Check with your extension service to see what is recommended for your area.

In addition to the once-a-season producers, which most of us grow, the everbearing varieties bear fruit for most of the summer. The one-crop bearers are best for commercial growers and for those who want to freeze a lot of berries, since the entire crop can be harvested within a few weeks. Everbearers appeal to people who like to pick and use a few berries each day all summer.

Strawberries do best on soil that is fertile, somewhat sandy, well drained, and fairly acid (with a pH of 5.5 to 6). The land should be thoroughly tilled, and all the sod completely pulverized. Even with the best soil preparation, you must weed frequently because strawberry plants are not at all competitive. Their roots are shallow, so that irrigation is necessary most years and cultivation must be carefully done to avoid damaging the roots. You can spare yourself much cultivation, hand weeding, and watering by using a generous mulch. We like shredded bark best, because it is weed-free and decomposes within a year so it can be safely tilled into the soil. Other materials such as straw, salt hay, leaves, and lawn clippings also make good strawberry mulches; but sawdust, wood chips, and shavings are not usually recommended because they do not break down quickly, and hay is likely to be filled with weed seeds.

The sooner you set out your plants in the spring, the more time they'll have to produce new runner plants to ensure a large crop the following year. Follow the planting directions that come with them,

THE BERRY PATCH

❖

and never let the young plants dry out, either before or after planting. Pack the soil firmly around each plant, and water immediately.

There are two main systems for growing strawberries. The most common is the matted row method, in which the plants are set at 20- to 30-inch intervals in rows spaced 3 or more feet apart (depending on how they will be cultivated). As the runners grow, they are trained so all the new plants will form along the rows, not between them. By mid to late summer, the plants should have filled up the rows. This method is productive, but usually only one large crop of berries can be grown before the patch becomes overcrowded with plants and must be replanted the next spring.

The hill method is rarely used commercially, but it works well for the home berry patch. The plants are set about 15 inches apart. The runners are cut off as soon as they start so that no new plants are allowed to form, and the original plants get very large. This method has many advantages: the berries are bigger, a bed can be kept in production for many years before being replaced, and more plants can be grown in a smaller area. Weeding and mulching are easier, too. You can set the plants into slits cut in large sheets of heavy black plastic to further simplify runner and weed control. The hill method also has disadvantages: more plants are needed, time must be devoted to cutting off the runners, and the plants are more prone to diseases and insects because they stay in the same soil for several years.

Next year's strawberry buds begin to form in late summer. Because they are very susceptible to frost injury, plants north of the Mason-Dixon line should be covered for the winter. A reliable snow cover can do this satisfactorily, but the plants are vulnerable if the ground is bare. You can help prevent ice damage by planting on a gentle slope, in slightly raised beds, or in hilled rows to encourage water to run off before freezing.

Straw was once the common cover for the plants. But straw may be hard to come by, since most grain is now threshed in the fields and the straw chopped and left there. Common alternatives include evergreen boughs, salt hay, shredded bark, and foam blankets made especially for plant protection. The timing of covering and uncovering the plants is critical. Do not cover them in the fall until the ground starts to freeze slightly; otherwise, the buds will not have become dormant and will continue to grow, making them susceptible to winterkill. In the spring, don't uncover the plants until the danger of hard frosts (those that freeze the ground) is past. Remove the cover on a cloudy day, if possible, to prevent any tender new growth that sprouted under the mulch from being "sunburned."

Because frost damage at blossoming time is a real hazard, and since the temperature often drops rapidly on clear spring nights, listen to the weather forecast and watch the thermometer carefully. If frost threatens, cover your beds with old quilts, blankets, straw, burlap, or newspaper if you can anchor them down. Sheets of plastic don't work well as insulators.

We like to cover the blooming plants in late afternoon, before the day cools, to preserve some of the ground heat that has accumulated during the day.

The Bush Fruits

Blueberries, currants, gooseberries, and elderberries are among our favorite crops. We value their reliability, too. We can nearly always count on them, no matter what the weather. They are ideal for the larger lot of a country home, and are inexpensive to start. Finally, they need less care than strawberries, and some will produce for years with no care at all. We have often found fruit-laden currant and gooseberry plants growing around old cellar holes in the back country. However, each plant bears bigger and better fruit and more of it, if it is pruned and mulched, and the area around it is kept free from weeds. Plants should also be given a generous helping of manure, compost, or other organic fertilizer each spring. Pruning is limited to removing wood that is over three or four years old, and thinning out branches that have become too crowded.

Birds can be serious pests, and growers find that in some areas the only way they can get any fruit at all is to cover the bushes with netting.

The bush fruits grow and produce in light shade, but they do better in full or nearly full sunlight. Set the plants about 5 feet apart, and if you have more than one row, keep the rows 6 to 8 feet apart. Water them throughout any dry spells the first season.

Whether or not you should plant the popular cultivated highbush blueberry depends on how well your soil and climate conditions meet its unique requirements. Blueberries need a very acid soil, so do not consider them as a potential commercial crop unless your soil tests approximately 4.5. Home growers can create an acid environment by mixing soil with cottonseed meal, peat moss, or composted oak leaves, and by mulching each year with pine needles. For blueberries to pollinate and produce fruit, you must plant at least two different varieties, and unlike most small fruits, it may be several years before they begin to produce sizeable crops.

Blueberries are less hardy than the other bush fruits, and need a long frost-free season to mature their new growth. Therefore, commercial growing is not recommended where the winter temperatures fall below −20 degrees F. and the growing season is less than 125 days. They are worth a trial for home use in Zones 3 and 4, however, if you plant the hardiest varieties and place them in sheltered spots out of the wind.

In most regions, pruning is a matter of thinning out branches and removing older wood. But in the North where the plants grow at a slower rate and seldom get more than 6 feet tall, pruning should be limited to an occasional thinning of the twiggy growth at the ends of the branches. Cutting back heavily results in a fast, prolonged regrowth which is likely to be winterkilled.

Currants and gooseberries are far more popular in Europe than in America, but they are beginning to catch on here, for several good reasons. All are hardy (even in the far North), fast growing, and accepting of ordinary garden soil. They grow on low bushes with attractive foliage, and are easier to raise than grapes. They often produce a few berries the same year they are planted, and the crop increases each year. Both are self-fertile, so only one bush is necessary for fruit, but you'll probably want more if you preserve them.

Gooseberries come in many colors, but we especially like the large red Welcome variety. They have a delicious flavor when made into preserves, desserts, and sauces, and when thoroughly ripe can be eaten fresh off the bush as well. Currants are smaller and usually not eaten out of hand, but cooked into jelly or made into liqueur. Although they can be dried, the dried currants you buy are actually small grapes and not to be confused with these members of the Ribes family.

Our Canadian neighbors raise large quantities of black Consort currants, and make them into delicious jams and sauces. Black currants are also good mixed into pancake batter, or made into a tangy juice for Christmas punch. We freeze our bright-colored Red Lake currants for use as food coloring and to add extra flavor to apple sauce and pies throughout the winter.

Tent caterpillars and other worms may attack both the leaves and fruit of currants and gooseberries, but these can be checked by spraying with Thuricide, a biological control. Mildew on currants is difficult to control once it is established, and sun and wind are the best preventatives. Set your plants in a sunny, airy place, and make sure the bushes never become crowded.

Some states have laws that prohibit planting gooseberries and currants near white pine trees. Both have long been reputed to be carriers of blister rust, a disease that can be fatal to these trees and other pines that have five needles in a cluster. Recent research confirms that black currant and wild gooseberry are the primary culprits, and most common garden varieties of these fruits have been absolved of harboring the disease. This verdict is not unanimous, so a nursery may need to check with the agricultural department of your state before filling your order.

For centuries the elderberry has been hailed as a healthful tonic and, fresh or fermented, was widely consumed for medicinal purposes. The fruits are stripped from their umbels and usually made into jelly, juice, and wine rather than eaten fresh. The lacy white blossoms are edible, too, either fried in batter or brewed into a punch. This beverage is made by putting the bloom clusters in a large glass jar filled with weak lemonade, and leaving the jar in the sun for a day. The elderberry drink is then strained and chilled.

Hybrid elderberry plants reach 6 to 8 feet in any good garden soil, but do especially well wherever it is moist (but not wet) all season. They have few insect and disease problems, but we always race with the birds to see who gets the bulk of the crop. Adams and Nova are our favorite varieties. Although elderberries are somewhat self-fertile, they produce better if two kinds are planted near each other. They often produce a few berries the year they are planted.

You may want to experiment with native bush fruits that are less well known and have little commercial value. The new varieties of saskatoon or juneberry (*Amelanchier alnifolia*) are popular in western Canada, and are an ideal bush fruit in those colder parts of the United States where blueberries may not grow well. The beach plum (*Prunus maritima*) is popular near the shore, where it thrives. The Nanking and other bush cherry-plums are planted widely in the North Central states, and edible varieties of bush honeysuckle and mountain ash are offered by some nurseries.

The highbush cranberry (*Viburnum trilobum*) has loyal fans, but

THE BERRY PATCH

107

❖

its flavor is far stronger than the commercially grown bog cranberry—so strong that the birds seldom bother with it. The berries mellow somewhat after the first frost, however, and then the juice can be mixed with apple juice to make a delicious jelly. Several named varieties are a bit larger and slightly better in flavor. We value our large bushes mostly for the looks of their foliage and berries, and use them in floral arrangements and to decorate Christmas wreaths. The bright red cranberries hang on the bush for most of the winter in dramatic contrast with the snow.

The Bramble Fruits

We'd argue that fresh raspberries and blackberries—eaten directly from the bush, or in pies, shortcakes, or ice cream—make any disadvantages of country living fade far into the background.

There are so many varieties of bramble fruits that one kind or another is suitable for nearly every backyard garden, and with a little care they come into production quickly and live for many years. Plants set out in the spring will produce a few fruits the next summer, and if growth has been good, by the following year they should offer a full-size crop.

The blackberry is too vigorous and competitive for small backyards, but one advantage of living in a rural area is that you probably have some acreage where you can safely let them take over. Choose a spot far from other plantings or one where you can keep them confined by mowing around them each week. It isn't easy to work among the prickly bushes, so gloves and a heavy jacket are in order.

Culture

You can buy berry plants through the mail or from a local nursery, but if you need a large number, you can save substantially by ordering through a wholesale nursery (see Appendix). Mail-order plants are shipped bare-rooted in spring or fall, while nurseries and garden centers usually offer a choice of bare-rooted and potted plants. The potted plants will cost more, but because they are already established and growing they give the fastest results.

Set bramble plants in soil that is prepared and fertilized as well as if you were planting a vegetable garden. Place red and yellow raspberries and upright blackberries 2 to 3 feet apart, and purple and black raspberries and vine blackberries (dewberries) 3 to 4 feet apart; space the rows 6 to 8 feet apart. You may want to keep a strip of lawn between the rows, rather than cultivate or mulch it, and the grass will help to keep the berries clean. Even though bramble plants sucker and may become invasive, they do not compete well with grass and weeds, so mulch or cultivate them to help them produce well. One foot of row should produce between a pint and a quart of berries during the season.

As soon as your bare-rooted plants are set in the earth and watered well, and the soil is firmed in around them, cut back the tops to 1 or 2 inches above ground level. (Leave the tops of potted plants unpruned.) Pruning encourages plants to produce the canes that will bear fruit the following year. Water them whenever nature does not provide rain, and supply liquid seaweed or fish emulsion once a week until mid-summer to encourage fast growth. Remove any canes that sprout up in the space between the rows.

The canes of the brambles are biennial, growing one year, producing the following year, and then dying. After the summer berry season is over, cut off at ground level the old canes that have borne fruit and are dying. It's best to burn them or take them to a landfill, since diseases and insects may overwinter in dead canes. Support the remaining canes with a strand of heavy wire, plastic cord, or boards fastened to posts, so they won't break over during the winter or when ladened with fruit.

Bramble fruit canes can be supported by strands of heavy-gauge wire.

THE BERRY PATCH

109

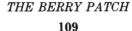

To avoid disease, buy only certified plants and choose disease-resistant varieties. If you take plants from a neighbor or transplant your own, be positive they are disease-free. Get rid of all the wild brambles growing within 200 feet also, because they are likely to be infected with mosaic and other serious diseases. Plant red and yellow raspberries at least 150 feet from black and purple varieties, since the latter may have an inherent virus and pass it on to the red and yellow varieties.

Red, yellow, and certain purple raspberry varieties propagate themselves by sending up suckers. You can dig these up in early spring and transplant them. Black raspberries and most purple ones propagate naturally by layering—the tall canes bend to the ground and the top ends take root. You can increase your planting by carefully bending over some of the newly grown canes in late summer and burying their tips in the soil. By the following spring, these tips will have rooted, and can be cut from the parent and planted. The new plants will begin to bear fruit in a year or two.

Besides the regular-bearing raspberries that ripen their crop in the summer, you can also raise those that produce two crops the same year. One crop ripens in the fall on canes that grew that summer, and another crop appears the following summer, on the same canes. These are sometimes called everbearers.

Fresh red raspberries sell extremely well and command premium prices. Because they are highly perishable, you can sell them only to the local market, but this means you will have little competition from elsewhere. If you decide to grow the two-season bearers commercially for the fall market, start slowly: people are not yet conditioned to buying fresh raspberries in September and October.

The common upright-growing blackberry resembles the red raspberry in its growth habits and the way the new plants are produced, so their culture is similar. Members of the vine blackberry (or dewberry) family, which includes boysenberry, youngberry, and loganberry, grow more like the black and purple raspberries, and are treated in a similar fashion except that they can be planted further apart. Their long canes need to be tied to a fence or trellis since they are too weak to support themselves. Most cultivated blackberries offered in catalogs are not as hardy as raspberries; vine blackberries are even more tender, and best suited to warmer climates (Zones 6 and 7).

Chapter 14

GRAPES ARE WORTH THE TROUBLE

Since Biblical times, grapes have symbolized fertility, and whether eaten or drunk, they were a part of the good life. A vine laden with fruit in late summer is a beautiful sight, and a table with a centerpiece lush with grapes makes any meal a banquet. So why aren't grapes more widely grown in North America? Perhaps because it is so often repeated that grape growing and winemaking are secret skills, shared by only a few devoted families, and that grape growing isn't for amateurs.

We can think of no good reason for the rural gardener to avoid grape growing. Grapes need little care, but to get the best results you should choose the right varieties for your climate.

The hundreds of varieties grown in North America can be sorted into four main classes:

1. American hybrids of the native fox grape (*Vitis labrusca*) were developed in New England and New York. The vines are hardy and productive, and the fruits are large and juicy. Many varieties inherited the pleasant, zippy flavor of the wild grape.

The *labrusca* hybrids are widely planted in the grape-growing regions of the East and southern Canada. Concord, Niagra, and Delaware were early varieties, but they now have many descendants. They are grown for juice, wine, and table use.

2. Vinifera vines are of European origin, grown especially for wine, raisins, and table use. These have a high sugar content, which

allows them to dry better without spoiling, and many seedless varieties have been developed. Because they are very sensitive to climate changes, they are grown mostly on the West Coast, and it is a challenge to grow them elsewhere in the country.

3. The Muscadines are grown mostly in the Southeast, where diseases make it difficult to grow other varieties. In places where root insects and diseases are particularly virulent, these grapes must be grafted on resistant rootstocks to be successful.

Muscats have a strong musky odor, and are suitable for table use and juice. Most, however, are made into wine, and a considerable wine industry has developed in recent years in the South.

4. The French hybrids were developed to combine the sweetness, fragrance, flavor, and winemaking qualities of the best of the European grapes with the hardiness, vigor, and disease resistance of the Americans. These grapes are used primarily for wine, and have enabled growers who don't live on the West Coast to produce vintages that compare favorably with the best of Europe.

Grapes thrive in heat, so choose a warm, sheltered spot for your vineyard, with a slope toward the south where there will be sun all day. If possible, pick a spot with light sandy soil, because it will warm up quickly in the spring and stay warm. Most grape varieties need a growing season of at least five months, free of frost and characterized by warm days and nights. For this reason, growers in northern climates should plant only varieties that are hardy and ripen in a short season. Grape leaves, flowers, and fruit are all very tender to frost, and it's difficult to cover them on cold nights. Fortunately, they leaf out and blossom late, so spring frosts are usually not a problem, but early cold snaps in fall may ruin the crop in almost any section of the country.

Check with your extension service and growers near you before selecting varieties. A grape vine should produce for many generations, so take care in choosing the one that is right for you.

Grape vines are lovely trailing over a backyard arbor, trellis, or pergola, and can create pleasant shady nooks for picnics, Italian style. We've seen them climbing over small trees—the Romans once cultivated them in this manner and the southern Italians still do. But for the best quality fruit and highest yield, the vines need maximum

This two-wire grape trellis can be supported with posts of pressure-treated lumber, cedar, locust, or redwood.

exposure to sunlight. One of the most common ways is to train them on a two-wire fence, spacing the posts about 8 feet apart. The wire should be smooth, about 9 gauge, with one strand 2 feet above the ground and the second about 3 feet higher. Plant one vine midway between each post.

Before planting, loosen the soil within a 4-foot circle to encourage the roots to grow rapidly. The hole should be about the size of a bushel basket, and nearly filled with a mixture of one-third topsoil, one-third rich compost, and one-third sand.

Culture

Some growers believe that poor soils produce some of the best wines. And it's true that too much nitrogen will produce excessive vine growth, putting plants at risk where early frosts are the rule. But a good soil is usually recommended. Avoid using fresh manure and chemical fertilizers; they affect the flavor of the fruit, and you are best off with dried or well-aged manure and compost.

Use mulches with care. They not only keep the soil cool, which northern growers don't need, but they can encourage shallow root development, which is not as good as a deep growing root system. To allow the soil to warm more quickly, don't use mulch until the days

❖

become hot and the nights stay warm. Commercial growers often plant clover or other cover crops and plow them under every few years to add fertility.

Because grapes produce a heavy growth of both vines and fruit, you'll have to do heavy pruning. A compact vine favors the growth of the highest-quality grapes, those closest to the roots. Greater vine growth does not mean a greater yield.

You can prune whenever the vine is dormant. In the North, however, early spring pruning allows you to remove any winter injury at the same time.

Treat your grape canes as if they were biennials. The second summer after planting, let only four strong canes grow from each plant and train one along each wire as soon as it is large enough. Allow each cane to bear grapes the following year, and then cut them all off. Meanwhile, during the summer when the old vine is producing, allow four replacement canes to grow parallel to the bearing ones. Because you want only the four canes and no more, it will be necessary to snip off a lot of extra sprouts. After you have cut away the four old canes in the fall, tie the new ones to the wires so they'll be in place to produce fruit the next season.

If a vine bears too many fruits, its energy will be depleted; so, don't allow it to overbear, or future crops will suffer. A vine that's at least four years old should be allowed to produce from 30 to 60 bunches, but no more. If too many flower clusters are produced in the spring, remove them.

Be patient at harvesttime. We picked our grapes too early the first year the vines bore, and they were unusable. The fruit should be allowed to ripen completely on the vine because, unlike apples, pears, and peaches, grapes do not continue to ripen after they have been picked.

Our plants have been free from insects and disease. In warmer parts of the country, however, growers may run into serious insect and disease problems. Commercial growers must be prepared to fend off a variety of trouble. Prevention is one of the best safeguards for home growers. Buy healthy vines and plant them away from any other grapes, including wild ones, that show infestations. Even with the best of care some pests may appear, so controls will be necessary. Use the safest ones you can find, and discontinue using them several weeks before harvesttime.

❖

Fruit of the Vine

Although we all enjoy eating table grapes, drinking juice, and eating raisins (dried grapes), the word "grape" has been synonymous with wine since early Egyptian times. If you cultivate a vineyard on your own side hill, you may decide to ferment part of your crop into table wine.

Winemaking from grapes is an ancient, precision skill, and many of our friends have been disappointed with their home attempts. To improve your chances of bottling a good vintage, read up on the techniques and equipment beforehand. Use only the varieties suggested for wine.

Commercial Possibilities

Growing grapes on a large scale is a demanding business. Not only should the climate and soil conditions be ideal, but a definite market is essential to justify the large investment in land, plants, machinery, and supplies. Fertilization, pruning, pest control, and harvesting must all be done with great care.

On a small scale, grapes can be sold at roadside stands in baskets, or made into juice or jelly. In the fruit-growing regions of the Northeast, many orchardists raise grapes to sell along with their tree fruits, and they often press some into juice for local sales.

Growing grapes for wine is especially demanding, because winemaking is such an exacting, competitive business. Most wine producers are large, and in order to supply the huge volume of fruit they require, they often plant hundreds of acres.

Chapter 15

THE HOME ORCHARD

Although it takes a lot of work to maintain fruit trees, our orchard is probably the last project we'd give up on our farm. "A thousand pleasant delights are attending on an orchard," said William Lawson in the early 17th century, and still today no country place seems quite complete without at least one apple tree in the backyard.

Judging from the people who came to our nursery for fruit trees each spring, we are not alone in thinking this way. Apples are by far the most popular fruit in the home orchard, but you will probably want a few plum, peach, and cherry trees, too. Pears are delicious, but because they are particularly susceptible to disease, you may want to forgo them unless you like more of a challenge. Apricots, nectarines, and quinces are well worth culturing if you live in a hospitable climate and have the proper soil conditions.

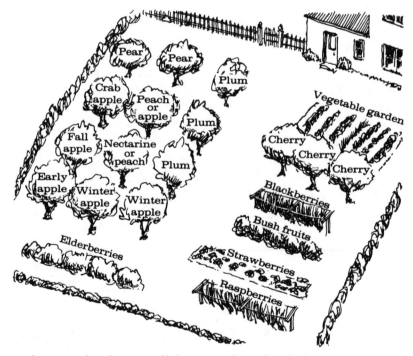

A suggestion for a small, home-scale orchard of tree fruits and berries.

If you haven't raised tree fruits before, don't make the same mistake we did when we began. We got carried away with tantalizing catalog pictures and descriptions, and ordered far more trees than we needed. Fruit trees, unlike shade trees, need a lot of care. We became aware that something was very wrong as soon as the trees began to bear. The fruits were tiny, wormy, and scabby. They looked nothing like the catalog pictures.

We now have an orchard of over a hundred trees, but we keep the trees small so that we can more easily fertilize them, control pests, prune them, and thin the fruit.

Shopping for Fruit Trees

Any fruit trees you buy are likely to be grafted, because named varieties cannot be grown from seed. If you were to plant a seed from a Delicious apple, for example, the resulting tree would not be a Delicious, but quite likely an inferior tree resembling its wild ancestors.

To get a true Delicious, a small branch of a Delicious tree must be grafted onto a rootstock (which may have been grown from a seed or taken from the division of a root clump). The kind of rootstock used in the graft will determine the ultimate size of the tree—dwarf, semi-dwarf, or full-sized.

If you choose dwarf or semi-dwarf trees, you can grow more trees, and a wider variety of fruits, in a small space. The smaller trees are easier to prune and spray, and harvesting is simpler too. They may be the best size for you, unless you live in Zone 3 or 4, where the rootstocks are not hardy. And because they are shallow rooted and tend to blow over easily, dwarfs and semi-dwarfs are not the best choice for a windy spot.

If you live, as we do, where dwarfs are unsuitable, you should plant standard trees instead. These grow between 15 and 20 feet high, so you'll have to perch on a ladder when working with them. But you can keep them to a manageable size by pruning heavily each year. They won't be as productive as when allowed to grow full height, but they will provide all the advantages of dwarf trees.

Location

Deep, rich, light, and loamy soil is ideal for an orchard. But if yours falls short, don't be upset. Poor soil can be improved by fertilizing, and by planting and plowing under cover crops (see Chapter 9). To succeed, a fruit tree needs nearly as much root growth underground as the limbs above. Make certain your tree will not have to grow horizontally because only a few inches of soil cover a layer of rock or hardpan.

Fruit trees tend not to grow well in wet soil, either, although plum trees that have been grafted on native plum roots can survive on soils that are moderately wet. Never plant the trees in a low spot where sudden rains or melting snow might cause water to cover their roots for more than a few hours at a time.

A gentle slope is the best location for an orchard, not only for water drainage but also so that cold air will drop to a lower level and be less likely to damage tree blooms on frosty spring nights. If late spring frosts are common in your region, you may want to avoid growing early blooming fruits such as peaches, cherries, pears, and plums and concentrate instead on apples and small fruits.

Whenever possible, buy trees that were grown, not merely sold, by a nursery with a climate similar to yours. This ensures that they will be acclimated. In the North, spring is the best time to plant bare-rooted trees because they will then have an entire growing season to get established before winter. If you live south of the Mason-Dixon line, fall planting allows trees to begin growing new roots before the top growth starts in the spring.

Potted and balled trees can be planted anytime the ground is not frozen, but it is best to get them in the ground at least a month before the soil begins to freeze.

Here are our suggestions for a home orchard of a dozen or so trees. For apples, choose at least one good cooking apple, an early eating variety, two fall-ripening kinds, and one or two of the winter keepers. (If you aren't familiar with the various kinds, the catalog descriptions or a good fruit book can help you decide which ones to plant.) Two different varieties each of plums, peaches, cherries, and pears should give you enough for eating fresh and some left over for preserving.

Follow the recommendations given in the catalog or at the nursery for varieties that will pollinate each other. You will probably need two different kinds of each species of fruit to ensure proper pollination, unless the catalog description states that one alone will produce by itself. Two trees in the McIntosh apple family, for example, cannot cross-pollinate, so you would need a second kind of apple to get fruit.

In our nursery business, we often try to talk people out of buying the so-called "all-purpose" varieties they know best, such as Red Delicious, McIntosh, and Golden Delicious apples. Although these fruits are good, they are primarily commercial varieties and need special care and lots of spraying. Less-known varieties are better for home gardeners because they are more disease-resistant, better flavored, and better suited for special uses such as cooking, eating, or cider.

Choose varieties of pears, plums, and peaches that are described as disease-resistant and suitable for your climate. All things being equal, we feel it is usually best to plant varieties that have been around for a while, rather than only the newest kinds. The oldies have stood the test of time, and are usually easier to grow for a beginning orchardist.

Planting

Space your trees according to the directions you receive with them, or according to the following table. Try to imagine these little trees as full-grown specimens, and allow them all the space and light they will later need.

The Home Orchard

	Number of Trees	Planting Distance (feet)	
		Standard	Dwarf
Apple	3–6	35–40	8–10
Apricot	1–2	20	12
Cherry (sour)	1–2	20	12
Cherry (sweet)	2–3	20	12
Peach	2–4	20	12
Pear	2–4	20	10
Plum	2–5	20	12

Carefully follow the planting directions you receive with the trees, and during the first month, water each one every day that it does not rain hard. The roots do not yet go deep enough to find by themselves the moisture they need. And for the first month, give them a weekly dose of liquid fertilizer such as kelp, fish emulsion, or manure mixed with water.

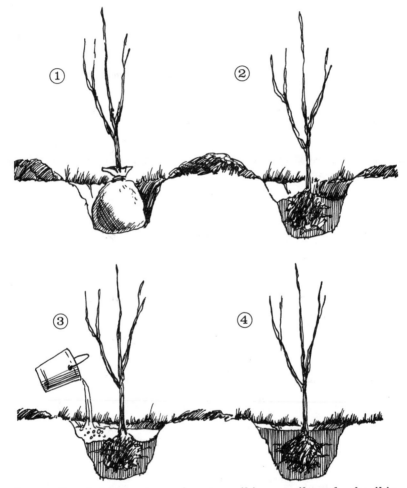

As you dig a hole for a tree, place topsoil in one pile and subsoil in another (1). Remove wrapping around trees balled in plastic (but leave burlap on). Fill the hole with a mixture of the topsoil and compost (2). Water generously (3), and continue to do so at least a couple of times a week unless the weather is rainy. A slight depression around the tree (4) will catch rainwater.

❖

Do not force a young tree to compete with grass and weeds for nutrients and moisture. Mulch it with shredded bark, lawn clippings, wood chips, or other organic matter to suppress competitive plant growth in the vicinity of the roots and to prevent the soil from drying out.

Orchard Care

It is best to prune fruit trees as little as possible until they begin to bear. Early pruning can make them grow excessively, which will delay bearing. It is important, however, to cut off any branches that form very close to the ground and those growing too close together. Try to let each tree have only one central stem, at least in early life, and remove any extra tops or limbs that might cause it to grow into a large bush instead of a tree. Inspect your new orchard frequently, so that you can pinch away a new branch growing in the wrong place rather than cut off a large limb later.

Once the trees begin to bear, you will have to prune annually. Unpruned trees are likely to produce a large crop of small, poorly colored fruit—and only every other year. Pruning decreases the number of fruits, but it increases their size and promotes annual bearing. By pruning to let more sunlight reach the tree's interior, you also ensure better color and flavor.

Do not neglect the annual spring fertilizing ritual. A large tree requires a lot of nutrients and moisture to produce its heavy growth of wood, leaves, and fruit. Be sure that the fertilizer contains a good percentage of nitrogen—one of the most important nutrients for fruit trees. Among the best are farm or dried manure (especially poultry manure), cottonseed meal, and blood meal. Greensand, bone meal, and phosphate rock have other important nutrients but little or no nitrogen. Mulch will decompose and add fertility, so add to it each year. Test your soil every three or four years and add lime or wood ashes if the pH is too low; apples and pears like a pH of about 6.5 to 7, and most other fruits prefer one of 5.5 to 6.5.

Although it takes time, we pick off perhaps 90 percent of the fruits when they are marble size, so that those that remain are about 6 inches apart. Like thinning vegetables, this procedure produces bigger and better fruit, and by saving all the energy that would otherwise go into producing extra seeds, helps the tree to bear a good crop every year.

Pests

Although some fruit tree varieties are more resistant to disease and insects than others, both problems are familiar to all fruit growers. The cool, humid climate of the North favors disease, and the warm weather in southern climates encourages a host of insects.

Orchard sanitation is the best method of control. Cut away all dead and diseased wood, and all diseased wild trees in the area. Remove nearby brush and board piles where insects can hide, and pick up all the unused fruit each fall so that insects and disease can't overwinter in it. Try to plant only disease-free and disease-resistant varieties, and fertilize and mulch the trees to keep them growing in a healthy fashion.

Although nobody likes to use spray, some sort of insect and disease control is necessary if you are to get good fruit. Dormant oils, insecticidal soaps, *Bacillus thuringiensis*, ryania, and insect traps go a long way toward thwarting pests. Your farm store or local garden cooperative can help you decide which are best for you, and tell you how to apply them.

Spray at the beginning of the season, and later on, only if you have a disease or insect problem. Discontinue spraying several weeks before the fruits will be picked. Organic gardeners prefer to put up with a minor amount of scab and insect damage, rather than eat fruit that is covered with spray. In addition to insecticides and fungicides, commercial orchards use a wide variety of chemicals that repel deer and birds, control brush and weeds, thin the fruit, and make it color earlier. They even use a chemical to prevent premature fruit drop and to ensure that fruit hangs on the tree until it is completely ripe.

Equipment

A small home orchard doesn't demand a lot of equipment. Most hardware or farm stores will be able to supply what you need, and check with the orchard supply firms listed in the Appendix.

You'll need pruning tools and a sprayer, and a ladder if your trees are full-sized. A cart or trailer for your tractor will come in handy for bringing in fertilizer and mulch, and carrying off fruit and prunings. We use a picking bag that fits over the shoulders and leaves both hands free, unlike a pail or basket. And, of course, you'll need boxes or baskets for the fruit, and a cool shed or cellar for storage until you use or sell it.

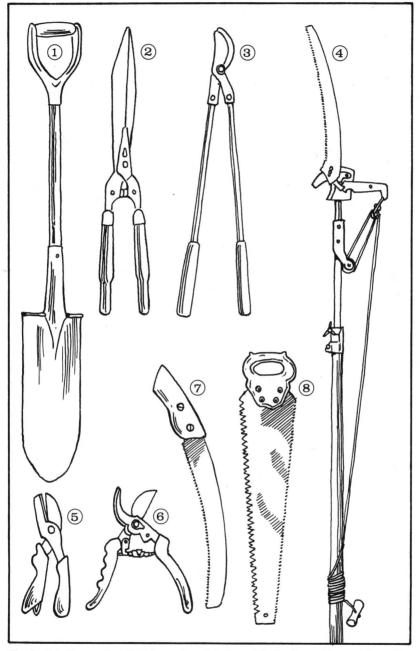

Tools for the orchard: (1) spade with long blade for root pruning; (2) hedge shears; (3) loppers; (4) pole saw with pruner; (5) hand pruner, anvil type; (6) hand pruner, scissors type; (7) pruning saw; (8) double pruning saw.

THE HOME ORCHARD

❖

After trying several types of sprayers, both gasoline powered and hand pumped, we have settled on a small trombone type sprayer that draws from a pail on the ground. It is easy to clean, has no tank to rust out or motor to give trouble, and fits the needs of our small orchard wonderfully.

If you live where deer are a problem, as we do, you'll need a high, tight fence. For a large orchard, it must be 8 or 9 feet tall to keep the vandals out. Don't count on an electric fence unless it has many strands and is the powerful sort used to contain sheep. If you have only a few trees you can surround each with a 6-foot-tall fence of chicken wire. You may also need to use a finer mesh of wire screening, or a plastic tree guard, to protect each trunk from mice and rabbits.

Reviving an Old Orchard

Many people inherit an old orchard when they move to the country. If you are one of those, you face a tough decision: restore it or convert it to firewood.

If the trees appear to be relatively solid structurally, and are varieties that bear fruit that you like, you may be able to bring the orchard back into shape in a relatively short time. Begin by cutting out all underbrush, dead and dying trees, dead and diseased limbs, and sucker trees bearing worthless fruit. Next, initiate a pruning program that you will spread over several years. You won't want to shock large, unpruned trees by trying to revitalize them all at once; they may kill themselves by rapidly generating new growth. Never remove more than one-sixth of a tree in any one year.

Gradually thin out old wood and branches that are growing too close together, and open up the tops to allow sunlight to shine on the interior branches. Fertilize the trees each spring, mow the grass and weeds, and start a regular disease and insect control program.

When the fruit begins to form in early summer, thin it to a distance of 6 inches from each other. By the second year, you should already see some improvement in the size of the fruit.

None of this work will be worthwhile if the trees in your orchard are in a decrepit condition or bear small, sour, hard fruit. In that case it is more prudent to turn the orchard over to the wildlife or saw it up for the wood stove. Fruitwood burns with colorful flames in the fireplace—a noble end for fine, old trees.

Commercial Fruit Growing

Many small orchards in our region sell their surplus fruit at health food stores, farmers' markets, and roadside stands. Larger ones also press cider and produce fruit pies, jams, jellies, grape juice, and honey from orchard hives.

But commercial fruit growers have a long wait between starting the enterprise and selling the first big crop. In the meantime you must invest a great deal of money and time. In addition to the initial costs, operating expenses go on every year, since trees need care whether they are bearing or not. You will need equipment for pruning, pest control, harvesting, grading, packing, fertilizing, mowing, hauling away prunings, and moving fruit. It requires nearly as much machinery to handle a 10-acre orchard as one of 100 acres, although small-scale orchardists can contract out jobs such as spraying and pruning.

Additional help is necessary at harvesttime, and probably for thinning, pruning, and grading as well. Fruit storage isn't a problem if the fruit will be sold within a few weeks, but if you store fruit for sale during the winter when prices are higher, you will need insulated buildings and refrigeration.

To ensure good pollination of the blossoms, you should have two or three bee hives for each acre of fruit. Although this is an additional investment in time and money, the honey can be a worthwhile addition to your merchandising.

If you grow a large number of fruit varieties your stand will be an exciting place to visit, and customers will drive long distances to get their favorites. For large-scale marketing in more distant markets, however, you will probably need to do like everyone else and specialize in the three or four commercial varieties that have skins tough enough to be handled several times without bruising.

Chapter 16
GROWING NUTS

Going nutting in the back country was a favorite sport when we were young, and each of us knew of big old trees we never told anyone else about. Even bird hunters often took along a bag in case they came across a special tree.

Most nut trees grow very large, and an advantage of a large lot is that you have room to grow these beautiful, edible ornamentals. (A note of caution: one of our neighbors wishes she hadn't planted a butternut in the middle of her front lawn, because it drops nuts in the grass and they have damaged her mower several times.)

Nut trees grown for home use seldom require spraying or pruning, and need little other care. Your climate may greatly limit the varieties you plant, though. Most species grow well only in Zone 5 or warmer, and some, such as almond, pecan, and English walnut, do best where there is little frost. Only the butternut, American hazelnut, and hardy strains of black walnut are suitable in Zones 3 and 4. All nut trees acclimate to their regions, so if you live in Zones 3 to 5, buy trees that were grown from seed that was raised in a similar climate. We have gathered butternut seeds near Albany, New York, only to have the young trees winterkill in our northern Vermont temperatures.

All the nuts—butternuts, pecans, walnuts, filberts, chestnuts, and hickories—are delicious and rich in protein. Most can be stored unshelled for several years without losing either their flavor or nutritional value. Squirrels, bears, and many birds enjoy nuts too, so the trees are excellent for attracting wildlife; we have to be right on the job to beat squirrels to the harvest.

If you want to make a long-range investment in the future, consider a widespread planting of nut trees. A few acres of black walnuts could grow into a fortune in lumber for your children or grandchildren, and produce many crops of nuts in the meantime. Black walnut, pecan, and butternut lumbers are all prized for paneling and for making fine furniture. In fact butternut is one of the strongest lightweight woods known—so strong that windmill blades were once made from it.

Nut trees are not for the impatient, whether you want them for their nuts or lumber. Most take at least five years to bear, and may not produce a large crop for a decade or more. Even after they reach maturity, some bear only every second or third year. Also, because the blossoms are sensitive to cold, a late spring frost at blooming time can destroy the crop.

Don't buy nut trees over 5 feet tall, because they may not survive if their long tap roots are cut or badly bent. Butternuts and black walnuts are self-pollinating, and a lone tree will produce nuts, but other species produce well only if they have a partner. If you plant several of the same species, be sure they are not all of the same variety, because more than one is necessary to ensure pollination. Almonds are pollinated by bees and can be planted farther apart, but the other species are pollinated by the wind, and must be within 100 feet of each other.

Harvesting is easy. Gather the nuts as soon as they fall from the tree, and spread them out on elevated window screens so that they can air dry. Ventilated greenhouses, garages, and attics are good drying places. Butternuts and black walnuts will keep for years if kept dry, and most others can be saved for a year or two if they are kept at 40 degrees F. or cooler.

Cracking the hard-shelled nuts, such as the hickories and black walnuts, can be a tough chore. To make it easier, pour boiling water over them and leave them to cool for 20 minutes. The shells then pop open easily, and the nuts come out intact.

Commercial Nut Growing

Pecans and walnuts are the most popular commercial nuts. You can sell them as gift items in attractive packages at a roadside stand or to stores and garden centers. Some nut orchardists sell them wholesale, in bulk; others market their entire crop by mail; and still others allow their customers to gather their own.

Chestnuts sell well during the Thanksgiving and Christmas holidays when they are roasted or added to the traditional bird stuffing. Black walnuts are used in ice cream, cakes, candies, and frostings. In our area, maple butternut fudge is considered a holiday treat.

The trees are useful for more than nuts and lumber. Charcoal made from nut shells is used in gas masks and for filters. Hickory is one of the finest firewoods, and the bark is used for smoking meats.

Income from nut production can be high, but the risks are great, too, since insects, disease, squirrels, and bad weather can take a toll on your profits. It is time-consuming to collect the nuts by hand, and mechanical equipment for shaking the trees and picking up the nuts is expensive. You'll need drying and storage areas, as well as grading and packing equipment. If you sell nut meats, you'll also need shelling equipment. As with many agricultural businesses, a small grower must invest nearly as much capital to get started as a large one.

Nut trees intended for lumber are planted much closer together than for nut production. Early care is necessary to ensure that the trees grow straight. Bottom limbs must be cut off so the log will be knot-free. Consult with a forester before committing your land to this venture.

Nut Species

ALMOND (*Prunus dulcis dulcis*), Zones 7 to 9
Almonds are grown mostly on the West Coast. The trees are in the same hardiness range as the peach, but almonds blossom very early and are so tender to frost that they can be grown only in locations with long frost-free periods.

The almond is closely related to the peach, and the nuts somewhat resemble the pits of the stone fruits. The trees need cross-pollination, so several different varieties should be planted together. Unlike most other nuts, pollination is done by insects rather than by wind, so the varieties do not need to be as near each other as is recommended for wind-pollinated trees. Named varieties are far superior to those grown from seedlings, and begin to bear as early as three or four years after planting.

CHESTNUT (*Castanea*), Zones 5 to 9
The Chinese chestnut (*C. mollissima*) is the source of most chestnuts sold today. The tree grows to 50 feet tall. It is about as hardy

❖

as a peach, but a long growing season is necessary because the nuts mature late in the season.

The Japanese chestnut (*C. crenata*) is a small tree, ideal for the home garden, but unfortunately it is hardy only in Zone 7 or warmer. The tree is not quite as resistant to blight as the Chinese, nor is the nut quality as high.

The American chestnut (*C. denata*) has been nearly extinct since the blight in the early 1900s, and only a few scattered trees remain. Hybrids between the survivors and other chestnuts include Central Square, Eaton, Sweet Home, and Watertown, all of which appear to be somewhat blight-resistant.

FILBERT (*Corylus*), Zones 5 to 9

The American hazelnut is a tasty native filbert, but the meats are small and it is of value mostly as a food for wildlife. European filberts (*C. avellana*) are the ones found in holiday nut assortments, and are a good size for backyard plantings—about like standard apple trees.

They are easy to grow, and should be fertilized little, if any. Many named varieties are now available. In Zones 6 and warmer, try Barcelona, Davoama (best for the Northwest), Bixby, Buchanan, Graham, Reed, Royal, and Skinner. Rush and Winkler are hybrids between the European species and the native hazelnut (*C. americana*), and they appear to be the best choices for Zones 4 and 5.

We are presently growing some Turkish filbert trees. They are usually grown as ornamentals, and the small, thick-shelled nuts are good for attracting wildlife. The trees appear to be hardy even in New England, and have survived several of our Zone 3 winters.

HICKORY AND PECAN (*Carya*), Zones 5 to 8

The native hickories are moderately hardy, and grown over a large part of central and eastern United States. The shagbark (*C. ovata*) produces the best nut of the native hickories, although it is seldom grown commercially. Its shape and loose rough bark recommend it as an ornamental.

Improved varieties such as Davis, Glover, Mann, Nielson, and Wilcox are easier to shell than their ancestors, and have larger meats as well. They are offered in nut specialty catalogs (see Appendix), but are rarely sold by nurseries and garden centers. Although their hardiness has not been widely tested, they appear to be best suited for Zone 6 or warmer.

The large, attractive pecan tree is a close relative of the hickory, but bears much higher quality nuts. Pecans require a mild climate to survive, and because the nuts need a long growing season to ripen they can be grown successfully only in the warmest parts of Georgia, Florida, and other subtropical states. The trees are usually planted about 30 to the acre. Improved papershelled varieties include Apache, Barto, Cherokee, Comanche, Major, Mohawk, Sioux, and Stuart.

Several recent hybrids of the hickory and pecan, including Burton and Geraldi, can grow up into Zone 6—good news for northern pecan lovers. Recently we heard of a tree producing nuts in Pennsylvania.

WALNUT AND BUTTERNUT (*Juglans*), Zones 3 to 9

The so-called English or Persian Walnut (*J. regia*) is by far the most popular nut. (Peanuts are not true nuts.) Ninety-seven percent of the walnuts marketed in the United States are grown on the West Coast, where the mild climate and long growing season favor the trees.

An important recent introduction is the Carpathian walnut, which is very similar to the English but capable of growing in all but the coldest sections of the country. Hybridizers have been hard at work, and varieties with larger meats are being introduced every year. These include Ashworth (one of the hardiest), Colby, Deming, Hansen, Morris, and Shafer.

The black walnut (*J. nigra*) and butternut (*J. cinera*) are native to the eastern United States and Canada and hardier than even the Carpathian walnut; the butternut thrives in Zone 3, and the black walnut grows well in most of Zone 4. Although varieties with thinner shells and larger meats are now available, they are nearly always less hardy than the natives. Improved butternuts include the Ayres, Beckwith, Craxeasy, Johnson, van Syckle, and Weschcke. Improved black walnuts are Burns, Elmer Meyers, Huber, Patterson, Snyder, Thomas, and Weschcke.

The roots of black walnut and butternut produce a toxic substance that kills off many other plants, so you may want to think twice before planting them near flowerbeds or other landscape trees. They are also vulnerable to diseases, which are difficult to control, spoil the appearance of the trees, and greatly shorten their lifespans.

Chapter 17
LANDSCAPING THE COUNTRY HOME

We suspect that our ancestors on this farm thought of a tree as something for an Indian to hide behind. Until 50 years ago, there were only a few large maples left standing about our home. As soon as we were in charge, however, we went a bit wild and planted shade trees, foundation shrubs, and windbreaks. Now, a large part of our landscape maintenance involves cutting out trees and shrubs that have become too large or overcrowded.

The prospect of landscaping a nearly treeless homesite can be intimidating. Consider postponing major landscaping decisions until you have lived with the property for at least a year. The delay will give you time to study the idiosyncracies of the site. You'll learn such things as the fastest route to the garden, the views you most enjoy in winter, where you will be driving tractors and trucks, which areas belong to the animals, and where heavy rain, snow, ice, and other vagaries of nature tend to alter the terrain.

Landscaping in the country does not stop at the edge of the front and backyard. We are presently cleaning up and beautifying a wooded area by our brook, cutting dead trees, moving rocks, and planting ferns and other shade-loving plants. Soon we'll have a good spot for walking and picnicking. You may want to lay out a riding path, snowshoe lanes, and a nature walk—long-term projects for your family and friends to enjoy.

With imagination you can make good use of what may appear to be a difficult-to-remove eyesore, or enhance a natural feature. One of our neighbors has turned the foundation of a long-gone barn into a beautiful sunken garden with trailing plants hanging over the stone walls. Friends of Adele Dawson, a well-known herbalist in northern Vermont, helped her build an authentic Japanese teahouse beside a dramatic waterfall behind her home. Other friends of ours cut a maze of paths through their woods for strolls, and one Halloween they set up a walk filled with cobwebs, skeletons, and wailing trees.

Consider just how many hours a week you and your family want to invest in your grounds. Obviously, if you love to work outdoors and enjoy gardening, a large lawn and an arboretum can be a pleasure to care for rather than a chore. On the other hand, you'd be frustrated if you devoted untold hours creating a gorgeous landscape that you have no time to enjoy. Remember that if you hire a professional landscaper, you may end up with a place that requires a professional gardener to keep in shape.

For your first plantings, select trees, flowers, and shrubs that take little work. You will find plenty of other outdoor projects that demand your time. Native plants tend to be better suited to a country home than exotics. They are also acclimated and usually more resistant to diseases and insects. We also like them because we can do much of our shopping right on the farm, digging and transplanting them to their new site on the same day. In taking plants from the wild, though, we have learned that it is best to give them the kind of exposure they had originally. We transplanted hemlocks and native yews from sheltered spots to our exposed hillside, and they were damaged by winter winds. Ferns and wild flowers were accustomed to partial shade, and objected strongly when we moved them into the sun.

The Lawn

One landscaping project you may not want to put off is the lawn. If you have built a new house, or extensive grading has been done recently, you should cover the bare ground as soon as possible to prevent erosion, dust, and mud. Although commercially grown sod is expensive, it is convenient because it produces an instant lawn and spares you the long seeding process. If you plant seed instead of installing sod, buy a variety recommended for your climate and make sure it contains mostly *perennial* grasses. Lawn seeding can be done anytime from spring until fall, if you keep the newly seeded area moist and covered with a light mulch of hay or straw.

❖

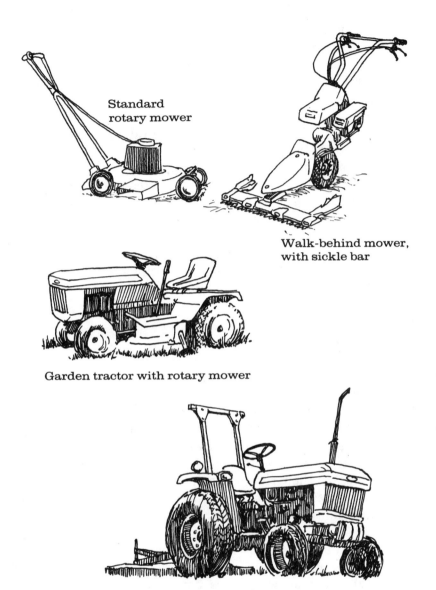

Standard rotary mower

Walk-behind mower, with sickle bar

Garden tractor with rotary mower

Small farm tractor pulling large rotary mower

Mowers for country-scale lawns.

Like most of our neighbors' lawns, ours was simply converted from a field. By mowing frequently, we got rid of the hay, and by attacking the weeds we now have a lawn that not only looks nice but also is able to stand heavy traffic. Although we drive loads of firewood over it and park cars on it, the rugged native grass still shows no sign of wear. Bluegrass wouldn't be able to take such treatment.

To revive a neglected lawn, add lime every two or three years and spread a balanced fertilizer each spring and fall. Your country lawn won't have to look as flawless as a suburban one, because there usually isn't pressure from the neighbors to keep it in top condition.

People we know in southern Vermont elected not to have a lawn at all, and planted their grounds entirely with shrubs and ground covers. They save the expense and trouble of mowing, but the plants require frequent attention. They have to keep weeds from crowding the ground covers, and they trim the shrubs. We confess that we would miss the open expanse of our lawn, and visiting children would miss the chance to play croquet and badminton.

Shade Trees and Shrubs

Country acreage gives you an opportunity to grow a wide variety of trees and shrubs. You can create a shady picnic grove on the edge of a pond, a row of fragrant lilac bushes lining the pathway to the barn, or a couple of shade trees just a hammock's distance apart. The hedges of arborvitae we planted years ago as a windbreak have delighted us each year with the unexpected bonus of nesting robins. We have friends who blocked their view of a neighbor's junk cars with a row of flowering crabapples. This privacy hedge also brings them flowers in the spring and many jars of bright red crabapple jelly each September.

Because shade trees take so long to grow, they should figure early in your landscape plan. Deciduous species such as maples, sycamores, flowering crabs, and dogwoods are among the most popular lawn trees. But spruces, firs, and arborvitaes cast a dense shade that keeps grass from growing well. Deciduous flowering shrubs such as azaleas, rhododendron, forsythia, hydrangea, and potentilla add bright color to what often appears to be an overly green landscape. In winter, when deciduous shrubs are bare and dead looking, we appreciate our evergreens. Group foundation plants imaginatively so that they won't have the symmetrical look found around suburban tract housing.

Look up, and to each side, before you plant anything. Our favorite front yard crabapple tree is growing into the power lines overhead because we failed to do that 30 years ago. Every few years we have to cut it back ruthlessly. Similarly, trees that were planted too close to houses rub against shutters and hold moisture that rots clapboards.

Other Plantings

After you have the basics in place, you may want to add some finer details to your landscape: wildflower plantings, clouds of daffodils or daylilies along a roadside, ferns in shady corners, groundcovers on banks too steep to mow, a rose garden, perennial border, rock garden, or a primrose path to the poultry house. Hedges are not as necessary for privacy in the country as in more populated areas, but they are useful for many other reasons. We planted arborvitae hedges to block our terrific north winds, and also to define the vegetable garden, backyard flower border and outdoor living area, berry patch, and orchard. Some of the hedges are sheared, but others are allowed to grow tall for greater wind protection and to keep plants from blowing over and drying out in the summer.

With lots of space, you are free to build terraces, pergolas, arbors, fences, and gazebos to enhance your grounds. We've seen water used imaginatively in pools and fountains. Our friends have a beautiful three-tiered pottery fountain in their shady wildflower garden. (The water is recirculated by an electric pump.) Other people we know pump water from their lake to create a babbling brook over a sloping rock ledge near their picnic area.

We often envy people who make furniture, or paint pictures; they can say, "Well, that's finally finished." With landscaping, however, you never seem to reach a point when you feel the job is completed.

Landscape Maintenance

Plants, trees, and grass need fertilizing, pest control, and mowing, pruning, or shearing to look their best. And sometimes plants must be taken out or moved if they are in the wrong place, and this may be psychologically challenging. Many people we know find it difficult to move a plant, despite the fact that it is unattractive, crowding its neighbor, or even threatening to fall on the house. Many of the plantings around the lake in our town have grown so large that views have disappeared, lawns, flowers, and vegetables no longer get enough sun to do well, and the windows of cottages get little sunlight.

We understand. It was a difficult decision to take out the large maple in front of our house that was planted when Lewis's parents were married, but it had become a hazard to the house, and to visitors' cars parked below. Unlike a favorite painting or a sentimental vase, our landscape is alive and constantly changing. We wouldn't have it otherwise, but sometimes it takes courage to do the right thing.

Chapter 18
THE FLOWER GARDEN

One of the joys of living in the country is that, even if you never plant a seed, nature will provide hundreds of different wild flowers each spring. Summer fields and roadsides fill with buttercups, clover, daisies, Queen Anne's lace, and other flowering plants. We enjoy ever-changing fresh native bouquets on our kitchen table, from the first pussywillows in late winter to the last asters of summer. Dried flowers and grasses take their place during the snowy months.

But we like to plant seeds, too. Our gardens of bulbs, annuals, and perennials give us great pleasure. We look forward each year to getting down on our hands and knees and working with trowel and clippers to encourage them to look their best.

If you are like many people, a primary reason for a move to the country is to indulge your passion for gardening, to transform a barren acre or more into spacious, curving beds of perennials, meadows of golden daffodils, and hillsides of lupine. Your country fantasies may include fern-lined paths winding through the woods, flowering hedges that lead from one garden to another, and borders of pungent herbs and brilliant annuals.

Gardening is refreshing and renewing, and especially so when you're doing it in a quiet rural setting. Accompanied by the nectar-loving hummingbirds, bees, and butterflies, the rural gardener easily slips into a restorative meditation.

Designing your country garden can be a real pleasure because you will probably have the freedom to choose from many possible sites. Will you concentrate on a plot near a brook or steep bank, or perhaps nestle a garden into an old stone wall or cellar hole? Like rural lawns and landscapes, country gardens tend to be less artificial and more informal than their urban cousins. You have great freedom to mix and match varieties and riotous color, as in an English cottage garden. And there is the very practical point that many soil-improving materials are readily available by the truckload—manure and mulch such as leaves, wood chips, spoiled hay, and spoiled fodder from a silo.

On the minus side, country flower gardens are prey to weed seeds that blow in freely from neighboring fields throughout the summer and fall. Dandelion fluffs and milkweed silks may look ethereal, but they grow into robbers of the soil's nutrients. Our current bugaboo is goldenrod, sprouting in every nook and cranny of the flower beds. A good thick mulch helps, but the seeds are only slightly deterred.

Another problem we should mention is trying to control your enthusiasm for transforming the nearly unlimited space at your doorstep. Many a large flower border has been started and abandoned for sheer lack of time and energy. Gardeners often paraphrase Keats: "A thing of beauty is a job forever."

Basic Blooms:
Bulbs, Annuals, and Perennials

We like to plant colorful annuals in nooks and crannies around our farmstead: in the center of an old granite millstone, in large iron kettles, a former cattle watering tub, old tree stumps, windowboxes, hanging baskets, pots on the terrace, and the perennial borders. Annuals provide constant splashes of color throughout the season if we remember to remove the fading blooms so they cannot produce seeds.

To get early blooms on your petunias, marigolds, and other annuals, you'll need to buy started bedding plants or start your own seedlings in late winter indoors. Set them out when the frost danger is past.

Although we start lots of our annuals inside, we also sow annual seeds in rows in the vegetable garden for bouquet cutting beginning mid-summer. Calendulas, cosmos, zinnias, bachelor's buttons, and strawflowers can be cut daily without concern about ruining the appearance of a well-filled flower border.

Biennials such as Canterbury bells, sweet william, and hollyhocks grow from seed the first year, but produce only leaves. In the second year, they blossom, ripen their seeds, and usually die, although with a short growing season like ours, some kinds may live longer. Because biennials often seed themselves and keep reproducing, their short lifespans may not be apparent. Even many wild flowers, such as black-eyed Susans, are of the biennial genre.

Perennial plants live for years, but most bloom for only a few weeks each year. One of the enormous challenges of gardening is to design a perennial garden that is ever changing, and offers blooms throughout the season. This requires you to understand the blooming schedule of each plant, and also its growth habits and lifestyle. Six-foot-tall delphinium need plenty of space in the rear of a border, but delicate dwarf astilbe would be lost if not situated at the very front. Few gardeners claim to be completely successful at this challenging occupation, and most of us spend a great deal of time moving our plants around.

Though you'd think that a perennial garden, once planted, might be work-free, that is not the case. The plants need an annual helping of compost or fertilizer, plus a thick mulch of organic matter. You'll also have to water them occasionally in dry seasons. In the fall they should be cut down after they have died back, and covered if winter temperatures fluctuate greatly. Most kinds, if they are to stay healthy and bloom well, must be divided at least every few years.

Flower Sales

You can profit from your hobby by selling garden flowers from your home, to florists, or at a farmers' market. One of our friends is busy throughout the summer providing flowers for special occasions, and is famous locally for her informal "country wedding" arrangements. She uses both wild and garden flowers, combined with the foliage of shrubs and grasses. She places ads in the local papers and on the community bulletin board at our local general store, but word-of-mouth is her best advertising.

Cutting gardens, including our rows of annuals in the vegetable garden, are often kept separate from the display flower bed. Because these flowers are grown in rows rather than beds, they can be cultivated and picked more easily. For long-lasting blooms, cut the flowers just as they are starting to open, and store them in a cool basement or large refrigerator. We have kept chrysanthemums and peony blooms for a month that way.

If you live within commuting distance of an urban area, you may have a ready market. New Hampshire friends of ours raise anemones, delphinium, and peonies and transport them in their van to the Boston wholesale market. Even in very rural areas like ours, people who don't raise flowers themselves will search out local cutting gardens to buy bouquets for special occasions.

Dried Arrangements

Arranging and selling dried flowers has become a brisk business in recent years. Winter bouquets, herb wreaths, potpourri, and pressed flower stationery are all popular at gift shops, craft shows, florists' shops and garden centers.

For bouquets and potpourri, many types of flowers may be air dried by hanging them upside-down in a warm, airy place out of the sun, such as a garage or attic, and stored in dust-free boxes or large paper grocery bags. Other sorts should be dried rapidly, with the help of white cornmeal, borax, and sand, or best of all, crystals of silica gel. Silica gel is available at florist and craft shops under various trade names such as Flower-Dri. It is relatively expensive, but can be reused.

Occasionally we press flowers or ferns to make our own Christmas cards, and others use them to make arrangements for framing or to decorate lamp shades. If you don't own a flower press, arrange the flowers between pieces of paper towel to absorb moisture and then insert them between the pages of a heavy catalog or under a pile of

❖

books. Ferns press well when they are laid flat between newspapers and placed under a rug for about a week.

You don't need to be a gardener to find an abundance of things for drying. If you wander around the countryside with a basket in summer or fall, you will come home loaded with treasures. Dormant grape vines can be dried and twisted into wreaths. Many grasses, cones, and berries dry well, and we use native nuts, berries, and seed pods both for winter arrangements and to decorate Christmas wreaths.

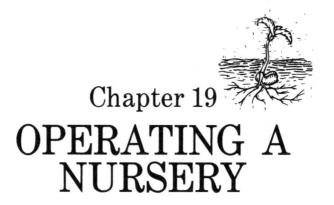

Chapter 19

OPERATING A NURSERY

For 40 years we ran a home nursery specializing in plants for cold climates, and in our statewide Plantsmen's Association there are nearly as many specialties as there are members: food plants, herbs, rock garden plants, wild trees for hedges, landscaping trees, and so on.

Many of us started because we enjoyed growing things and soon found our places overflowing with all the extra plants we had produced. Since we couldn't bear to throw good plants away, we opened a nursery and turned our hobby into a cash crop. A nursery can be started with only a little good land—in fact some are less than an acre in size. And it's wise to start off small until you know what you are doing. Selling plants and flowers is rated as a high-risk business, and many failures come within the first few years. Not only is weather beyond control, but an uncertain demand for the varieties you raise can also affect your success. A thorough knowledge of the plants you grow and sell is important, as is experience in insect and disease control. And, of course, an understanding of merchandising is essential.

Patience and the willingness to work hard are valuable assets to anyone who plans on working with plants and people, because the nursery business can be very demanding at certain times of the year. You must be able to cope with customers who arrive in force just as you are frantically doing your own propagating, planting, and maintenance. You'll also find that many customers like to pick up plants outside their working hours, so your days will be long, and holidays and weekends are likely to be your busiest times.

Although potted nursery stock can be planted safely all summer and fall, most gardeners are conditioned to spring planting, and lose interest in buying plants after the weather warms. So it is that most nurseryfolks we know are utterly exhausted by the end of spring. (One year we turned the calendar ahead three days early, because it felt so good just to tell ourselves that May was finally over.)

If you have limited training in horticulture, visit growers in your area and, if possible, work with someone already in the business. State universities often offer short courses in horticultural subjects through the extension service.

Growers in most states are well organized. If you raise perennials or trees, operate a greenhouse, or do landscaping, you may be interested in joining a group with similar interests. Trade magazines will help you keep up with current trends, give sources of plants and supplies, and list useful books.

Before you begin selling, your state department of agriculture will have to inspect and certify your nursery or greenhouse to ensure that your plants are free from harmful bugs or diseases. If you ship plants out of state, a copy of your certification must accompany each shipment.

Most small nurseries specialize in only a few popular plant species. Even if you choose to sell a wide variety, it is best to become well informed about one group of plants and feature them. If you choose varieties that are in demand and do well in your climate, your reputation should spread rapidly. You may not get rich, but we predict you'll find the work rewarding, and the customers nice. Another benefit is the knowledge that you are working with nature to beautify the world.

Investment and Equipment

A small nursery requires little more equipment than does a vegetable garden. If you buy plants from wholesale growers to resell, you can usually get short-term credit. This means you can sell at least part of the merchandise before payment is due.

A large nursery can be very expensive to equip, however. A field-growing operation requires tractors, trucks, and special machinery for tilling, planting, cultivating, and digging and moving the trees. Refrigerated sheds may be necessary for winter storage, and if you ship plants you'll need equipment for packing the stock. If you grow and sell plants in containers, you'll need to invest in soil mixers, potting machinery, and fork lifts for moving the plants. Landscapers need equipment for grading, moving large trees, building lawns, and pruning trees. A computer will be invaluable, too, in keeping detailed tabs on the operation.

In any type of nursery business, you will need a large, unfailing supply of water, and probably automatic irrigation. To propagate plants you will need a greenhouse with a mist system for starting cuttings. Required also are lath houses or shade frames, for growing seedlings and for hardening off cuttings started inside.

If you think in terms of high tech, you may want a laboratory where you can clone plants by culturing them in test tubes. Tissue culture is becoming a popular method of quickly producing disease-free plants in tremendous volume, but it is still rather impractical for a small-time operator. To build and equip a laboratory and greenhouses for growing the small explants, as they are called, may cost hundreds of thousands of dollars. Cloning also requires very strict control of temperature, pH, and humidity, since each plant needs a special culture. Few hospitals have such sterile conditions as a tissue culture laboratory; all the water and air entering the area must be purified of bacteria, germs, molds, and spores.

Field-Grown Nursery Crops

Nursery stock is usually grown by planting (lining out) small trees or plants (called liners) in rows in a field. Field-grown plants are dug by hand or, on a large scale, by mechanical diggers. Large nurseries dig their plants after they've become dormant in the fall, and store them over the winter in insulated refrigerated buildings.

❖

The plants are sold bare-rooted in the spring, or planted in pots and sold. Evergreens and large deciduous trees and shrubs are usually dug while dormant, with a ball of earth; they are wrapped in burlap or plastic, and sold as B and B (balled and burlapped) stock. Small nurseries usually dig their plants before they begin to grow in the spring, and either pot them or sell them wrapped in peat moss or other material.

Field growing of nursery stock is practical only if the field is relatively flat and the soil is deep and free from stones. Each crop of balled trees takes with it some 100 tons of topsoil per acre, and this must be replaced by trucking in new soil or by building it with heavily fertilized cover crops.

Container Gardening

By growing outdoor plants in containers rather than in the ground, you can sell your trees, shrubs, and perennial plants throughout the season in full leaf and in flower. Container gardening allows you to raise a large number of plants in a small space, and since feeding and watering can be better controlled, growth is faster and the plants are more uniform in size. Less labor is involved in selling, because if the plants are well labeled the buyer needs little attention and, as in a department store, can browse and make a leisurely selection. The customer also stands less risk of losing a plant because, unlike bare-rooted stock, all the roots are intact and undisturbed.

Container growing also has disadvantages. Pots, especially large ones, are expensive. They're heavy when filled with plant and soil. Potting mixtures must be carefully prepared according to the needs of the plant, with the proper pH and a good balance of soil, humus, sand, and nutrients.

Daily watering is necessary whenever rain doesn't do the job. Although automatic watering is a great convenience, no system is foolproof: overhead sprinklers are likely to supply too much or too little water, and tube waterers often become plugged. In our small nursery we always watered by hand because we liked to look over every plant each day and check for insects and disease. This duty meant that our life was regulated around watering, just as the day of our neighboring dairy farmers is centered around barn chores. Daily watering also means that the nutrients are rapidly leached from the pots, so a strict program of fertilization must be maintained.

Another problem for container growers is that the plants become root-bound after a year or two if they go unsold. They must either be planted in the field or transplanted to larger pots.

Propagation

You'll probably buy some wholesale plants for resale, but your highest profit will come from those that you yourself start and raise to selling size. The most common methods of starting plants are by (a) seeds, (b) cuttings or slips made by cutting off a branch and rooting it in sand or a vermiculite-perlite mix, (c) division of the parent plant into smaller plants, (d) grafting (surgically attaching a branch) or budding (attaching a bud), and (e) layering, in which a branch is bent down and partially buried in the soil to take root.

Nursery Projects

Bedding plants. Annual flower and vegetable plants—from petunias to cabbages—grown for spring planting are ideal crops for a beginner because you need so little investment in equipment, seeds, and containers. The plants are ready to sell in only a few weeks. Annuals can be started on a small scale in a corner of the house in late winter and then grown to saleable size in a greenhouse or cold frame. One friend in this business says he likes to grow and sell plants, but he also likes the fact he can do all his plant business in the spring and then have the freedom to collect antiques during the rest of the year.

Herbs. The recent interest in herbs has resulted in a market for all kinds of flavoring, medicinal, fragrant, and purely ornamental plants. We know of many successful herb growers, in businesses that include mail-order seeds and retailing everything from anise to yarrow in small pots. Like bedding plants, herbs are easy to raise and take little equipment or skill. If you are growing annual herbs to sell, you'll need a greenhouse or hotbed, but we know growers who sell only perennial herbs and dig plants for customers on the spot.

Perennial flowers. The demand for perennials appears to be increasing each year. Some plants come and go in popularity, but ever-popular species are daylilies, hosta, iris, lilies, peonies, ground covers, wild flowers, water plants, ferns, and rock garden plants. The initial plants may be a large part of your investment. Since most plants are grown and propagated outdoors, a greenhouse isn't necessary. You don't need to pot them either, unless you decide to do it as a convenience to your customers. Most perennials can be dug, wrapped in a newspaper, and safely taken home and planted. A former hobby gardener in our town has developed a wide following among both wholesale and retail customers by enlarging her private gardens and selling a wide range of flowering plants. Her husband, who thought they had retired, has become her partner, and they are both as busy now as when they had full-time jobs.

Woody plants. These plants—shade trees, flowering shrubs, ornamental evergreens, hedge plants, bush fruits, fruit trees, and berry plants—obviously require more growing space than bedding plants and perennials. They also take longer to grow. Your initial investment can range from very modest to something your banker may find questionable; the variables are the size of your operation, whether you buy small plants to grow for a few years or propagate your own, and the speed with which you want to get into production.

Tree seedlings or transplants. Some nurseries specialize in growing large numbers for Christmas, forest and highway plantings, windbreaks, erosion control, and alcohol production. You'll need level land with fertile sandy-loam soil, shade frames, irrigation, digging equipment, and a source of quality tree seeds. Be sure there is a market before you start this kind of operation, because the trees must be sold as soon as they reach planting size. The market fluctuates widely as demand rises and falls, and to do business on a large scale you will probably have to ship them outside your area. You may also find you are competing with state nurseries that are able to sell at prices lower than you can manage profitably.

Specialty items. Growers of such specialties as antique fruits, roses, rock garden plants, Alpine plants, wild flowers, and aquatic plants sell at roadside stands and through small magazine ads. If you grow these plants for fun, you may be able to expand your hobby into a profitable business. (An interesting fringe benefit of this kind of enterprise is that you are likely to meet a lot of people with similar interests.)

Indoor plants. Popular items include African violets and other flowering or foliage plants, orchids, and novelties such as bonsai or parasitic and insect-eating plants. The market extends to full-fledged interior landscaping in motels, shopping centers, and even private homes.

A greenhouse is a necessity for growing these plants on a large scale, and their propagation and care is demanding. Plan on being tied to the business 24 hours a day, and be prepared to diagnose all manner of plant illnesses and to offer professional advice to your customers.

Sod. Ready-made lawns are in great demand now, and sod growing is big business. You'll need fertile soil in a level, rock-free location, as well as equipment to till, seed, fertilize, dig, cut, and load the sod rolls. You will also need trucks for delivery, since sod is difficult to ship by common carrier.

Bulbs, tubers, or corms. Most tuberous begonias, cannas, daffodils, dahlias, gladioli, and lilies are raised by large growers on the West Coast and in Europe, and most retail nurseries buy their bulbs from them. As a small grower you can have fun growing these plants, however, and may find them profitable, especially if you can produce unusual varieties. Tulips and hyacinths are difficult to propagate successfully, and require a cultural climate that's hard to find outside of Holland.

Services

Exterior landscape design and planting. A bona fide landscape architect needs a degree and considerable training. But a great many self-taught people with skill in plant culture and a feel for design have forged successful careers in this field. Landscapers not only draw blueprints for placement of trees, shrubs, and gardens, but also grade building sites and install walks, terraces, pools, walls, fences, farm ponds, orchards, and gardens. A lot of equipment is necessary if you provide such a wide range of services, but the demand continues to increase as people spend more leisure time in the country.

Property care and management. Many enterprising rural dwellers provide lawn maintenance, tree pruning, garden care, and pest control services, especially where there are vacationers and older citizens. Retirees who want to keep busy and share some of their horticultural skills may work part-time caring for grounds and gardens.

Interior landscaping and maintenance. Offices, stores, restaurants, motels, hospitals, banks, and indoor shopping malls are all markets for designers who install and care for indoor plantings. This specialized field requires a great deal of knowledge and training; but the investment required is likely not to be large unless you raise your own plants or carry a large inventory of those you buy.

Gathering native wild plants. Some landscapers and nurseryfolk sell plants they dig from country pastures and the woods. These are popular because they are hardy and less expensive. Great care and skill must be taken in digging and caring for the plants, because they are not likely to be as well rooted as nursery grown trees, and customers should be made aware that they need to feed and water the plants more frequently.

The most popular collected plants in our area include evergreens for hedges and small shade trees, such as birch and maple. Others gather ferns, shrubs, and un-endangered flowers from the wild. One friend, who has permission to collect wild flowers from dozens of farms, claims the whole state of Vermont is his nursery!

Collectors usually pay the landowner a set fee for each tree they dig, but some landowners give away the plants because they want the area cleared. If you dig, be aware that some plant species are endangered and should not be moved, and gathering plants anywhere must be done only with the consent of the owner. Plants on public lands and roadsides are not considered free for the digging, either.

Chapter 20

THE GREENHOUSE

Like a yacht or private railroad car, a greenhouse was once considered something only the very rich could afford. New building materials have changed that, and today most of the serious gardeners we know wouldn't be without one.

We built our first small greenhouse in the early 1950s. It was constructed of poles we cut from our woods, covered with the newly available polyethylene, and warmed with a wood stove. It appeared crude, but we were thrilled to begin gardening two months earlier.

Today, six greenhouses later, we consider our small homemade buildings more valuable than ever. By lengthening the growing season, they make it possible to have plants that we couldn't have grown otherwise. We're also glad of a refreshing taste of spring when winter blizzards are raging outside. We've found that working for a few hours in our warm flower-and-greenery filled greenhouse on a sunny wintry day is an excellent substitute for a tropical winter vacation, and a wonderful antidote for cabin fever. It's great spot to bake away a winter cold, too.

We are amazed at how fast the late-winter sun turns the seedlings into good-sized plants. And it is a joy to transplant there on a sunny day. One sunny day, Lewis was working there as it got warmer and warmer. He took off more and more winter clothes, then absent-mindedly left to run to the house for something. He realized the true season with a profound shock.

A greenhouse not only lengthens the season, but also can be heated to allow gardening year-round. A large number of plants can be

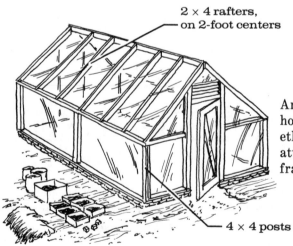

2 × 4 rafters, on 2-foot centers

An easily constructed greenhouse, covered with polyethylene. This plastic skin is attached to the structure's frame by ¾" × 1" lath.

4 × 4 posts

grown in a comparatively small area, and they grow quickly because they are in a controlled environment. And a "hot house," as it was once called, is a good place to dehydrate food, ripen tomatoes and pumpkins, and dry seeds, nuts, firewood, clothes, and paint.

We installed an above-ground pool in one of our greenhouses a few years ago, and used it for its intended purpose and to raise the humidity, water the plants, and provide a reservoir in case of fire. It was better than a hot tub.

The term "greenhouse" can refer to anything from a plastic covered lean-to built over your cellar door, to an elaborate glass-covered structure in which watering, heat, and humidity are automatically controlled. If you want only to stretch the growing season a few weeks, a simple, inexpensive structure will do. The covering may be transparent plastic film, clear plastic panels, or fiberglass. In it you can grow your vegetable and annual flower plants, pansies, and herbs, and if you wish, start perennial plants, root softwood cuttings, and grow early crops of lettuce, tomatoes, and other vegetables. Many people in our area use such a greenhouse each spring to start a few vegetable and flower plants, and root geraniums for their window boxes. Others use one to grow a crop of early lettuce, melons, or tomatoes.

A year-round greenhouse allows you to do all of these things and more. You can grow houseplants, including geraniums, gloxinias, African violets, and unusual foliage plants. One of the most beautiful home greenhouses we've ever seen is filled from top to bottom with extraordinary orchids. It adds a year-round tropical paradise to this New Jersey house. Some gardeners grow fresh, pesticide-free greens and other vegetables throughout the winter. And if you like to propagate new plants, you can root hardwood cuttings and bench-graft fruit trees and evergreens.

For year-round use, be sure the greenhouse you buy or build is made of durable materials such as aluminum and redwood. Mount it on a solid permanent foundation that won't move with the frost, and cover it with glass or one of the long-lasting ridged plastic glazings. Many ready-built greenhouses are on the market (see Appendix), to be installed by you or with help.

You have a wide choice of heating systems. Some people attach a small greenhouse to their home so that the furnace can keep it warm at night and on cloudy days; and the greenhouse can return the favor

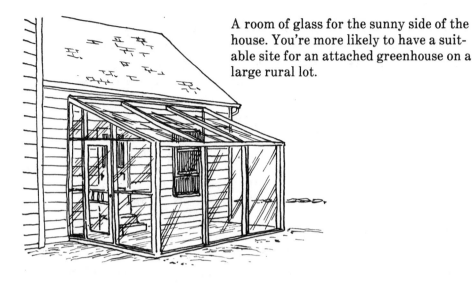

A room of glass for the sunny side of the house. You're more likely to have a suitable site for an attached greenhouse on a large rural lot.

and heat the house on sunny days. Mary and Caleb Pitkin, who live in a nearby town, have attached a greenhouse to their dairy barn to take advantage of the free heat and carbon dioxide produced by the animals during the winter.

A free-standing greenhouse needs its own source of heat. Oil or gas-fired hot-water systems are the most popular because they produce an even heat, cost less to operate than electric heaters, and take less work than required for wood or coal fired heaters.

We burned wood in our earlier greenhouses, but gave it up. It was hard to regulate the heat; the stove produced a flood of creosote that was bad for the plants; and on cold nights we had to get up to stoke the fire. A fellow nurseryman in a town north of us used to sleep in his greenhouse during the worst weather.

We try to make our greenhouse as tight and as efficient as possible to save both labor and fuel. If you live in a cold, windy location, you may want to have an insulated wall rather than glazing on the north or northwest side of the house. Some growers cover the interior walls on those sides with aluminum foil, to reflect light from the roof and other sides.

Before you build a greenhouse you may not be happy with, read all you can about greenhouses and visit others in your area. Be sure the greenhouse is an efficient size; is orientated to catch the most sun during the months you are using it; and has trouble-free heating and watering systems. Automatic fans and possibly roof vents will be necessary to circulate air and to remove the tremendous heat that can build up on sunny days, even in mid-winter.

The climate and growing conditions in a greenhouse can be controlled to allow plants to grow like crazy. But these artificial conditions mean that you must give careful attention to ventilation, watering, and pest control. Any insects or diseases that start are likely to spread out of control. Keep junk from accumulating, and weeds from growing under the benches, and sterilize all flats, pots, and transplanting tools. Avoid buying any plants unless you are sure they came from clean greenhouses, and use only artificial or sterilized soil.

A greenhouse is very demanding, and even with automatic heat and fans, we could only be away for a few hours at a time when the house was full of bedding plants.

The Potting Shed

If you possibly can, build a potting shed on the nonsunny northern or northwestern end of your greenhouse. A shed saves valuable space in the growing areas, and is a fine place to store pots, soil, fertilizers, flats, hoses, and other supplies. It should be equipped with a wide bench for potting, transplanting, bench grafting, making cuttings, and writing labels. Experiment a bit, and construct the bench at a height that is most comfortable for you. The potting shed can also act as a buffer zone: if you include an outside door you can enter the greenhouse through it on a wintery day without letting a lot of outside air in on your plants.

A Commercial Greenhouse

Greenhouse growing has changed considerably over the years. Early in this century, practically all of the winter flowers used in the Northeast were grown in glass houses, sometimes covering many acres. Now, it may be cheaper to fly cut flowers from South America or

California than to grow them in the North. Many other types of operation are thriving, however. Plants are still grown in year-round greenhouses for holidays, and great pains are taken so that poinsettias, lilies, roses, or whatever will be at their very best at Christmas, Easter, Mother's Day, Memorial Day, June weddings, proms, football games, and other occasions.

Greenhouse growing is often combined with a nursery operation, so started vegetables and annual flowering plants can be offered along with regular nursery stock. The buildings are also used for starting perennials and trees from seed, for rooting cuttings, and for grafting fruit trees, evergreens, roses, grapes, cactii, and gypsophillia.

Some retail florists also operate greenhouses so they can grow part of the greenery and blooms they use in bouquets, corsages, and arrangements. They also use them to display azaleas and other potted plants that have been brought in to sell.

The investment both in starting and operating a large greenhouse can be high, so be sure of a profitable market before you undertake this project. Besides the building, you'll need automatic watering, humidity, ventilation, and heating systems. A soil sterilizer, mixer, screener, fertilizer injector, and possibly a potting machine may be necessary, too. Consider setting up some method of moving plants throughout the building, additional lighting for those plants that need it, and shading for the ones that must have the daylight hours shortened in order to bloom.

Horticulture is big business, and wholesalers are ready to provide you not only with equipment, but also with plants, seeds, pots, flats, fertilizers, peat moss, labels, and much more (see Appendix for names of suppliers).

Because many plants of the same species are usually grown together in the confined environment of the commercial greenhouse, the risk of disease and insect devastation is very high. Growers must fumigate often, and be especially careful not to bring any infected plants into their buildings. As with the nursery business, a certificate from your state department of agriculture is necessary before you begin to sell plants, and you should expect annual or more frequent inspection.

Chapter 21
HAY AND GRAINS

Do you like the smell of new-mown hay, or do you get hay fever?

Your answer may help you to determine whether or not you'll raise hay. If you are not allergic, you may find many good reasons to do it. Hay is a practical crop for keeping large amounts of land open and productive. You can use hay not only for animal fodder, but also for bedding, mulch, and building up the soil to grow other crops. It is one of the best ground covers for stopping erosion, and needs no cultivation. If long-lived grasses such as timothy are kept fertilized and limed, reseeding is necessary only occasionally.

A hayfield may not always be practical, even if you want to keep your land open. When we gave up raising cattle, we were faced with what to do with the acres that had once been pastures and fields. Since our land is rough and rocky, our farming neighbors were not interested in renting it. Even on paper we couldn't justify the investment of a new tractor, mower, baler, rake, wagon, fertilizer, and spreader, to say nothing of the labor involved in growing and harvesting hay, so we planted it to orchard, nursery, and Christmas trees.

Our nearby neighbors, on the other hand, had a different experience. They had purchased an abandoned farm, but, unlike ours, it had large, flat, and fertile acreage. They had no haying equipment either, but they rented the fields to a farmer with excellent results. It is now well managed, and they have the open land they want.

If the hayfield that came with your property has been fertilized and cut regularly, it is probably in good condition and you should be able to find plenty of uses for it. You might grow hay to sell, produce mulch for your other plantings, raise fodder and bedding for your livestock, or rent the fields to a farmer who will agree to keep them productive. But if you neglect them, and fail to give them annual applications of fertilizer, within a few years they will deteriorate into an unsightly patch of weeds, and perhaps become a fire hazard.

If you acquired no haying equipment with your farm, renting out your fields may be the best move, provided you can find someone nearby who wants them. Although the arrangement may not be highly profitable, it can help pay your taxes and keep your property neat. Before making an agreement, talk with others in your neighborhood about the current rates and types of arrangements, and perhaps check with your extension agent or a lawyer to be sure how to handle it. Whatever you do, get the deal in writing, and signed by both of you. Gentlemen's agreements are apt to create problems after a few years, if one party or the other misunderstands details of fertilizing, trimming around the edges, and maintaining fences. It is customary in our area for an agreement to run for five years, with provisions for renewal.

If your fields come to you worn out and uncared for, the grass growth is probably short, thin, wiry, and intermixed with weeds and brush; and the fields may need a great deal of work before they will produce a worthwhile crop. If you are unable to find someone who wants to take them over, you may opt to keep the fields open only for the scenery; by hiring someone to mow them and leaving the hay on the fields as a mulch, the soil will rebuild itself.

Obviously, a lush hayfield doesn't automatically happen, so if you decide to put a worn-out field back into production yourself, get professional advice. Your county agent or a nearby farmer should be able to explain plowing, harrowing, liming, and fertilizing. Ask for recommendations about the best combination of seeds, and the best "catch" crop, such as oats or barley, to grow fast and cover the soil while the slower sprouting hay seeds are starting. Because the machinery required for many of these operations is not likely to be used often, you will find it to be cheaper and much easier to hire a farmer or contractor to do most of the actual work.

Haying

Most hay grown today is composed of perennial grasses. Among them are timothy, redtop, reed canary grass, smooth brome, and cocksfoot. Trefoil, alfalfa, and clover aren't true grasses, but are often grown as hay, too; although their growth habits are similar, they have different characteristics, nutritive values, and soil preferences. Most hayfields are composed of several varieties, some having been deliberately planted, and others seeded through manure or by the wind.

In recent years, alfalfa has become one of the most-grown fodders because of its high nutritive value and its ability to produce several crops a year where the seasons are long enough. Alfalfa is often grown for ensilage, because it loses much of its nutritive value if rained on after being cut and then reworked to dry. Good weather is necessary to producing high-quality alfalfa hay.

Hay used to be mowed by a hand scythe or horse-drawn mower. If your lot is small and you want only a little hay for animals or mulch, you can cut it with a two-wheel sickle-type power mower, rake and fork it by hand into a cart, and haul it to the barn or a haystack with a trailer or small truck.

Modern hay harvesting is so mechanized that one person can do much of the work sitting on a tractor, stopping merely to change machines and attachments. The first step is a mower which usually also crushes the hay so it will dry faster, followed by a rake, baler, bale loader, and trucks or trailer to haul hay bales. Unless you sell hay directly from the fields, as some do, you'll also need a barn for storage, and perhaps an elevator to stack the bales inside. You'll need to be prepared, too, to devote many of the best summer days to cutting, drying, and putting the hay into the barn.

Hay for forage should be cut early in the season, when it is at the leafy vegetative stage and before early bloom, if the food value is to be at its peak. If you allow hay to grow past its prime, it deteriorates in value each day it is left standing in the field. The production of good hay requires not only skill but luck with weather. "Make hay while the sun shines" is not just a clever saying.

Hay must be dried carefully. If it is too dry, it has lost much of its nutrition; if not dry enough, it will ferment in storage. Fermenting hay not only spoils, but gets very hot in the process. Each year many farmers around the country lose their barns as fermenting hay combusts and bursts into flame spontaneously. To better cope with wet summer weather, many farmers in our area have installed electric hay dryers in their barns.

Rather than dry and bale their hay, many farmers chop it when it is only partially dry, and store it in trenches, silos, or large plastic bags. The resulting silage, when it has been processed properly, loses less nutritive value to weathering than does hay. Rowen, as later cuttings are called, is often made into silage, because drying conditions tend to be less favorable in late summer. Many grasses bloom only once, so rowen is likely to be thinner in content and lower in energy than the earlier cuttings. Making it into silage is the best way to preserve what nutrition there is.

In our area, small landowners sell hay to nearby horse or goat owners, or to organic gardeners who value it for mulch on gardens and berry patches. Spoiled hay is also sold to cover newly seeded lawns, roadsides, and ski trails.

Grain

The story of mankind is closely tied to the raising of grain. Wheat and corn (in the West) and rice (in the East) have furnished much of the diet for humans and domesticated animals since the beginning of history. You are partaking in an ancient ritual if you raise your own grain, and thresh, clean, and grind it into a flour for bread.

Grains are grasses with edible seeds. Corn, wheat, oats, buckwheat, and millet are most commonly grown by the small farmer, although barley, rye, flax, rice, sorghum, and triticale (a cross between wheat and rye) are raised in some places. Soybeans, baking beans, and sunflower seeds are sometimes called grains, although technically they are not.

In years past, homesteaders nearly always grew small patches of grains for food and fodder. In the early 1800s, Lewis's great-grandfather's gristmill on our brook was kept busy grinding the corn and wheat his neighbors brought in throughout the year. A half-century later, however, farms became more specialized, and the grains they ate and fed their livestock were raised only on large acreages in regions where they grew best. Dairy farmers now grow grain primarily for animal forage and as cover crops for building up the soil. But many part-time farmers have recently begun to plant small patches of grains so they and their animals can enjoy organically grown, herbicide-free food.

Most grains are planted in the spring, except for winter rye and winter wheat, which are planted in late summer or early fall. First, it is essential to thoroughly prepare the soil, and fertilize it well. Plant at the rate recommended by your farm store or county agent, or see

Planting Amounts and Yields for Grains (in lbs.)

Grain	Plant per 1,000 Sq. Ft.	Plant per Acre	Yield per Acre
Barley	1¼	70–100	1,900
Buckwheat	1¼	35–50	2,000
Oats	3	80–120	2,000
Rye	2–3	90–100	1,500
Wheat	3	90–120	1,800
Corn	½ per 75 hills	8–10	200 bushels

the table above. Seeding may be done by flinging out the seed by hand, using a crank-operated hand seeder, or with a tractor-drawn seeder. If the crop is to be used as forage, it may be either cut while green and chopped and put in a silo, or dried and stored. If it is to be used as grain for human consumption, it is allowed to ripen and is harvested as soon as the kernels have become fat and mature.

You can grow a small amount of wheat, buckwheat, or millet for home use with a minimum of equipment. Just till and fertilize the soil as you would for a garden, and sow the seed by hand. Cut it with a scythe, dry it, and thresh it by beating it with a stick on a clean barn floor. Finally, winnow it clean by pouring it from bucket to bucket in a light breeze. Store it in a dry cool place, protected from rodents and insects.

Although some of our homesteading friends grind their grain with a hand grinder, we like our electric one very much. It works well on wheat, and we can adjust it from a coarse grind for cereal to a fine setting for baked goods. We made the mistake of not getting one rugged enough to grind dried corn, however, so we have to have that done at a health food store.

If you want to raise grain on a large scale, either to sell or to feed to animals, get advice from your county agent on such matters as varieties to plant, fertilizers, and likely diseases. You may be able to hire someone to plant and harvest it for you, and thus spare yourself the purchase and maintenance of expensive equipment. And in many areas, there are mills where you can take your grain to be ground.

Wheat.　Wheat is the grain most used for human consumption in this country, and it is usually the first chosen by those who want to raise most of their own food. One Vermont agronomist, Win Way, raises more than enough wheat to supply his family all year on just a tenth of an acre. Ohio writer Gene Logsdon reports that one acre of wheat can support a pig, a milk cow, a beef steer, and 30 chickens. Many other backyard farmers grow small amounts of wheat and grind it as they use it as cereal, pasta, and bread. Unground grain will keep for several years if it is securely stored in a cool, dry place.

Wheat can be grown successfully on a small scale nearly every-where that corn can be raised. But a commercial-scale effort will be difficult where growing seasons are short and the harvest season is cool and damp. The kernels may fail to fully develop or to dry enough to be threshed and stored without spoiling. Also, the time between when the kernels ripen and when they shatter and fall to the ground is short, so the weather must be nearly perfect during the harvest period. Unless you can be sure of a growing season of at least 150 days, with the likelihood of little rain at harvesttime, you'll be better off buying grain from a health food store and grinding it yourself.

Most wheats grown in North America are of five types: hard red-seeded winter wheat and hard red-seeded spring wheat (both grown mostly west of the Mississippi); durum (grown in the North Central Plains and used for pasta); soft red winter wheat (grown mostly in the East for pastries); and soft white wheat (grown in the Northwest and Northeast and used for bread).

Oats.　We grew up playing a game to the tune of a little ditty:

Oats, peas, beans, and barley grow,
Oats, peas, beans, and barley grow,
Do you or I or anyone know,
how oats, peas, beans, and barley grow?

Oats are easier to grow than wheat, and will ripen successfully almost everywhere in the country. They make good food for livestock and poultry, and are one of the most nutritious grains, especially high in protein. Unfortunately, the kernel is enclosed in a hull, and special equipment is needed to remove it. That's why oats are seldom grown on a small scale for home consumption. They are one of the best grains to use for mulch, soil building, and a cover crop, however. The

❖

unthreshed stems make good food for livestock and the straw remaining after threshing makes excellent bedding and mulch.

Buckwheat. Although buckwheat is nutritious, not everyone enjoys the flavor. We do, especially in buckwheat pancakes smothered in maple syrup. The grain is a favorite with Northerners who find raising wheat much too challenging, since it grows well nearly everywhere and ripens early for easy drying.

We value buckwheat as a soil conditioner. It builds nutrients in the soil, and thoroughly chokes out weeds and quackgrass with its broad leaves. But we've found, as have others, that buckwheat should be harvested before it scatters its seeds or it, too, becomes a weed as bad as those we are trying to choke out.

Corn. When conditions are right, corn grows rapidly. Newcomers to the country are apt to be fascinated when, after a rain on a quiet, warm, summer night, they can actually hear the noise of corn growing in a large cornfield. It is an eerie, unforgettable sound.

Of all the crops the early settlers found the Indians growing in the New World, corn was the most valuable. It is the most widely grown grain in the United States, and used primarily for fattening animals. We especially like growing corn because we don't need expensive equipment to raise and process the small amount we need.

Many different types of corn have been developed: sweet corn, grown in home gardens for its tasty ears; fodder corn, the whole stalk and ears of which are chopped and stored in silos to feed dairy and beef cattle in winter; field corn, grown for the ears, which are picked off the stalks and husked by machine, dried in large corn cribs, then shelled and ground into cornmeal for poultry, animal, and human food; ornamental Indian corn, used mostly for decoration; and popcorn.

If you are raising corn for animal or poultry fodder, check with your county agent about the amount required for a herd or flock of your size in your particular climate, and the type to plant. Corn has been hybridized to such an extent that professional advice is necessary to determine the best strain for each soil type and climatic conditions.

Although corn is a valued crop, few grains deplete the soil faster, so a well-planned program of fertilizing and crop rotation must be carefully followed if you are to continue to get good production. Because it grows so tall, corn requires that plenty of humus and nutrients must be available in the soil. The soil should be deeply tilled so the heavy root system that supports the tall corn stalk can develop.

We used to save some corn each year for planting, but now we buy new seed each year. We prefer the new hybrids because they are far better in quality and are more frost-resistant—but they don't come true from seed.

Unlike other grains, corn is planted in rows and kept cultivated. If the seed has been planted too thickly, it must be thinned like a vegetable crop. The soil is usually hilled up around the plants soon after they come up, both to support the tall plants and to warm the soil for faster growth.

Corn can be a profitable crop for a small farm. Fresh sweet corn is always in demand, especially early in the season. Many people depend on farmers' markets for their supply to freeze. Some gardeners like to raise a bit of field corn to dry and feed to their animals, or to grind into cornmeal. The demand for popcorn, one of the most nutritious snack foods, continues to increase as viewers consume it while watching movies, TV, and VCRs.

You may want to consider raising a few plants of colorful Indian corn as decoration for your home or to sell at a roadside stand or farmers' market. In earlier times, farmers often planted a few seeds in with their field corn, and it was traditional if a man found a red ear of corn at a husking bee, he got to kiss any girl at the party.

Chapter 22
WILL YOU HAVE ANIMALS?

Spring was the season we enjoyed most on the farm as children. We could get out of our heavy winter clothes and run around on the bare ground once more, and best of all, it was the time for new life—new leaves, new flowers, and the birthing of baby chicks, geese, ducks, pigs, calves, kittens, turkeys, and occasionally a colt.

Our country ancestors depended on their horses and oxen for work and transportation, and counted on their flocks and herds for milk, honey, butter, eggs, chicken, steaks, pork chops, bacon, sausage, hamburg, lamb, mutton, and the holiday ham, turkey, or goose. The animals also supplied raw materials for their sweaters and blankets, sheepskin coats, mittens, sleigh robes, feather beds, pillows and comforters, tallow candles, beeswax, and even goosegrease for their illnesses. Animals were indispensable for a family's comfort and survival.

Few of us today care to raise our entire supply of protein, clothing, and bedding; but a pastoral setting seems to invite the sight and sounds of grazing cattle and horses, bleating sheep, cackling hens, crowing roosters, gobbling turkey toms, honking geese, and buzzing bees.

Keeping small numbers of animals and poultry is easier now than it was a few years ago. Farm stores are far more willing to supply the needs of the small farmer, and even cater to us with an excellent assortment of equipment, seeds, and animal feed.

Whether your animals will be pets, food, additional income, or motive power, carefully consider the act before buying so much as a chick. Animals and birds are much more demanding than plants and trees. A friend of ours, after trying several animal projects, says he hated having them dependent on him; the only animals he will have around now are his two hives of bees. Scott and Helen Nearing state a similar thought in their book *Living the Good Life*. They refused to have animals on their farmstead, reasoning that "No man is completely free if he raises animals." But, we might add, no man is completely free if he raises children, or takes on a job, or any other responsibility. Your livestock may be worth far more to you than the freedom to go away for the weekend.

If you decide to keep poultry or animals, expect to provide daily attention, shelter, food, and water. Cows or goats need daily milking, chicken and duck eggs must be gathered twice a day, and horses should be groomed frequently. In most of the country, poultry and animals must be kept in a tight barn for the winter, and sometimes all year. Shelters need to be cleaned out periodically. (This was one of our most detested chores when we were young.) Large animals can break down fences, eat the neighbors' garden and chase their children, butt down barn doors, and break windows, causing repair bills and even lawsuits. They may also get sick at odd times, have trouble producing their young, or get struck by lightning. And there's always the possibility of being confronted with a half-ton cow that dies in the barn in the midst of a winter blizzard. No matter what animals you own, you will probably soon memorize the phone number of your veterinarian.

Another problem is that a livestock animal may become a pet. Pets are very difficult to sell or eat, even if grown and no longer cute. Large-scale farmers seldom have this dilemma because they aren't likely to become attached to hundreds of steers, sheep, or turkeys. But if you have only one pig, a lamb, or a few ducks—beware. We've learned that it is unwise to give names to turkeys, capons, rabbits, beef animals, pigs, or lambs, or to frolic with them when they are young, unless we are absolutely certain we can be hard-hearted when the time comes. Life will be easier for you and your children if you make pets only of your dog, cat, horse, milk cow, or breeding geese that will be a part of your family for many years. Some friends of ours have such strong feelings against eating their animals that, as soon as an animal is butchered, they put all the meat in the freezer. Several weeks later, they find they can deal with the freezer in a more impersonal way.

The chapters that follow should help you decide which animals will suit you best. Poultry, rabbits, and bees are popular because they can be raised easily with little space or investment, and we will cover them more fully than cows, pigs, sheep, and horses.

Summer Meat Projects

Many people we know limit their animal raising to the summer months, thereby avoiding the problems associated with keeping animals indoors—winter feed, weathertight housing, and the increased likelihood of disease. In spring, they buy a couple of young calves, pigs, or lambs; a pair of rabbits or turkeys; or a flock of young roosters, geese, or ducks. They keep them for a few months and then butcher them. Although most livestock need shelter from rain and sun, they spend the great part of their lives outside. The result: in one season you can produce tasty veal (although this is usually raised inside), spring lamb, roasting pig, broilers, fryers, duckling, goose, rabbit, a Thanksgiving turkey, as well as all the usual cuts of pork and beef.

Pigs, veal, rabbits, ducks, and chickens must be fed twice a day, but beef cattle, lambs, goats, and geese grow well with only a good pasture and constant supply of drinking water.

If you buy a male pig, sheep, calf, or goat, it should be castrated at a young age. Unaltered older males tend to be dangerous not only to each other, but to their owners and anyone else who comes into their territory. Also, the meat isn't as good as that of a "steer." This operation may have been done before you purchase him; if not, your vet can do it for you, or you can buy elastic bands at a farm store that will do the job quite painlessly and bloodlessly.

Registered Animals

Purebred animals, from dogs to palominos, can be registered, and their pedigrees recorded at the headquarters of that breed. If you intend to show the animal at fairs or shows, or plan to sell breeding stock or offer stud service, you should buy registered stock. Be prepared for a lot of paperwork if you sell the animals, because exact pedigrees are very important.

If production of meat is your primary concern, you will find that mixed breeds and quality grade (unregistered) animals and birds are usually just as good as the purebreds—and usually they are healthier and less highstrung. They cost far less, too.

Butchering

It is easy to butcher small animals and poultry. Butchering larger animals takes more equipment, and is much more complicated, however. If you raise cattle, pigs, sheep, or goats for meat you will be faced, sooner or later, with transferring a live animal into groceries. If you are a do-it-yourselfer who wants to be in control of the entire operation, there are good books on the subject. Still, no how-to manual is a substitute for a lesson from an experienced neighbor. Unskilled butchering can cause suffering for the animal. If not done properly, it is a smelly, dirty job, and can ruin a lot of meat. You can take your animals to a nearby butcher shop, or if your state permits it, call a traveling butcher who will do the job at your farm.

Fences

When the land was cleared initially, one of the first things the settlers did was identify their claim by building fences—with stone, rails, boards, dug out stumps, or poles stood on end.

Modern fences may also be built to delineate boundaries, but in the country we use them mostly to keep domestic livestock in and wild animals out. Most are made of woven wire, barbed wire, or smooth wire charged with high-voltage electricity. Woven wire comes in many styles. Tight-meshed hardware cloth is used for game birds and fur-bearing animals. Lighter poultry fence wire is designed for poultry and rabbits. And sheep and cattle are contained by a permanent fence of heavy-gauge wire. Barbed wire works well to contain cattle, but is usually not effective for sheep, and is dangerous for horses.

Electric fences are useful as temporary fencing and for holding in sheep, pigs, and other animals that are difficult to contain. They have the advantage of being easy to move when grazing areas need to be rotated, and are less expensive and easier to install than woven or barbed-wire fences. Electric fences use a transformer that produces an extremely high voltage, but the amperage is low, and the shocks come at spaced intervals, so the jolts are painful without being dangerous. An insulator is needed on each post so that the wire won't be grounded. Occasionally check to see that nothing has fallen onto the fence to short-circuit it.

If wooden posts are used, they should be of a rot-resistant wood or a wood that has been treated with preservative. Your farm store or county agent can advise what is available in your area.

Chapter 23
CHICKENS

The prospect of fresh eggs and high-quality poultry meat is so appealing that a flock of chickens is a common feature of many country places—in spite of the fact that little money is saved.

Time required: 5 to 10 minutes a day for a small flock of laying hens or meat birds, 30 minutes every week or so to clean the pens.

Incubation time: 3 weeks.

Poultry Glossary

Broiler—Young cockerel killed for meat at about 9 weeks
Brooder—Heated unit for raising baby chicks
Broody hen—One ready to set and hatch chickens
Chick—Newborn poultry
Cock—Male chicken
Cockerel—Young male chicken
Foul—Bird over a year old
Fryer—Cockerel meat bird, slightly larger than a broiler
Hen—Adult female
Incubator—Unit for hatching eggs
Molt—The annual, or oftener, process of losing feathers
Pullet—Young female
Roaster—Older male chicken grown for meat
Rooster—Adult male

Raising chickens takes less time, investment, and heavy work than most animal endeavors, and they're ideal for children. Your place may already have a small shed that can be converted to a poultry house, or perhaps you can build a suitable room in an existing barn. If not, a weatherproof shelter can be built easily and cheaply. You won't even need running water, because a small flock drinks so little that you can easily carry water to it each day. The daily chores of filling the feeders and waterers and gathering the eggs take only a few minutes, and you can clean the henhouse and nests on weekends.

When you add up the cost of the birds, equipment, grain, and your own time, it may be difficult to justify the enterprise in your account book, but you can write off your labor as recreation and exercise. And then there's the value in knowing that those eggs, broilers, fryers, and roasters are tastier than any you could buy at the store for any price.

If you let your chickens run loose, don't expect to train them to stay out of the road or off the front porch. We are convinced that chickens were the most stupid of all the creatures on our farm, but once they got out of their yard they would invariably find the garden and scratch it up. And they quickly learned to go into their shelter during a storm—something we could never be sure the turkeys would have enough sense to do.

Six-sided brooder house, and nesting box of 1-by lumber.

Breeds of Chickens

If you are interested only in producing eggs, buy a lightweight breed such as White or Brown Leghorns. Both are excellent layers of large white eggs, and they eat less grain than the heavier breeds. They tend to "talk" a lot and cackle loudly after laying, but the noise is a happy sound; an elderly aunt of ours referred to it as singing.

If you prefer to raise both eggs and meat, choose a heavier poultry breed such as Rhode Island Reds, Plymouth Rocks, or White Rocks. These are also good layers of brown eggs (which despite local preference one way or the other, are the same quality as the white). The cockerels (see box, "Poultry Glossary") of these breeds are raised for meat, and the layers are often sold as meat fowls after their best egg-laying days are over.

Since a good laying bird can supply from four to six eggs a week, from four to ten pullets should supply all needs of a small family, unless you eat a lot of angel food cake.

In addition to the Leghorns and heavier breeds, we see many flocks of Bantams around the countryside. Because these birds are only about half the size of ordinary chickens, they are a practical choice if you are keeping poultry for egg production rather than meat. The colorful Bantams require less room and less grain than larger birds, and they are very cocky and fun to watch. Some are bred primarily for showing, so if you want eggs, be sure to buy birds that are noted for being good layers. Bantam eggs are identical to hens' eggs in quality and flavor, but are smaller, so you will need more for an omelet.

Getting Started

When buying chicks, you have a choice of starting with all pullets, all cockerels, or "as hatched." Pullets are the most expensive, especially in the lighter Leghorn breeds. Although we usually raised our own, whenever we bought them we sought out Barred Rocks, one of the heavier breeds. We bought 50 "as hatched" and they usually came out about half pullets and half cockerels. Although there were always a few losses during the first weeks, we planned on keeping about 15 pullets for laying eggs. We selected out the pullets that were poor layers and the cockerels as soon as we could identify them, and raised them separately for meat.

Hens normally lay for nearly a year, and then begin to molt. A few weeks after molting, they grow a new wardrobe and begin to lay again, but fewer eggs this time. Hens *can* be kept for two or three years; but most growers prefer to replace them each year because it costs as much to feed a hen that takes a month's vacation and lays three eggs a week as it does to keep a younger one that lays six.

Early spring is the best time to start your flock. You can order chicks from one of the mail-order firms that advertise in farm magazines or from your local farm store. Day-old chicks are the least expensive and the most fun, but "started" birds, four or more weeks old, are far less demanding, and of course, begin to lay faster. Pullets start to produce small eggs when they are about five months old, and after a few weeks their eggs increase to full size.

If you buy day-old chicks, have their food and brooder ready for them when they arrive. Brooders come in different sizes, so choose one that will be large enough to hold your chicks until they have grown to a four-week size, and have it warm when they arrive. Day-old birds require a temperature of 95 degrees F. during the first week. After that the temperature can be lowered 5 degrees each week until it reaches 70 degrees F. The unit will have a thermostatically controlled heater, but you should keep a thermometer in it to make sure that the thermostat is accurate and the heater is working properly.

For our 50 chicks, we made our own brooder by building a pen about 2 feet high, 4 feet wide, and 6 feet long. It was built of light plywood, and we suspended an infrared heat bulb about 18 inches above the floor in the center. We kept an extra bulb on hand in case the one in use should fail. The bulb allows the chicks to move to and from the heat as they wish, and there is less danger that they will become too warm or be suffocated by crowding if too cold. The heat bulb, when burning round the clock, provides light so that they can eat and drink at night, and consequently, they grow faster.

When baby chicks arrive, they are mere balls of fluff and unbelievably cute. They will be hungry and do a lot of peeping. Feed them a special starting grain mixture from your farm store and provide lukewarm water. You may need to dip a few beaks into the water dish to teach the first chicks to drink, but the rest will learn quickly. Your flock will need fresh water and food within reach at all times.

We didn't often buy baby chicks on our farm. Instead, we kept one rooster for our flock of 15 to 20 pullets so we could have fertile eggs. Every spring, two or three "broody" hens decided to set on the nest all day and night rather than lay eggs, so we gave each one about 10 fertile eggs in some out-of-the-way nests. In three weeks each delighted mother produced a flock of lively chicks. We supplied them with chicken starter feed and water, but the mothers kept them warm so we didn't need a brooder.

One year no broody hens appeared, so we hatched eggs in a small incubator borrowed from a neighbor. We could watch the fascinating hatching process as, one by one, the chicks pecked their way out of their shells. With this method, there was no protective hen to object to an audience.

Some people keep a rooster, even if they don't hatch their own chicks, because they believe fertile eggs are more nourishing. The eggs don't keep as well in storage, however.

The Chicken and the Egg

By the time the birds are four or five weeks old, they are well feathered out, so if the weather is not still cold they can be moved from the brooder into their permanent house. Enormous factory-type commercial chicken houses seem a travesty to poultry lovers, and you can provide a far more pleasant home for your flock with little expense. It should be draft-free, and tight enough to exclude weasels, rats, foxes, and other poultry eaters. The experts recommend a space of about 3 square feet per bird, but we prefer to allow even more room—about an 8 × 12-foot space for 20 birds. It should have windows to provide plenty of light and ventilation whenever needed. Cover the floor with dry straw, hay, or wood shavings, and remove and replenish it when wet or dirty.

During the summer we let the birds out into a small yard enclosed with chicken-wire fence so they could add grass and insects to their diet. They had to be confined to keep them from scratching up the garden and from messing up the front yard. And in our area, the fence was necessary to keep out wandering dogs and foxes.

You'll need to provide roosts in the henhouse because, unlike ducks and geese, chickens don't like to sleep on the floor. These can be

❖

poles about 2 inches in diameter, laid horizontally from 2 to 3 feet above the floor. Allow about a foot of space for each bird to sleep, and install the roosts so that you can easily remove them to clean below. You'll also need to buy or build nesting boxes. They should be about 1 foot square, and placed 1 or 2 feet above the floor along an inside wall of the henhouse. Since hens often want to lay their eggs at about the same time, install six to eight nests for 20 birds so that they won't need to lay them on the floor while waiting. Line the boxes with clean hay or shavings.

Gather the eggs at least twice daily, more often in hot or cold weather, and keep them cool. If you leave eggs in the nest for long periods they are likely to be broken, and they lose flavor if they are kept warm by other hens laying more eggs in the same nest. An added incentive to pick up the eggs frequently is that if a number of eggs pile up in a nest, the hens may instinctively decide it is time to stop laying and start setting.

If you keep the nests clean, you shouldn't need to wash the eggs; but if you do, never use cold water, because it will cause the eggs to spoil more quickly. Use warm water (about 100 degrees F.) and dry them before refrigerating.

The average hen will eat from 85 to 110 pounds of feed a year, depending on her weight. Feed the growing mash suggested by your extension service or farm store until the birds are about five months old, or just before they begin to lay. Hens are creatures of habit, and dislike any sudden change in their diet, so before changing completely to a laying mash, give them a mixture of the different feeds for a week. You can supplement the grain mix with your homegrown grain, table scraps, or greens; but an exclusive diet of such food will not supply enough nourishment for good egg production.

Keep feed and water available at all times, and plan on their eating more in cold weather. Because grain is costly, we learned to use long narrow feeders so the birds couldn't jump into them and scratch the feed out on the floor, as is their nature. The hens need calcium to produce strong shells for their eggs, so keep a dish of ground oyster shells or calcite crystals (available at farm stores) near the feed dish. They will help themselves. It always seemed that our hens never ate much, but if we ever accidentally ran out, we soon became aware of it because the eggs appeared wrapped in a rubbery membrane instead of a shell.

If you keep your birds indoors, provide a small box of coarse sand to supply the grit needed in their gullets to grind food. Grit is particularly important if you supplement the hens' diet with cracked corn or other hard, unground grain.

Meat Production

Commercial producers of poultry meat raise their birds in wire cages in order to conserve space and automate their feeding and cleaning. Home flock owners usually prefer to give their birds more room, and permit them to be outside during the summer. Most do not allow them a wide range, especially as they get nearer the butchering stage, because the more a bird uses its muscles in walking, the less tender the meat will be.

You may be able to find someone who will butcher a number of birds for you at a reasonable price if you don't care to do the job yourself. Dressing off a chicken is simple, although the initial one may take longer. If possible, watch someone with experience butcher before you try it alone. You will probably find, as we did, that the process is somewhat repulsive at first, but proficiency comes quickly. Most poultry raisers prefer to butcher a number of birds at once and freeze them, rather than each time they want a chicken dinner.

You can make the cleaning easier if, for 24 hours before butchering, you give the birds plenty of water but no feed. Commercial growers use either a specially made, awl-like killing tool that pierces through the chicken's mouth into the brain, or a guillotine-type instrument that beheads it cleanly. Home producers traditionally cut off the bird's head with a hatchet or light axe. You can do this alone, once you get the hang of it. Grasp the critter by the legs with one hand and the axe with the other. Drape the head over a block of wood, and sever it with a quick blow. Hang the bird up by a string tied to one leg to allow the blood to run out freely. After the blood stops, dip the bird completely in very hot water to make it easier to pluck out the feathers. Don't leave it in the water more than 20 or 30 seconds, or the meat will begin to cook. Cut an opening on the lower part of the body below the tail so you can remove the entrails easily, and cut off the feet. Finally, wash out the cavity thoroughly with clean cold water, and allow the bird to cool naturally for an hour or so. As soon as the body heat is out, the meat is ready to cook, refrigerate, freeze, or can.

❖

Eggs to Sell

It is difficult to match your flock's production exactly with your needs, although you may find yourself using more than otherwise when the eggs are fresh and readily available. You can sell extra eggs to neighbors, or swap them for other food or services. Our neighbors keep chickens primarily to teach their children the responsibility of caring for animals and to give them the experience of running their own little business. Many farm wives, in times past, depended on their "egg money" for the little extras the farm income couldn't otherwise provide.

Federal regulations allow you to sell small numbers of eggs to friends and neighbors, or at a roadside stand, without a license. However, if you have 3,000 birds or more, and sell to stores, restaurants, and bakeries, your business is subject to state and federal laws.

Can you make money selling eggs? Unfortunately, the answer depends to a large extent on factors that are beyond your control. The price of grain fluctuates greatly, and your profits will seesaw with it. Markets can be equally uncertain, because large producers quickly increase their production whenever a shortage develops.

Chapter 24

GEESE AND DUCKS

Geese and ducks were once a part of every farmstead in Europe and America. They not only furnished a varied diet, and feathers for pillows, comforters, and beds, but added to the family income when the surplus birds were sold at the village marketplace. These days we're seeing more and more geese and ducks around country homes. They are attractive, lively creatures, fun to have around and a source of outstanding meals.

❖

Time required: Small flock of ducks and other poultry, 10 minutes a day, 30 minutes a week to clean out. Geese outside with water available will require almost no care.

Incubation time: Geese, 30 days; ducks, 28–35 days.

Goose and Duck Glossary

	Goose	*Duck*
Adult female	Goose	Duck
Adult male	Gander	Drake
Crowd	Gaggle, flock	Flock, brace
Young	Gosling	Duckling

Both geese and ducks take less work than turkeys; and they are less likely to get disease or to injure themselves. They are not as demanding about living arrangements, either, and can comfortably spend the winter in a shed that is warm enough so their water doesn't freeze.

Both like to be outdoors when the weather is mild, and it is nice to let them roam free if you have a good place. They do leave large, moist droppings everywhere, however, so you're not likely to enjoy them frequenting your lawn or front porch.

A pond isn't essential for these water birds, but even a small one will add greatly to their pleasure and yours. Don't let them swim in a pond you use for swimming, though, because they mess up the water, badly. They shouldn't be invited into one where you raise water lilies or frogs, either, because they have large appetites for green matter.

A Gaggle of Geese

We once had a pair of African geese named George and Gertrude, and without doubt they were the most fun of all the creatures on the farm. Geese are monogamous and like to stay with the same mate for life, which may be three decades or more. The couple had great personalities, talked all the time, and answered to their names. Everyone admired their style—the way they played in the small pond and fearlessly chased away dogs and other animals that were curious about their goslings.

Your geese will probably become pets, too. They are intelligent and curious, will be good weeders in the berry patch, and are apt to follow you around like puppies. They are also capable of devouring your garden, and of terrifying man and beast with their threatening hisses and honks. Because of their keen hearing, geese are excellent watch birds, and the United States Army is now using them to replace some of their guard dogs.

Before we got our geese, we were told that a goose ate everything in front of it and poisoned everything in back of it. There may be some truth to this, but we are fond of them, and their droppings do make a great fertilizer. They are among the most undemanding livestock you can raise, and they provide delicious meat and large eggs. In summer all that is essential is a small backyard space for them to graze and a shelter where they can sleep at night protected from coyotes, bobcats, foxes, and dogs. Although they are heavily insulated, in winter they need a dry shed or cabin.

You will want a fence to keep the birds confined to their grazing area and out of your garden and yard. They kept flying over our five-foot fence until an old-timer told us to clip back a few inches of the ends of their wing feathers with pruning shears. Although they screamed all manner of fowl remarks during the operation, it didn't hurt them a bit, and it did successfully lower their lifting power.

Since geese are grass eaters, they will find most of the nourishment they need if allowed into an orchard or pasture. You should supplement their foraging, however, with cracked corn or the type of poultry pellets used for raising broilers.

We originally bought our geese to use as weeders in our strawberry patch and nursery. They did a good job, but we found that if the weeds were in short supply, they would eat the berry plants as well. Also, we had to take the birds out of the patch well before the fruits formed, or they would consume them without even waiting until they were ripe. Geese are also good weeders along raspberry rows and in the orchard, particularly because they don't scratch off the mulch to

❖

eat the worms, as chickens do. They have their limits, though. One man we know heard about their weeding ability, and since he was tired of hoeing his garden, let his geese in to do it. By the time he got around to check on their progress, they had devoured nearly every row.

Getting Started

To get started with geese you have a choice of buying a goose and gander from a breeder; buying fertile eggs and hatching them in an incubator or under a broody hen; or buying day-old or month-old goslings from a hatchery or farm store.

If you want a year-round flock so you can raise your own, start with a goose and a gander. Buy year-old birds in the fall, if possible. It takes two years before a goose is mature enough to breed, and since they are planning on a lifetime match, they'll need time to become well acquainted before the mating season in the spring.

One year we bought some fertile eggs from a neighbor and hatched four little goslings under a Rhode Island hen. It was fun to see how frantic the hen became when her newborn offspring promptly jumped into the first mud puddle they found, and how quickly they outgrew her, even though they still all ran around together.

To get a flock in a hurry you can buy day-old goslings, and instantly become the surrogate parent of a flock of delightful little birds with their loud "peeps." Build a pen with sides 2 or more feet high in a draft-free barn, and cover the floor with dry shavings or sawdust. Provide heat either with a brooder or an infrared heat bulb as suggested in Chapter 23. Keep the temperature at approximately 90 degrees F. the first week, 80 degrees F. the second, and 70 degrees F. the third and fourth weeks.

As soon as the birds arrive give them food and plenty of water. Use the same starter feed as for ducks, but never feed them chick ration because it contains a medication that can be fatal to goslings. After a couple of weeks, change to duck pellets—the most practical feed for geese since there is less waste than with mash. They'll also need some sand or grit, which you will have to provide when they are confined inside; but they will find their own once they are in a yard or pasture.

Fill a container with water that is deep enough for the baby birds to dip their heads into entirely, but not so large that they can get into it, which they'll instinctively try to do.

Hatching Your Own

Our two geese, George and Gertrude, lived in a small coop about 8 feet square with a window and door. The only furnishings were a water bucket and a box for their grain. We left the door open during the day except in the winter, and shut it at night to keep out the wild animals.

We spread hay on the floor for bedding and warmth, and made a nest about 2 feet square and 1 foot high, except in front where it was 4 inches high for easy entrance. This was also filled with hay. They lived comfortably there throughout the winter, and as soon as spring arrived we let them outdoors during the day.

Since geese like to breed in water, the small puddles caused by the spring rains and melting snows furnished them plenty of opportunity, and soon Gertrude was producing one enormous egg nearly every day.

A goose wants to set as soon as she has produced a nest full of eggs; we took away the eggs as soon as they were laid, because we didn't want the goslings to appear while snowstorms were still likely. We always left one egg in the nest to encourage her not to give up, and we marked it so we could be sure to always leave the same one. After about two weeks, we let Gertrude fill up the nest with a dozen eggs, and she began to set full time. Each day she left the nest to go outside for food, water, and exercise. She always splashed around in a puddle or her water dish, and carried moisture back to the nest on her feathers, which kept the eggs at the right humidity. We were intrigued at how carefully she turned over every egg each day. During the laying period we had provided a source of calcium—ground oyster shells or calcite crystals—so the shells would be hard enough to withstand the rough treatment. In four weeks we had a nest full of chipper little goslings.

Although George took an immense interest in all the proceedings, he let his mate do all the work. He did stand guard against our curious dog and cat. Geese are ordinarily friendly, but both male and female are protective during the mating, egg setting, and especially when raising their young. Leave them alone during these periods because they may become dangerous—hissing, biting, and striking with their powerful wings at anyone who approaches. Few newborn creatures are cuter than baby goslings. Mother will provide warmth for them, but you must supply food and water in low pans that the small birds can reach easily. You'll enjoy watching them grow, but beware of becoming attached to them emotionally if you're raising them for the roasting pan.

The Dressing Off

Goose meat is moist and dark, and a special treat on your Christmas dinner table. Geese typically are slaughtered when they weigh 11 to 15 pounds, at five or six months of age and after they are somewhat free of pinfeathers. The process is much like dressing off chickens, except for removing the feathers, which are difficult to pluck because of the oil in them. The easiest way is to soak the goose for a few seconds in very hot water after it is killed, and wrap it in an old blanket soaked with equally hot water. Once the blanket has cooled, the feathers will come off quite easily. Some gourmets prefer the more laborious method of picking the bird dry, because the hot water turns the skin slightly red. If you are saving the feathers for a pillow or comforter it is best to pick it dry, because the feathers will not be in the best condition if they are soaked.

A Flock of Ducks

Like geese, ducks are water birds, but they are less independent and require more care, better shelter, and greater protection from wildlife. They are also smaller, less intelligent, and not as easy to train. We raised ducks on our farm long ago, and it was fun to watch the ducklings and their mother swim around in our little pond. We also appreciated their ongoing supply of eggs.

Breeds

Of the many breeds of ducks, the White Pekin and the Muscovy are most often raised for home use. White Pekin is especially good as a meat producer since the birds reach 7 pounds in only two months.

Muscovies come in a variety of dark colors as well as white, and the birds hiss rather than quack, which makes them easier to live with than the noisy Pekins. They like to fly, so you'll need a high fence or have to cut off the ends of their wing feathers to keep them at home. Meat from the young birds is excellent, but it tends to be tough if the birds are over five months old. Drakes weigh 10 pounds at maturity and the females somewhat less.

If you raise ducks primarily for the fun of it, you may want to keep two females and one drake through the winter. The females will lay an egg nearly every day if you keep the eggs picked up regularly. Then, when you are ready for them to raise a family, let the duck fill up the nest. In about a month each female should hatch out a dozen or so little ducklings.

If you want ducks primarily for meat, it is less trouble to order newly hatched or four-week old ducklings from your local farm store or from a hatchery listed in a farm magazine in the spring, rather than feed and care for the birds all winter. Keep the newly hatched ducklings under a heat lamp or brooder the same as suggested for chickens. They will be hungry when they arrive, so supply them feed and water immediately. Follow the feeding recommendations of your farm store. Baby ducks should have one kind of ration, the fattening birds another, and the laying and breeding ducks still another. When we had ducks, however, we fattened them primarily on cracked corn and other grains that we raised on the farm, and they did very well. As for geese and turkeys, keep grit and water where they can get it at all times.

Like geese, ducks grow quickly, so provide plenty of room for them in their shed or barn. They should each have ½ square foot of floor space initially, 2½ square feet by the time they are two months old, and 5 to 6 square feet ultimately, if they are a breeding flock. Spread wood shavings or other litter over the floor, and change it frequently because the birds will get it dirty very fast.

If you keep your ducks beyond the usual ten-to-twelve-week period, you can put them out to pasture for the summer when they are about a month old. Although they still need to be given food, water, and shelter, you'll have far less work if they live outdoors because their pen won't need cleaning out.

We let our ducks roam loose, but this is not a good practice if you live near a highway. Ducks enjoy strolling about together and will saunter casually across the road, as if daring cars to hit them. We have friends who live on a dirt road, across from their small farm pond. They told us they kept ducks until their children were grown just to slow down the passing traffic. Everything seems to stop for a mother duck trailed by a flock of fluffy little ducklings.

Ducks love a small pond or pool, but water is not necessary, and if you're raising them for meat, they fatten up faster and the meat is more tender if they don't have the additional exercise a pond gives them.

If you are raising ducks for their eggs, separate the sexes as soon as you can identify them. You can tell the difference because the females honk and the males make an odd belching sound. Drakes of colored varieties are also more bright-hued than females. The females mature and start laying eggs when they are about seven months old.

Ducks lay over a longer season than geese, sometimes nearly all year. The eggs are larger than hens' eggs and taste almost the same, but dedicated duck fans claim they are much better for cooking.

If you want eggs for hatching, provide one drake for each six females. Set up a nest for each broody female, and supply a shallow pan of water if the birds are not allowed outside each day. Like geese, the mothers-to-be must get their feathers wet daily to add humidity to the nest and make the eggshells soft enough to allow the young to break out easily. It takes 28 days for domestic ducks to hatch their eggs, and 35 for Muscovies.

Although White Pekins are especially good layers, they have a tendency not to brood, so their eggs usually must be hatched in an incubator. Because our flock was small, we often hatched the ducklings under a cooperative hen, who was always startled when she saw what her efforts had produced.

Roast duckling is considered a gourmet treat, and the meat, like that of goose, is all dark. Ducks are usually butchered when they are no more than three months old because they then stop growing, molt, and develop pinfeathers that are hard to pluck.

The butchering directions are the same as given for chickens, but since their feathers are oily like those of geese, follow the recommendation we gave for plucking geese.

The demand for duckling meat is greater than that for goose, and if you are enterprising you can probably build up a good market for surplus birds at local stores, restaurants, and hotels. Pekins are the breed most often grown commercially. Be reasonably sure of your market before you start heavy production. If you can't sell them at the right time, it is expensive to continue to feed the birds after they have reached their prime weight.

Chapter 25
RAISING RABBITS

The people we know who raise and eat rabbits have difficulty understanding those of us who don't. Their thinking is that if more people raised their own meat, they would be healthier and spend a great deal less money for food.

Time required: One buck and two or three does, 5 to 10 minutes every day, 30 minutes for cleaning once a week or so.
Gestation time: 31 days.

Rabbit Glossary

Buck—Male	Hutch—Home
Doe—Female	Kindle—To give birth

They have a point. The Malthusian odds are certainly in their favor, since the capacity of rabbits to reproduce prolifically is legendary. One rabbit doe can give birth annually to from 30 to 50 bunnies, which translates to 70 to 100 pounds of white meat. Rabbit meat is higher in protein and mineral content and lower in calories and cholesterol than almost any other. With one buck and two does you should be able to count on 100 pounds of meat for a family each year, with only a small investment in equipment and feed. Rabbits grow so quickly that a 3-pound fryer can be raised in about two months. Rabbits older than two months can be eaten, but most people prefer the younger, more tender fryers or roasters.

Although you must provide food and water, rabbits are not big eaters, and a lot of their feed can be grass from the lawn and surplus vegetables from your garden. You can probably get by with only 20 or 30 hours of work on your project each year, although you will probably want to spend more because rabbits are fun to watch. You need only a small area to keep a rabbit hutch, and zoning regulations usually do not forbid them since the animals make no noise and their odor is not offensive when they are well cared for.

Most people raise rabbits at home for meat. But you may find other reasons for having a rabbitry. They can be raised as show animals, and they make good pets for children. They produce a "cold" manure which can be used fresh on the garden without burning the plants. Their soft, warm skins can be marketed or home-tanned for hats, coats, slippers, and mittens. The soft hair of Angora rabbits is a favorite of hand spinners and knitters.

Although rabbits are not as difficult to confine as chickens or pigs, they need to be kept under control or they can devastate a garden or flower bed. Children in a nearby town accidentally let their small herd loose one night, and the people along their street didn't forgive their parents for years.

Getting Started

Rabbit growers are well organized on the national and state levels. The American Rabbit Breeders Association publishes books, pamphlets, and lists of breeders, clubs, and supply houses. Your farm store may also be able to give you names of local breeders who can supply stock.

There are more than 70 varieties of domestic rabbits in a wide variety of colors. They range from the petite ones, which weigh only 4 pounds at maturity, to giant 15 pounders. New Zealand Whites and Californians, both medium-sized, are the most popular and practical for meat production. Fryers of these types can be grown to 4 pounds in about two months, and reach roaster size in eight months.

If you want to produce meat for your family, you can get a good start with two to four does and one buck. In most areas, you'll have a choice of buying inexpensive two-month-old bunnies that have just been weaned, more expensive does that have already kindled, or medium-priced young does that have not kindled but are nearly ready for breeding. Choose those that are lively, bright-eyed, and friendly, with shiny coats.

When you bring them home, put each one in an individual hutch. Rabbits are hardy and can be kept in outdoor housing all winter in the warmer parts of the country, but in a cold climate they'll need indoor housing during the winter, with protection from cold drafts. A moveable hutch is ideal because it can be used outdoors in summer and then moved into a shed or barn when the weather turns cool.

Plans are available for construction of a rabbit hutch from your state extension service. Farm stores sell special hutch wire—½ × 1-inch mesh for the floor and 1 × 2-inch for the walls. Each cage should be at least 3 feet square and 18 inches high. Most designs call for a sloping roof, with a door large enough for easy access to the rabbit and for cleaning. Each cage must be cleaned and disinfected at least once a year with a strong germ killer such as Lysol or Chlorox to prevent disease. Disinfect any equipment that has been unused for awhile and is being put back in service.

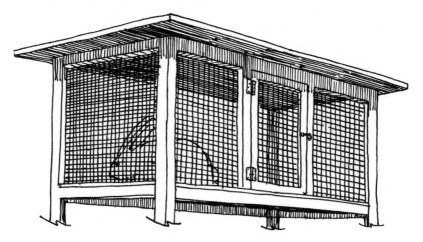

Rabbit hutch covered with hutch wire.

An outdoor hutch should be placed in a shaded spot. Some people grow earthworms beneath them. Worms work in the waste that falls through the mesh, converting it into more worms and fertile worm castings; both are marketable, but you may decide to use the rich castings in your own garden or potting soils.

Place a feeder and a waterer in each hutch. Because cleanliness is important, the best type of containers hang on the exterior of the cage, with openings on the inside. Special feeders and waterers are available at supply houses, or you can make your own. Metal feeders are best, since rabbits like to nibble on wood. A dandy waterer can be made from a large soft drink bottle hung upside down, with a sipper tube purchased at a farm store.

Supply your pregnant doe with a nest box with hay bedding for at least a week before the bunnies are due to arrive. She will not only use the hay, but also pull out some of her own fur to line the box. Nest boxes are available from rabbit supply houses, or you can easily make your own from plywood. The usual size is 1 foot by 2 feet, and 6 inches high.

Rabbit Culture

The doe of an average-size breed is ready to mate for the first time when she is about six months old. Always take the doe to the buck's cage, since she will not welcome him as a visitor in her domain. When he falls over, the deed is done, and you should remove the doe. Do not leave her in his cage for long, or he may harm her. The mating causes eggs to be released, and in six to eight hours you should return her to his cage for a short period, to ensure fertilization and increase the size of the litter. Seven to ten baby bunnies will be kindled 31 to 32 days later—hairless little creatures whose eyes will not open for 10 days. Twenty-four hours after the kindling, divert the attention of the mother and inspect the litter to remove any malformed or dead offspring. Some people prefer to raise only the strongest six or seven, and cull the rest, since the mother will have trouble feeding more than that satisfactorily.

She will nurse her young for two months. At that time they will weigh three or four pounds ("fryer" size) and be ready for butchering. Don't remove all the young from their mother at one time, however, because this is too hard on her, and her milk supply should be allowed to dry up gradually.

The doe can be rebred from six to eight weeks after each kindling, but many growers prefer not to have litters during the coldest winter months. Although it seems cruel by human standards to keep a doe always pregnant, it is much healthier for her, and she may continue raising young for five to six years. If she is allowed to "rest" for several months or more, internal fat will grow around her reproductive system, and she is likely to become infertile. When a doe is no longer productive, she should be replaced by a strong young doe from the most productive of your female bunnies. Inbreeding is not harmful among rabbits.

Even if your family consists of only three breeder rabbits, you will want to keep records of each animal's breeding dates, rate of growth, production, mortality of the young, and even the personality, to be able to make the best replacement selections. If you raise rabbits to sell, be even more attentive to breeding details because the generations follow each other so rapidly.

In addition to keeping excellent records, you should be well informed of your breed's characteristics, methods of selection and culling, and the results of inbreeding (mating of closely related animals), line breeding (mating of distantly related animals of the same breed), and crossbreeding (breeding of two different breeds).

Food and Drink

The rabbit is a vegetarian and thrives on a combination of commercial pelletized feed and fresh greens. Bucks and does that are not nursing need 4 to 6 ounces of pellets a day, but nursing does should have as much as they will eat. Since commercial pellets are not all the same, ask your grain dealer to help you choose the proper feeds for growing rabbits, nursing does, and bucks and does that are not nursing. Do not overfeed them. Unless they are nursing they should be fed only as much as they will eat in a half-hour.

Whenever you introduce new food into their diet, do it gradually so it will not upset their digestive systems. Supplement the pellets with lettuce, beet greens, carrot and celery tops, potato and apple skins, and table scraps of toast or cereal. Their favorite foods include green grass and root vegetables, especially carrots. Keep clean, fresh water and salt (preferably in block form) available at all times.

Diseases

Diseases are not usually a problem in a small backyard rabbitry as long as you start with healthy rabbits, shelter them from extremes of heat and cold, and keep the hutches extremely clean. Liver coccidiosis is a common parasitic disease that often occurs when conditions are unsanitary. Diarrhea can be controlled by proper feeding; and rabbit snuffles (colds) sometimes must be treated with penicillin. Isolate any rabbit that appears ill to prevent the spreading of the disease.

Butchering

Rabbits are probably the easiest animal to butcher, and for this reason the job is usually done at home rather than by a slaughter house.

Kill the rabbit by hitting it on the head with a small club. Cut off the head immediately, and hang the carcass up by one rear leg until the blood is drained. Then cut off the legs and tail, and make a small cut in the skin at the center of the spine. Put your fingers into the cut, forcing them under the skin, and pull in opposite directions. The skin will split in half, and come off easily with no hair on the meat. Of course, if it is important to save the skin, you must be more meticulous and cut it in such a way that you can remove it in one piece.

Eviscerate the rabbit by making a small cut in thin skin over the stomach, being careful not to cut into the intestines. Remove the entrails, and rinse everything thoroughly with cold water.

Chapter 26
PONDS
FOR MANY REASONS

One of our neighbors told us recently that she and her family had never completely enjoyed their country home until they built an acre-and-a-half pond in back of their house. Now, instead of driving many miles to enjoy the swimming, boating, and fishing they love, they just run out the back door.

A pond can also provide fire protection and may lower your insurance payments. By raising the water table, it may encourage nearby trees and plants to grow better. A pond also supplies water for irrigation and livestock. Finally, it can be a home to water lilies, ducks, and frogs.

We should caution that a pond that is badly built, poorly maintained, or misplaced will become a headache. It may degenerate into a smelly swamp, filled with reptiles, mosquitos, and slimy green algae.

Before you start to draw your pond on graph paper, decide how you want to use it. No one pond can effectively provide all of the things listed above. Murky water grows the food that fish like to eat, but is unattractive to swimmers. A pond shallow enough for water plants will not be deep enough for trout. Ducks and geese do not coexist well with aquatic plant life. Your needs and desires should determine the size and depth of the pond you build.

Location should be your next consideration. Never choose a spot solely on the basis of whether or not a pond would be beautiful or useful in that spot. Get expert advice from a pond specialist—either a private engineer or someone from the Soil Conservation Service—who is familiar with the terrain in your area. By boring into the ground, the specialist will be able to judge the prospective sites on your

Sources of water for a pond.

property. A clay soil is best for a pond, but you may be able to bring in clay from a spot nearby if your soil is sandy or gravelly. Although rock ledge below the pond sounds good, it may not be ideal because of cracks that are likely to leak. Swampy land may appear to be a logical site, but swamps often dry up in summer, or prove to be difficult to excavate.

Year-round springs are the best source for a pond because they keep it supplied with fresh, cool, well-aerated water. Natural runoff from a slope is second best, but it is dependent on rain and melting snow, and is likely to carry a lot of silt with it. The slope should be covered with grassy sod, because silt will run off a poorly covered slope. Make sure, too, that the slopes have not been treated with agricultural chemicals that are harmful to fish.

If you have a stream, you may be advised to locate the pond adjacent to it so that water is available, but will flow into it only when needed. If you dam a stream, the flow of water will be difficult to control, especially in a flood. Also, a pond made from a dammed stream collects undesirable fish species, fills up quickly with silt, and will likely need to be drained and re-dug from time to time.

No matter where you build, the pond should have an overflow pipe or concrete spillway to handle runoff; otherwise, surplus water will run over the dam and erode it. Don't count on a heavy grass cover to be an effective soil holder. The soil will start to wash loose if even small amounts of water run over it for more than a few hours. Check with your Soil Conservation Service before you build, too, because rules involving building ponds vary from practically none in some regions to rather stringent regulations in others.

If you intend to stock your pond with fish, you will want to investigate the requirements of the various species. It is recommended that ponds for bass and bluegills be a minimum of an acre in size for the best results, but trout will thrive in a half-acre of water if it is deep enough so that the water stays cold for most of the summer.

In the South, ponds for warm-water fish need be only 4 or 5 feet deep, but in the North, because a pond of that depth is likely to freeze nearly solid, it must be much deeper for fish to survive. Twenty feet is recommended for trout, with 12 feet a minimum for other fish.

Construction

Don't try to save money by getting a neighbor to build your pond with a bulldozer or a few sticks of dynamite. It is a job for experts only. A crane with a dragline is the best way because the machine can dig from a distance without disturbing the land around it. A bulldozer with an experienced operator is a less expensive alternative, and in our area many excellent ponds have been built that way.

If your contractor has a reputation for building ponds that have remained in good shape for many years, you and he or she can probably plan one together successfully. But if the contractor is new at the job, get an expert from your soil conservation district or a good pond engineer to work closely with him or her.

The sides of the pond must be sloped properly. Algae and weeds will grow if they are too gradual, but the banks will quickly erode if they are too steep. The dam and spillway or overflow pipe is an especially vital part of the construction, and both the upstream and downstream slopes of the dam must be planned and constructed carefully, so heavy rains won't wash them out.

Expect to do some annual maintenance, even if your pond is well built. Remove the weeds and brush at the water's edge. They encourage algae growth in the water, and without them you'll be better able to quickly spot erosion along the sides. Immediately fill in eroded areas, and keep an eye out for animal activity. Beavers often plug up spillways and overflow pipes; muskrats enjoy seeing water run, so they like to make holes in a dam. If you find any suspicious signs, ask your local game warden about trapping and moving the animals to another area.

You can plant evergreen trees and shrubs a short distance from the water, but keep them off the dam itself because the roots may weaken the structure in future years. It is not a good idea to have deciduous trees near a pond, because their leaves will blow into the water, discolor it, and cause algae growth to deplete the oxygen.

Raising Fish

Swimming and raising a few fish can go together well in the same pond, and most of us who live in the country like to do both. If you choose to raise fish on a large scale, however, you will probably have to forego swimming in the same pond, because the water would be more murky than you'd enjoy due to the increased amount of aquatic plant life that fish need for food.

In a cold, deep pond you can raise either rainbow or brook trout, or both, but you should not add other kinds of fish. In a warmer pond, bass and bluegills are a popular combination because the bass eat the bluegills if they get too numerous. These species are often stocked at the rate of 50 to 100 bass and 500 to 1,000 bluegills per acre. You may choose instead to raise catfish, carp, crappie, goldfish, muskellunge, or northern pike. Check with other fish farmers or the state extension service to find what is best suited for your locale and conditions. The state fish and game service will be able to furnish you with the names of hatcheries in your area, and will also provide information about the size of fish to purchase and the length of time it will take for them to reach maturity.

Although you can buy commercial food for your fish if you wish, the fare supplied by the pond should be sufficient. You can encourage aquatic plant life by adding fertilizer to supplement the nutrients supplied by lightning, rain, soil, and other natural means. Nitrogen, phosphorus, and potash are all necessary for good growth of algae. Here is a simple rule of thumb: if a white golf ball can be clearly seen at a depth of one and a half feet, the pond probably lacks one or more of the nutrients necessary for maximum fish growth.

A natural fertilizer mix of approximately 8-8-5 formulation can be used at the rate of 100 pounds for each acre of pond surface. Apply whenever the golf ball is visible. Some growers fasten ropes on burlap or loosely woven plastic grain bags filled with manure, and suspend them just under the surface of the pond. These bags should be shaken from time to time as the water clears, and they'll need to be replaced occasionally. Too much fertilizer can be as bad for the fish as too little, so be careful not to overdo your feeding.

If your main interest is swimming, you can keep the water clearer and discourage algae growth by feeding the fish a commercial food or freshly washed earthworms.

Restocking

If your pond functions perfectly, and you catch just the right amounts of fish, you may never need to restock it. This isn't likely to happen though, so inspect your pond to see that it is neither too empty nor too crowded. If the fish appear to be too numerous you have a legitimate excuse to take a few hours off for a fishing expedition and a cookout. Under favorable circumstances, certain species, such as bluegills, breed so rapidly that heavy fishing is necessary to keep the pond population healthy. Others, such as trout, reproduce slowly and need an occasional restocking. Do not wait until the pond is completely devoid of fish before adding more, since an assortment of various sizes and ages is necessary to assure you a continual supply.

Fish Enemies

In addition to human poachers, which you will have to handle in your own way, animals and birds steal fish. Gulls, herons, kingfishers, bears, and fishers all help themselves to home-raised fish as shamelessly as they do those that nature provides. The best protection is to locate the pond close to your home. Barking dogs help, and commercial bird scarers that make startling noises can be used if you and your neighbors can stand the racket.

Like all forms of life, fish may be bothered by pests and disease. When stocking your pond, buy only from a reliable commercial hatchery so you will be sure of getting disease-free fish, and make sure that children or well-meaning friends do not contribute any wild fish they have caught elsewhere. Buy only high-quality fish food, and store it as directed so it will not become contaminated by parasites. Make sure that water does not enter the pond from polluted sources such as old farm dumps, ancient wells, or badly functioning septic systems.

If you find numerous dead fish, or if those you catch appear unhealthy or wormy, ask your local game warden or other expert for advice. It may be necessary to drain the pond, refill it, and start over.

Chapter 27
BACKYARD BEES

The first year we had bees, an old-timer told us that bees could not winter outdoors in our climate, and not wanting to lose our colony, we dutifully fastened the various parts of our hive together, and started to carry the heavy thing down the cellar stairs. Halfway down, the hive came apart.

Bee Glossary

Apiary—Collection of bee colonies
Drone—Male bee
Frame—Support for the honeycomb
Hive—House for bees
Queen—Fertile female
Super—Extra hive sections where honey is stored
Swarm—Crowd of bees that have left the hive
Worker—Sexually undeveloped female

Thousands of bees poured out, quickly filling the house with bees, and it was some hours and many stings later before we got all the bees out of the house. After that, the bees wintered outside. They liked it better, and so did we. And we learned not to pay too much attention to all the old wives' tales we heard about bees.

Even with such misfortunes, bees are still our favorite livestock project. They require no daily chores, actually preferring to be ignored, and need almost no attention in the winter. They do swarm occasionally, and ours seemed to sting at the slightest excuse, but they never stomped through the herb bed or broke down a fence. Quite uncomplaining, they work long, long hours at producing their delicious, natural sweetener, and they are endlessly fascinating to observe.

We were also delighted that their fast pollination often allowed us to get a crop of apples, plums, pears, or strawberries we might otherwise have missed. Because the bees pollinated the blooms on the first warm day they opened, the flowers were able to resist the frost that frequently came a few days later and would have damaged the flower so the pollen couldn't enter.

Beekeeping requires only a few square feet of land, and compared with most other livestock enterprises, takes only a few hours of work each year. On the other hand, it does take some savoir faire to successfully establish a hive of bees, prevent them from stinging and swarming, keep them healthy, and bring them through the winter in good shape.

About Your Colony

Italian bees are most frequently raised in this country, though Caucasian and various hybrids are also kept. A 3-pound order of bees will include approximately 12,000 individuals, and one queen—enough to start one hive. Within ten weeks, if all goes well, they may number more than 75,000. One of these, and only one, is the queen, a female who is constantly cared for by the worker bees. Her sole function is to lay eggs, which she does nearly around the clock during the height of the season. She can be readily identified because of her large size and the circle of attendants that always face her. The workers can raise a new queen anytime by feeding a bee larva a special diet, and they do so whenever the old queen becomes less active, or when the hive begins to get too crowded. Because two queens will not co-exist in the same colony, the older one will either kill the new queen or lead a swarm from the hive.

Besides laying the fertilized eggs which hatch into workers, the queen also lays a few unfertilized eggs which hatch into males. These are called drones. They do no work, and are larger than the worker bees but not as large as the queen. A drone's sole function is to mate with a new queen in a short lively courtship high in the air, after which he dies. The queen guards her supply of sperm throughout her lifetime, and fertilizes the eggs as she lays them. As winter approaches, all the drones in the colony are either killed or driven out.

The workers are undeveloped (and unliberated) females that are incapable of laying eggs. They gather all the nectar, do all the housework, and cure the nectar into honey, often fanning it with their wings for hours. In fact, they work so hard that those that hatch during the honey-gathering season wear out their wings and die within a few weeks; those hatched in the fall may live six to eight months.

The nectar they gather is similar to a sweetened water when it is brought to the hive. There, it is evaporated, modified, and converted to honey. Actual weighings have shown that it takes 20,000 bee-loads to accumulate 1 pound of nectar, which will be processed into only a ¼-pound of honey!

Getting Started

You can get underway, as we did, with a beginner's kit from a beekeeper's catalog. This will include a standard hive, which consists of a brood chamber where the bees will live and raise their young, a base and cover; supers (extra stories where the honey is stored above the brood chamber); frames and wax foundation to insert into the hive and supers, upon which the bees will make honeycomb; a hive tool, to take apart the hive sections after the bees have sealed them together with wax; a smoker, to calm the bees when you are working with them; a veil; and long gloves.

Since your kit will contain only the bare essentials, also order additional honey supers and wax foundation so you will be ready when the principal honey-producing flowers, such as clover, begin to bloom.

Your kit will also include a booklet of instructions, so thoroughly read it or another beekeeping guide before you assemble your hive, and study it again just before the bees arrive.

Buy the kit and extra supers in the fall or winter. This will give you plenty of time to assemble everything and paint it white so it will reflect the sunlight and keep the bees and honey cool. In addition to assembling the brood chamber and frames, and the honey supers and frames, you will need to secure a sheet of wax foundation on each frame. The bees will use these wax sheets as patterns for the honeycomb they use for brood cells, and as storage compartments for honey.

Place the hive in a sunny spot, with its entrance facing the morning sun, if possible. The hive should get shade after midday if you are in a warm climate. Put it where it will be sheltered from strong winds (you won't want to move it for winter), and away from human traffic. Since bees need fast, unhindered bee-line access to the front of the hive from all directions, make sure no nearby trees or buildings obstruct this movement. Mount the hive on bricks or cement blocks to keep it off the ground and prevent rotting.

Bees need a source of fresh water somewhere in the vicinity, so if none is available, install a bird bath or small pool.

Your bees will probably be shipped to arrive at the right time for your region—early enough so they will be ready to get underway as soon as the first fruit trees and dandelions begin to bloom. Check to see that a certificate of inspection is on the box that the bees are in, to indicate that they are disease-free, and follow the directions for installing them in the hive. Because nectar sources will be limited early in the season, you'll have to provide a sugar-water syrup with the feeder that comes with the hive. Continue feeding it until the bees stop eating—an indication that they are finding plenty of food on their own.

The lower section of the hive (and in a two-story hive, the two lower sections) make up the brood area where the queen raises her young. The wax foundation in this section has wires to help support the heavy weight of the larva bees. These sections are left undisturbed year after year, unless something goes wrong.

Above the brood area are the honey supers, which come in different heights. The shallow units are light and easy to carry, but the deeper ones provide more honey storage. The queen must not

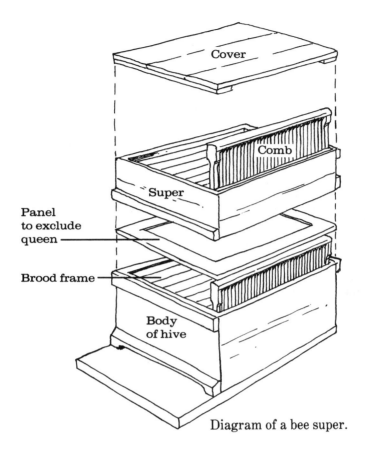

Diagram of a bee super.

invade this area to lay eggs, so a queen "excluder" is sometimes placed between the brood area and these sections, allowing only the smaller workers to pass through.

The term "busy as a bee" is meaningful to anyone who has been near a hive or a fruit tree on a sunny day during the blossoming season. In a vintage honey season (in the North, a rainy June and a hot July and August), each colony may collect from 6 to 10 pounds of cured honey a day.

Keep an eye on the amount of honey being stored, and each time the bees have filled half the frames in a super, remove that super, replace it with an empty one under it, and place the half-filled one on top. In a good year, there may be five or six supers on your hive. Near the end of the season, remove most of the supers that contain the better grades of honey, such as clover, and leave the darker grades (goldenrod, buckwheat, etc.) for the bees to eat during the winter.

Precautions

A mistake we made the first year with our bees was to give them too much attention. Bees don't like to have you look in the hive every day, or to show them off to your friends, and they express themselves clearly. They not only produced less honey, but we got stung so much that some sort of immunity must have developed because, by the end of the summer, a sting was barely noticeable to us. Most beekeepers pay little attention to the stings after a few seasons. Well-known apiarist Charles Mraz, who has been selling honey since 1931 in Middlebury, Vermont, is among the many who contend that the stings reduce the suffering from arthritis. You might call it a natural form of acupuncture.

The sting is the bee's defense mechanism, and when you are working around the hive, move slowly and never slap at the bees. To reduce the likelihood of being stung, open the hive only when the weather is sunny and warm and the bees are preoccupied with gathering nectar. Wear a veil, gloves, and close-woven, light-colored clothing that is tight at the ankles and wrists. Use a smoker to quiet them, directing the smoke gently into the entrance of the hive.

The venom of honey bees is not as painful as that of yellow jackets and black hornets, but if you suspect you might be allergic, consult a doctor before working with bees. When you are stung, pull out the stinger carefully, trying not to press the attached sac so you won't squeeze more venom into the sting. Then, to relieve the pain, immediately place mud onto the sting, and when you get a chance, apply aloe. We've tried these old folk remedies and they work.

The Sweet Harvest

Honey harvests vary greatly from year to year, depending on the strength of the colony, the weather, and the crops grown in your area. After leaving 75 to 100 pounds of honey for the bees to consume over the winter, the yield per hive can vary from almost nothing to 200 pounds or more.

You will need to uncap the honeycomb so the honey will flow out, and an electric knife works well for this procedure. In a warm room you can drain most of the honey simply by inverting the uncapped comb over a pan for a time. If you have several hives, you should invest in a honey extractor, however. Its spinning motion extracts the liquid honey rapidly. Work carefully, because after extracting, the undamaged comb should be returned to the super, to be refilled by the bees.

Swarming

The workers respond to a crowded hive by raising one or more new queens, but they may also raise one even when the hive is not overpopulated. Unless bees appear to be overflowing your hive or the old queen appears unhealthy, don't allow queen cells to hatch. Check the brood frames each week and cut out any queen cells you find. They're easy to spot—large and shaped like a peanut shell.

On the other hand, if your colony appears too crowded, losing a swarm may be a good thing. The lost numbers will be quickly made up. After a swarm leaves, check the hive to see if other queens are being raised, and cut their cells out. If you lose additional swarms, your hive may be decimated.

A bee swarm is quite a sight. About half the colony sides with the old queen and it leaves with a loud roar. The swarm hurtles through the air like a punted football, and usually alights on a nearby tree or shrub for a few hours while scouts search for a hollow tree, old building, or another place to set up housekeeping.

If a swarm lands on a limb within reach, you can start a new colony in an empty hive that has been outfitted with brood frames and wax foundation. Remove the cover and half the frames, cut off the limb with the bee cluster, and, with a quick jerk, shake the swarm into the empty space. Then quickly put on the cover. After a day the bees will have spread throughout the remaining frames, and you can replace the frames you removed. Your chances are good of escaping a sting through all of this excitement, because the bees gorge themselves with honey before leaving the hive and are usually too stuffed to sting.

We learned the first year that only early swarms are worth saving, because in our climate a late summer swarm cannot build up enough brood or store enough honey to get it through the winter. According to the old beekeepers' saying:

A swarm of bees in May, is worth a load of hay,
A swarm of bees in June, is worth a silver spoon,
A swarm of bees in July, is not worth a fly.

Overwintering

Follow the recommended directions for overwintering bees in your area. In most places it is best to leave the hives outside in a sheltered spot. Narrow the hive entrance to keep out the cold, but don't close it because the bees like to fly outside on mild sunny days. It is difficult to guess how much honey is enough to overwinter the bees, so check occasionally in late winter and throughout early spring to see if they are running out of food; if necessary, feed a sugar-water solution until spring flowers begin to bloom. Budget some extra money for this, because in a poor honey year you may need to supply up to 40 pounds of sugar per hive. It will still be cheaper than buying replacements, and much easier than cleaning out a hive filled with thousands of dead bees.

Problems

The best defense against bee diseases is to start with healthy, certified bees, and to use new or carefully sterilized equipment. Make sure, too, that there are no old infected hives around that the bees might visit. Keep the hives well ventilated, and watch the colony closely. If you notice signs of dead bees or larvae in the hive, you may have a disease called foul brood, so contact the official bee inspector in your area. Your extension service will help you locate him or her.

Insecticides may affect bees when they visit the flowers of recently sprayed orchards, gardens, and farms, or when aerial spraying drifts near the hives. Use only the safest methods of pest control for your own plantings, and encourage your neighbors to do the same.

Most animals leave bees alone, but a bear once devastated the dozen hives of a friend. Although our friend had previously been defensive of all animals, he had no trouble forming a posse to round up the culprit and convert him into a parlor rug. If bears are frequent visitors to your area, you may need to keep a watch dog, build a strong fence, or install a noisy alarm system.

If you make more honey than your family can consume, you should have no trouble selling it with a roadside sign or at a farmers' market. Premium comb honey is sold in small boxes consisting of a single comb. Liquid honey is strained and pasteurized and sold in glass jars, or sold unpasteurized as creamed honey. Some beekeepers we know like to sell their entire crop at once, and their friends appear at extracting time bearing gallon jars and cans.

Bee colonies, whether they are kept as a business or for home use, must be inspected by the state each year, so as soon as your bees are well settled, ask your extension agent to put you in touch with the proper authorities.

Many beekeepers fail because they become too enthusiastic. They set up more hives then they can care for, or more than their area can support, which encourages the bees to steal honey from each other. If you want to expand your apiary beyond the number of hives that the flowers in your neighborhood can supply, you can often find people in other locales who will be glad to provide a spot for several of your hives in exchange for a little honey and excellent pollination benefits. Whether you have one hive or many, we advise you to concentrate on maintaining strong colonies. A few vigorous colonies are invariably far more productive than a lot of weak ones.

Chapter 28

THE FAMILY COW

Early in this century, you probably would have kept at least one cow if you had lived in a rural area, a village, or even in a good-sized town. About the time the automobile replaced the horse, the family cow was also retired. Dairy products were delivered to the door, and became easily available from the neighborhood store.

Time required: Depending on your setup and time of year, 30 minutes or more twice a day, more in winter; 60 minutes on weekends for cleaning, getting supplies, etc.; additional time for getting hay, building fence, etc.

Gestation period: 284 days.

Cow Glossary

Bull—Adult male
Bullock—Young male
Calf—Less than a year old
Cow—Adult female
Dry—The period before calving when the cow
    gives no milk
Fresh cow—Cow that has just freshened
Freshening—Giving birth
Heifer—Young female
Herd, Drove—Crowd
Steer—Altered male
Yearling—Between one and two years old

It is undisputably easier to buy milk, cheese, butter, yogurt, and ice cream than to cope with a cow. But we can come up with several good reasons to keep one. If you own a barn, have at least two acres of good pasture land, can produce your own hay, and use a lot of dairy products, a cow can reduce your family grocery bill. On the other hand, if you must buy all its feed and evaluate your time at executive rates, a cow is not cost efficient.

A family cow can provide benefits that can't be bought. It will be a friendly pet, offer lessons in life to children, and keep land open by grazing. It will produce an ongoing supply of manure for the garden and for speeding up the production of rich compost. And, of course, there is the supply of untreated milk and cheese. Even the by-products from making butter and cheese have uses. Buttermilk and whey can be fed to pigs, veal calves, chickens, and even plants. Finally, the family cow can provide offspring that you can sell or raise for meat.

Although these bonuses may tempt you to rush out to a farm auction and buy a dairy cow, anyone who has chosen to live in the country to be "independent" should know that cows are very demanding. We are acquainted with a number of people who once owned a cow and have given it up, and without exception they cite daily chores as their major reason for abandoning the venture. Twice a day, every day, at 12-hour intervals, you must milk the cow. You may choose the hours, such as 5 A.M. and 5 P.M., or 8 A.M. and 8 P.M. But you should not vary the times to fit a change in your own schedule, because it is not good for the cow and milk production will suffer. Consequently, unless you have regular help or willing neighbors, you won't be able to spend the weekend at the lake with friends, go to a wedding at milking time, or sleep late on stormy Sunday mornings.

Other chores that may wear you thin after a few months include washing the milk pail and cream separator, feeding and watering the cow, putting her in and out of the pasture in summer, cleaning out the barn, and pasteurizing the milk daily (unless you consume it raw). All eat into the time you might have planned to use reading the newspaper or working in the garden. The list of additional tasks is long, too: grooming the cow; hauling sawdust or other bedding; repairing the water system, fence, or window that the pushy animal has wrecked; hauling grain and hay; moving manure; and coping with diseases, injured teats, worms, lice, and fleas. You may also need to stay up all night with her when she is sick or assist with a birth that doesn't go well.

Producing Milk

"City kids think milk comes from a plastic carton or gallon jug!" we've heard said in a joking way. No one is that naive, of course, but cousins of ours, new to the country, did seem surprised to learn that the cows they saw grazing in the fields didn't produce milk year-round.

After a heifer is mature, at about 2½ years of age, she begins to get racy about once a month for two or three days. She is bred with a bull during those periods, or artificially inseminated. About 9½ months later she will produce a calf, and then give milk for about 9 months—the largest amount at the first of the period, and gradually less. Two to 3 months after freshening she can be bred again. After 9 months of producing milk, she is gradually "dried off" by taking less and less milk. While she is dry she is fed a special ration to nourish the calf growing inside her. This means that from 3 to 3½ months of each year, a cow produces little or no milk.

Starting with a Cow

Unless your predecessors on your place kept a cow and left you the equipment, home dairying will require a substantial investment, so you don't want anything to go wrong. Before you begin, read everything you can about dairy cows, and talk with people who have them. If you do not already own a barn or shed that can be remodeled, plan your new one carefully. Design it so that feeding, milking, and cleaning out manure can be done as quickly and easily as possible, and install an automatic water bowl so the cow can drink whenever she wants. The barn must have room enough for a stall for the animal, and plenty of room to store hay, grain, milking equipment, and other supplies.

The barn temperature should be kept above freezing so the cow's water should not freeze. An automatic water bowl will enable the cow to drink whenever she wants, and save the watering chore, but you still should let the cow loose nearly every day so she won't get stiff from lack of exercise. The barn should be weathertight for winter use, and ventilated on warm days through operable windows.

In a home dairy, a cow can share a barn with horses, poultry, sheep, goats, pigs, and rabbits, as long as each is in a separate pen or stall and kept clean so the milk won't pick up manure odors. The more animals, the warmer the barn will be in winter.

A cow stall needs a feeding rack to hold hay and a grain box that cannot be tipped over. Provide a rope and halter for hitching and leading the animal, milk bucket, curry comb and brush (for grooming), milk strainer and filters, emergency medical equipment, and a milking stool. Many of these items, as well as a hay fork, manure fork, large flat shovel, and barn broom, can be picked up second-hand.

Large animals mean big hauling jobs, and you may want a small tractor and trailer to move manure, hay, and bedding. If you plan to harvest your own hay, you must also invest in haying equipment unless you can rent it conveniently or hire a farmer to do your haying.

If you decide to process your milk, you may want a cream separator, butter churn, cheese maker, pasteurizer, ice cream freezer, and yogurt kit.

Ask your county agent how much hay a cow will need over the winter in your climate. If possible, store a supply that will last for the entire winter, so you won't run out during a bad storm or when there is a hay shortage and you can't buy any. A cow will eat from one-half to three-quarters of a bale each day. (An average bale weighs 50 pounds and a ton consists of about 40 bales.)

To graze a cow during the summer, you need a pasture that produces lush grass without a lot of weeds, and it should have a brook or other supply of clear water. To confine your milk factory, enclose your pasture with an electric or barbed-wire fence. As long as there is enough feed, and no hostility, a cow can share a pasture with horses, goats, or sheep.

In addition to pasture grass in the summer and hay in winter, a commercial grain mix is supplied by most farmers, using one kind of mixture while the cow is producing milk, and another when she is dry and developing her calf. If you always give her the grain at milking time, it will lure her to the barn at the right hour and prevent having to chase her around the pasture. Keep a block of mineralized salt where the cow can lick it whenever she wants, both winter and summer.

Some people do not believe in feeding commercially prepared grain at all, because it is difficult to find any that is not grown and processed with chemicals. Instead, they provide a lush pasture in summer and high-quality hay throughout the winter. They supplement the cow's diet with homegrown forage such as millet or green oats when the pasture is short in late summer and fall, and give her ground homegrown grain when she is dry.

To keep the cow dry and comfortable, provide clean bedding for her at milking time, when she is in the barn having her calf, and all the months she is confined inside during the winter. Hay, straw, sawdust, and shavings are all good bedding, as are dry leaves if you can get enough of them.

Keep records of the breeding and calving times so you will know precisely when to "dry her off," when to expect the calf, and when to breed her again. You may also want to record milk production and all expenses to evaluate the practicality of your operation.

Buying a Cow

Milk cows are not cheap. When shopping for one, as in buying a used car, *caveat emptor*. If you are not a good judge, let an expert help you make this important decision. A cow may sell for any price, from less than a hundred dollars for an aging critter to the million-plus which was paid in 1985 for a heavy-producing Vermont cow whose new owner hoped to transplant the embryos into other less-talented cows. Since extremely high production is not likely to be your goal, you should be able to get a good one in the vicinity of $300 or $400.

The breed preferred for commercial dairy production is the black-and-white Holstein. It produces the most milk, usually 3 or more gallons at a milking, is healthy, docile, and since it is a large animal, valuable for meat when its producing days are over. The smaller brown or tan Jersey is more popular as a family cow, however. Although it gives less milk (1 or 2 gallons at a milking) than the Holstein, this is more than enough for an average family, and because the milk is richer it produces more butter and cream.

Other good breeds are the yellowish red-and-white Guernsey, the red-and-white Ayshire, and the Brown Swiss. A Milking Shorthorn is sometimes chosen as a family cow because it is a good animal for both milk and beef. Each breed has its champions, and loyal owners defend their choice as vigorously as some car owners tout theirs.

There is no good reason to purchase a cow with a pedigree for mere family use. A good crossbreed or an unregistered animal will produce enough milk for the family and is less expensive.

You may want to buy your animal from a neighboring farmer or cattle breeder, at a farm sale or auction, or at a commission sale, where farmers bring surplus animals to sell each week. A cow that is fresh will cost more, but will give you milk immediately. If you are in no hurry, you can save money by buying a heifer calf and raising it to producing age, or a bred heifer and get both cow and calf.

Milking

The amount of milk your cow produces depends a great deal on her ancestry, of course, but it will also be influenced by how you handle her. Treat cows gently, because they are sensitive creatures of habit that respond favorably when things happen calmly and predictably. Like people, however, they vary widely in temperament, and the gentlest of them can jump or kick when surprised by a fly bite, an unfamiliar person or animal, or a loud noise. Legend tells us that the reason cowboys sang around the campfire was to calm the herd at night. Some farmers play soft music in their barns at milking time, claiming it increases production and makes the cows more manageable. We once had a hired man who sang loudly when he was in the barn, but this couldn't have had a calming effect unless the cows all happened to be tone deaf.

Hand milking is more practical for a family cow than machine milking since it is time-consuming to clean a milking machine twice a day. If possible, watch someone milk before you try it, and don't be discouraged if the first times are difficult. You will use finger muscles you didn't know you had, and the cow will probably be nervous if she isn't accustomed to old-fashioned ways.

Milk absorbs bacteria and odors easily, so keep the equipment clean at all times, and always wash your hands and the cow's udder before milking. Strain the milk through filters, and either immediately cool it or pasteurize it first and then cool it. Your farm store can supply you with the necessary materials.

Opinions vary on the need for the pasteurization of milk. One side warns of the diseases caused by drinking raw milk, while the other claims that clean, fresh raw milk is much more healthy than the pasteurized and homogenized variety. You will have to make this decision for yourself, but if you opt for pasteurizing, buy a unit, because it is difficult to do a good job on the kitchen stove or in a microwave oven.

What to do with extra milk? Before you sell it, check the laws of your state. In some states, small amounts of raw milk can be sold if customers pick it up at the farm, bringing their own containers. Regulations involving commercial dairying are strict everywhere, however, and it is hard for a small producer to comply because of the expense of the necessary milking and refrigeration equipment.

Cow Problems

You no longer have to fear the once-dreaded tuberculosis, brucellosis, and hoof and mouth diseases, which wiped out entire herds only a few generations ago. But scours, milk fever, mastitis, and other diseases continue to plague both large and small dairies. The best way to prevent troubles is to start with a healthy animal from a herd known to be relatively trouble-free, keep her in clean, comfortable surroundings and feed her well, and do not visit dairy barns that might have a disease you could carry home. Read up on signs of cattle illnesses, and notify your vet whenever your cow has symptoms that you can't readily identify and treat yourself.

Breeding and Calving

As we mentioned, a cow is usually bred from two and a half to three months after calving. You can usually tell when she is in heat by the different noises she makes, and the uncomfortable way she acts. You will probably see some blood on the urethra, too. Artificial insemination is an excellent method for the one- or two-cow farm, since it is impractical to own a bull or bring one in for breeding on short notice. Be sure to contact your local artificial inseminator well ahead of when you expect to need the service, so you will know how to locate him or her when the time comes. A cow is in heat for only two or three days, so it is important to have her bred during that time. A month of milk production will be lost if you have to wait until her next period.

Feed your cow a special grain mix during the time she is dry to build up her health and provide the additional calcium necessary to prevent milk fever at calving. Your veterinarian may suggest other mineral supplements, too.

A cow views birthing as a private matter, and if she is in a pasture she may break out and flee to the far corners of a nearby woods at the critical time. Bring her into the barn a day or so early to ensure that she and her calf will be safe in a warm, dry stall or pen. Keep a close watch, because the calf can arrive at any hour, including the middle of the night, and you should be on hand to act as midwife or call a vet if the calf becomes twisted inside its mother and cannot make it out by itself.

A calf is born active and hungry, and soon after it arrives it will be ready to stand awkwardly and nurse from its mother. This first milk is called colostrum and it contains a conditioner that is essential for the good health of the newborn.

❖

Your new offspring should weigh from 50 to 100 pounds, depending on the breed. You can sell it immediately to a local cattle dealer, or feed it for a time and get a better price. If it is a bull, you may decide to raise it for your own meat supply (see Chapter 30); if it is a heifer you may decide to raise another milking cow for yourself or to sell.

Commercial dairy farmers feed large amounts of grain to their animals so they will produce the maximum amount of milk; and they seldom keep cows for more than 6 or 8 years before selling them for beef. Home animals, if they are raised more naturally, often produce milk well for at least a dozen years out of a potential lifespan of 20 years or more. The animal can then be used for meat, which, although it may not be the best quality, is perfectly usable.

Renting Cows?

In some regions dairy farmers will rent one of their cows. Usually they are low producers that are not of great value to the farmers, but ideal for a small family that doesn't need much milk. Sometimes the owner will take the cow back during the dry period, and exchange it for a producing one. The farmer collects rent on the cow, attends the calving, and keeps the calf. Where such rentals are available, this may be a good way to have a family cow, especially if you are uncertain about the wisdom of being in the home dairy business.

In another arrangement, a family we know owns a cow and a good pasture, but not a weatherproof barn, so they keep their animal during warm months and board it with a neighboring farmer during cold months in exchange for the milk.

Chapter 29
GOATS

Relatives of ours bought two goats to raise for milk, and were surprised when the animals immediately became a part of the family. The father had grown up on a dairy farm and expected the goats to be like small cows. Instead, they followed everyone about like dogs, ducked into the house whenever they got a chance, and frolicked with the children. Contrasted with the cows he had known (he described them as aloof and rather stupid), the goats were friendly, intelligent, and quick to learn.

Goat Glossary

Billy—Adult male	Kidding—Birthing
Crowd—Herd	Nanny—Adult female
Kid—Young goat	

Friends in our town, on the other hand, found goats disagreeable, and gave them up. One day, the animals broke loose and ate their entire young orchard; another time, they consumed most of a neighbor's shrubbery. And visitors to their home were not pleased to find a goat proudly standing on top of their car.

In the United States, the cow is synonymous with milk, but in much of the world goats are its primary source. They are more efficient than cows in converting feed, even low-quality feed, into milk—one of the many reasons a couple of goats may be more practical for your family than a cow. One lactating goat produces from 3 to 5 quarts per day, a more reasonable amount for a small family than a cow's 10 to 20 quarts. Like cow's milk, you can make it into cheese, butter, ice cream, and other dairy products. Because goat's milk is naturally homogenized and the fat globules are easier to digest than those in cow's milk, many people who have trouble digesting milk can use it. The milk is whiter than cow's milk and has a slightly different flavor that not everyone likes. You may want to try some before you invest in goats.

The animals have the edge on cows, too, because they are far cheaper to buy and feed, need less pastureland, and can get by with smaller quarters. They are also less susceptible to disease; breeding fees are likely to be less; and transporting a goat, if necessary, is far easier than moving a cow. Like cows, they provide an ongoing source of manure for your garden and compost pile.

Some people are prejudiced against goats because they associate them with impoverished and backward agriculture. The animals also have the reputation of being smelly, dangerous, destructive, and noisy, but no goat lover would concur. In fact, the animals are intelligent, and many people keep them mostly as pets for their children. It is true that male goats produce a bad scent during the breeding season, and are prone to butt things around, but few families keep a male.

Goats have a well-earned reputation for browsing fruit trees, landscaping, flower beds, and vegetable gardens, and they don't discriminate between yours and your neighbor's. They will pull clothes off a line, and are so curious they do not hestitate to explore the interior of the house or car.

Goats enjoy the company of humans, and especially of other goats, so don't plan to own only one or it will be lonely, bleat noisily, and be less productive. Keep two, and they will assure your family of a continuous supply of milk, since you can milk one when the other is dry. The creatures often get so attached to their owners and surroundings that they need a period of adjustment after moving to a new home, so don't be surprised if milk production decreases the first week you acquire a lactating goat.

Getting Started

The best time to buy a goat is in the spring when newborns abound. If you can't locate a source in your area, place an ad in a local newspaper or contact your state's goat association. If you are new to goat husbandry, take along an experienced friend or neighbor when shopping for your first animals.

Most part-time farmers find that grade animals (part purebred and part crossbred) are less high strung than purebreds, and calmer animals are better as milk producers. If you plan to raise breeding stock to sell or to show at fairs, however, start with registered animals. The leading breeds are French Alpine, La Mancha (the only important goat breed developed in America), Nubian (an English breed with a Roman nose and short hair), Saanen (known as the Holsteins of the goat world, developed in the Swiss Alps), and

Toggenburg (a brown animal that Vermont owners keep confined during deer hunting season). Saanens are the heaviest milk producers, but their milk has less butterfat than some of the others. Nubians produce less milk than Saanens and Toggenburgs, but their milk is richer in butterfat. Two less-common breeds are the Pygmy, a dwarf animal, and the Angora, raised primarily for its long silky hair that can be knit into sweaters.

Goats need the shelter of a small barn or warm shed in the winter. For each animal, provide a box stall of about 20 square feet, a clean pen for birthing, and a pen in which to eventually separate the new kids from their mother. Add bedding of sawdust, hay, or straw to keep the animal warm, and replace it whenever it gets dirty. Because a goat is so short, you will need a raised stand for her when you are milking. You can easily build it yourself.

It is possible to keep goats without giving them pastureland, but a pasture saves greatly on your feed bill and dispenses with the extra chores of feeding, cleaning the barn, and exercising the animal. You'll also have happier goats if they are free to browse. Since they eat almost any green material, don't pasture them near poisonous weeds such as hellebore or plants such as tansy that can cause abortions. Goats eat paper and boxes, so keep the animals away from farm dumps that might have containers of agricultural chemicals and other hazardous materials. Because they also chew on wood, don't build their stalls or fences of wood that has been treated with preservatives.

Make sure you can securely confine your goats. High stone walls are best, followed by stockade walls. An electric fence will do if it has three strands of wire, 12 to 18 inches apart with the bottom one 6 inches from the ground. When pasture feed is in short supply, you may need an even tighter fence, however. If you have no pasture, give them a pen for exercise or tether them to a post outside.

For better milk production, give them grain twice a day, about 2 pounds per feeding, and about 1 pound a day of special feed during pregnancy. Your farm store will be able to make recommendations. Place a mineralized salt block in the barn or pasture, or add trace-mineralized salt to their grain each day. Surplus garden vegetables are another good addition to their diet. Make sure that clean water is available at all times, since they need to drink a large amount to produce their milk. Because goats are extremely fastidious and will not touch food that they have fouled, always feed them hay from a rack and keep the grain in a secure box. In a year, each goat will need approximately ½ ton of hay and 1,000 pounds of grain, in addition to its summer forage. Store the feed supply out of their reach, because goats do not know when to stop eating and may kill themselves by over-indulging.

The Life of a Goat

A doe gives birth to her kid, or more often, twin kids, after a gestation period of only five months. Female kids may be bred when they are about ten months old. You may want to sell these, or you can raise them for milkers or meat. Meat animals are often butchered at about six months of age for the sweet, tender meat (chevon). Their hides are valued as fine leather (kidskin). Never keep a male newborn for the purpose of breeding within your own herd, because the mating of related goats results in weak and unhealthy offspring.

Goats, unlike cows, can be bred only between late August and February when they are in heat, from 1 to 3 days every 21 days. You can arrange for breeding by artificial insemination, by renting a buck, or by taking your doe to a buck at another farm. You can tell when she should be bred by the uncomfortable way she acts, and the different noises she makes. Note the date carefully, and after 21 days observe her to be sure the insemination worked. If not, have her bred again. If you miss the last period in January, you'll have to wait until the next fall for another chance.

A lactating doe must be milked twice a day without fail, and dried off before the last two months of her pregnancy so all her energy can go into nourishing her developing young. Be on hand during the birthing to help out, but only occasionally is there need to call a vet. A doe usually takes good care of her firstborn, although if she has twins all the attention may go to one, so you may have to dry off the other and make sure it also gets an immediate feeding of the colostrum—the first milk the mother produces. Many a goat owner has spent a frigid mid-winter night, bottle feeding a newborn kid beside the kitchen stove.

Your animals should be dehorned within the first week of life before the horns begin to grow, both for your own safety and that of the other goats. Use caustic paste or a dehorning iron. Young males that are raised for meat should be castrated with a band castrator. You can buy these products at a farm store or from a veterinarian. If you are nervous about performing these unfamiliar tasks, get a neighbor or vet to work with you the first time.

Even if you do not plan to show them at the county fair, your goats will need grooming. You'll have to trim their hooves (they grow like toenails), and brush and clip the long hairs around the udder so that dirt and manure will not accumulate.

For more information on goat husbandry, read extension service publications and the books recommended in the Appendix. You may also want to subscribe to the *Dairy Goat Journal*, P.O. Box 1808, Scottsdale, AZ 85252.

Problems

Goats are less prone to diseases than most other farm animals. Parasites are one of their most common afflictions. Internal parasites can be treated with worm medicine, and external pests, such as lice, can be combated with a louse powder. Foot rot may trouble goats kept in a wet or muddy area. You can recognize mastitis, an inflammation of the udder, by the clotted, stringy milk the goat produces, as well as by the udder's swollen appearance; treat it promptly with antibiotics to prevent permanent damage. Milk fever is a paralysis caused by a low calcium level in the blood at the time of kidding, and an immediate injection of a calcium solution must be given to prevent death. Ask your veterinarian or farm supply store for medications to have on hand for such emergencies.

❖

Chapter 30
THE BEEF AND VEAL BUSINESS

Beef cattle were once almost as rare in our dairy state as buffalo, and as children we saw them only in Western movies. In recent years though, we have seen various breeds throughout our area. Most places have only one or two animals, but herds of a dozen and more are not unusual. And we know of many part-time farmers who are raising veal calves in their barns and sheds. A retired ex-urban couple in a neighboring village raises several calves each year to eat and sell, and they enthusiastically claim that the meat is far superior to any they have ever bought.

Time required: Small herd of beef, almost none in summer, ½ to 1 hour per day in winter. Veal, 1 to 3 animals, up to 45 minutes a day.

Beef Cattle

Commercially raised beef animals are usually pastured through-out the summer, fed through the following winter, and allowed to graze again during the next summer. During their second fall they are fattened with grain and should weigh from 900 to 1,000 pounds. Those raising beef for their own use find that such a large animal provides too much meat for a family, and choose to butcher them sooner.

Part-time farmers often raise beef animals instead of dairy cattle because they are less demanding. They do not need to be milked at regular times twice a day, and while in summer pasture they can feed and water themselves for several months. You need far less equipment for raising beef than for dairying, and less skill, too. They do require good pastureland and fresh water, and if they are kept over the winter in a cold climate, they also need shelter and daily care.

Although large beef cattle may frighten people who aren't accustomed to them (and the bulls may be dangerous), steers and females are usually gentle in spite of their powerful mien. This project may appeal to you if you like to have a freezer full of delicious beef which is free of growth hormones, antibiotics, and feed additives. Even one animal can keep a great deal of land open, and it will fertilize as it eats.

Although one steer may be enough to provide all the meat your family needs for a year, the animal will be more content if it has a companion, and both will grow better. Some people buy a couple of weaned calves in the spring, pasture them during the summer, and sell the extra animal at butchering time; others get together with neighbors, and share the costs of pasture, feed, and butchering.

Most beef is raised primarily for home consumption, but some people have cattle primarily to keep their land open. One small herd nearby is owned by a man who says quite frankly that he keeps them because he likes the authentic Western look his white-faced Herefords give his "ranch." They go well with his cowboy hat and boots, too.

Some of the less common breeds—Scotch Highlander, Brahma, Limousin, and Simmental—are often raised especially for exhibiting at fairs and beef shows. Quality registered animals earn big prize money at county fairs and shows. We have farming relatives who, when their children were growing up, spent two months each summer showing cattle at local and state fairs. They had a travel trailer for themselves and another for their cattle. The children spent many hours grooming their favorites, parading them around the show ring, and enjoying the company of others with similar interests. It was sort of a summer camp with a profit, as they brought home lots of blue ribbons and prize money that went into their college fund.

Large beef herds are raised both by ex-dairy farmers who have housing and land available and by newcomers who have bought farms and want to keep their land productive. Some specialize in producing breeding stock, and others sell their animals for beef.

Unless demand increases and prices rise, most farmers in our area of the North will not find commercial beef raising a profitable enterprise. That's because of the extra labor and feed required during the long winter when most beef animals must be kept inside. Shorter and milder winters, however, may allow a profit. If you are considering beef cattle as a business, check out the situation in your area. Unlike dairying, which provides continuing revenue, beef profits are realized only one time, when the animals are sold.

Breeds: What's Your Beef?

Each breed has its champions. Black Angus, Polled Hereford, Charolais, Shorthorn, and Longhorn are some of the most familiar. In the South, Brahmas and their crosses with other breeds are particularly popular because they can stand a warmer climate. In the North, Scotch Highlanders, a prehistoric-looking longhorn from Scotland, are chosen because they are hardy enough to stay outside in cold weather.

To satisfy the public's current preference for beef with less fat and fewer calories, new breeds have been introduced recently. Among them are the Beefalo, a cross between the bison and a Hereford or Angus; the Brae, which was developed by feeding Black Angus a special diet; and the Chianian, a descendant of a breed raised in the Chiana Valley of Italy since Roman times. Many of these new breeds grow quickly, resist disease, and seem to do well when fed only on grass, with little or no grain.

If you plan to raise registered animals or have a large herd, you may want to join one of the beef associations in your state, receive their literature, and attend meetings. Most are active groups that welcome new members and are eager to help each other.

Getting Started

If you are an inexperienced cattleperson and want to raise only two or three animals for your own food supply, you will not need an expensive registered animal. In fact, many people we know who raise beef for their own use buy a Holstein bull calf from one of the neighboring dairy farmers. Holsteins and other heavier dairy breeds can be raised successfully for beef. Many dairy farmers have their heifers bred artificially to a bull from one of the smaller beef breeds so that their first calf will be smaller and more easily born to a young heifer. These Holstein-beef crosses are good family beef choices for part-time farmers.

Both dairy bull calves and crossbreeds can often be purchased at reasonable prices, either directly from a farmer or at livestock commission sales in dairy country.

If you decide to raise more than a couple of animals, see an established beef breeder or go to a beef auction. The price will vary greatly, depending on supply and demand; the age, weight, and condition of the animals; and the bargaining skill of the owners. You may want to begin by buying a few cows with young calves in the spring. (A beef cow produces only half the milk of a dairy cow, and the calf will drink it all.)

While they are young, the bulls should be converted into steers (castrated). Call in a veterinarian, or do it yourself with the elastic bands you can buy at a farm store. Steers not only tend to be more docile, but also their meat is better. If you keep the animals more than one season, you should also dehorn them while they are young, either with a dehorning iron or caustic paste. Long, sharp horns are not only dangerous to the owners, but to other animals as well, especially when they are crowding around a water tub or feed trough.

Land Requirements

Beef cattle spend a great deal of time eating, sometimes up to eight hours a day. The amount of pasture you need will depend on the age, size, and maturity of your cattle. A mature beef cow can eat an average of 50 pounds of grass each day, which means from one to two acres throughout the season if the land is good, and far more if it is not. Check your pastures frequently at dry times of the year, especially in late summer, and if they appear to be overgrazed, provide supplemental hay or other fodder.

Beef animals, like all cattle, are experts at finding weak links in fencing. Although one strand of electric fence will usually suffice, two are better. Many small ranchers like electric fencing because it is easy to install and can be easily moved. More permanent fences of barbed wire should consist of three or four tight strands. Whichever fence you use, walk along it periodically to check for damage.

If your pasture does not have a brook, you must supply a water tub or other source of pure fresh water at all times—one animal may drink up to 12 gallons a day. Also provide a block of trace mineralized salt. Your veterinarian may advise other feed supplements if you raise calves or if there are mineral deficiencies in your area.

Winter

If you keep a beef animal through the winter, you'll need plenty of high-quality hay. In the northern states you should plan on 100 bales or more (about two acres' worth) for each beef animal. The animals must be fed from two to four months longer in the North than in the South, which adds considerably to the labor and expenses of beef ranching in that region.

Beef cattle have heavy winter coats, unlike dairy cattle, and do not mind subfreezing temperatures. But in any climate, you should provide shelter from wind, snow, and freezing rain. Where temperatures don't fall much below freezing, the shelter needn't be more than a roofed, three-sided structure with an opening to the south. You'll need to provide a heater to keep their drinking water from freezing, however, and you'll also need an adjacent building to store hay.

Some people keep their beef in a dairy barn during the winter, but it's easier to remove the manure from a structure that has no stalls or partitions. If you build a new structure, ask for plans from your state extension service; you also will probably be able to get plans for feeding pens and the headgates you'll need when you or the vet work on the cattle.

The Finishing

To "finish the steer" is to get it ready for slaughter. A steer is fattened to produce a maximum amount of weight and the proper marbling of the meat. The process takes one to three months, during which the steer is confined and given a grain ration containing 14 to 16 percent protein, as well as corn and hay. In a small home operation the finishing is often done after frost has killed the grass in the fall, when the steer is about 18 months old.

When you read "baby beef" on your restaurant menu, the chef is not supplying calf meat, but meat from prime animals that have been fed an especially formulated grain mixture so they will keep their baby fat. The meat makes delicious eating, but is not cheap to produce.

Not everyone believes in this finishing process, and baby beef is not as popular as it once was. Organic farmers try to avoid feed mixes that contain growth stimulants, disease controls, and other chemicals. Many raise their animals entirely on grass and hay, although some supplement this with their own ground wheat, corn, or other grains.

Veal

If you do not have enough room to house or space to pasture large beef animals, you may still be able to produce veal. This is a high-quality meat that is low in fat yet high in protein. Veal is the meat of a calf, either male or female, butchered when it is between the ages of 5 and 15 weeks old. Veal calves are not raised on beef cattle grain mixes, but given a special diet, and kept in a barn rather than put out to pasture. The food, plus the confinement, prevents muscle development, so the meat is extremely tender. Veal can be produced either from a milk calf such as a Holstein or Jersey, or from a beef animal such as a Hereford or Black Angus, or from crosses of beef and dairy cows.

The calves are raised in pens about four feet square, and the bedding must be changed often to keep the area dry. Feed the calf with its mother's milk for the first three to six days. (Colostrum is essential because it contains antibodies that protect the calf from infection.) Then twice a day it is fed a commercial milk replacer powder, mixed with water according to the directions on the package. You will probably need about 200 pounds of starter, which is available at farm stores, to raise a calf to 14 weeks. Veal raisers do not feed any other food, such as hay or grain, or even additional water unless the weather is very hot. Excess water will make the calf bloat and drink less milk.

If you have milk available from your own dairy cow or goat, you may use it as an alternative to the milk replacer. Start feeding about a gallon a day, gradually increasing the amount until you are giving the calf all it wants. If it develops scours (loose bowel movements), immediately cut back on the amount and gradually work up again. The veal will be a darker shade on this diet.

Many farmers feel that keeping the animal confined is unfair, so they let the animal outside in a small pen for short periods. The appearance and flavor of the meat is not the same as when grown in confinement, but the owners believe it is of better quality, and their conscience feels better, too.

Problems

Because beef cattle are outdoors so much of the year, they tend to have fewer health problems than dairy animals. Still, they are susceptible to illness during their winter confinement. Veal calves, on the other hand, because of their limited diet and confinement, are more disease-prone than cattle that are fed normally and allowed outside. To lessen the chance of disease, keep the area immaculately clean, and feed them only freshly mixed formula and clean water.

Whether you are raising young calves or large beef cattle, keep the stalls clean, draft-free, and dry to discourage ailments such as lice, itch, barn sores, and pneumonia. Prevent sudden changes of temperatures by making sure cold winds and rains can't blow in open windows or doors. If possible, do not let other farmers who may be carrying disease into your barn, and do not visit theirs. Scours is a particularly contagious disease that can be spread by humans from one barn to another.

Butchering

Unless you have skill and the proper equipment, butchering veal and large beef is best left to the experts. Your extension agent can direct you to a government-inspected slaughterhouse. Ask if charges are in terms of live weight or bled weight, hanging or dressed. Establish whether or not you want to save the hide and organs, including heart, brains, tongue, sweetbreads, liver, and bones for soup stock or for your dog. If the meat will be cut and ground, you may be expected to prepare a list detailing the thickness of the steaks and the weight of the hamburger packages.

Chapter 31

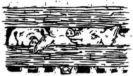

PIG POSSIBILITIES

Pigs suffer from an image problem, in spite of the popularity of Miss Piggy. People label pigs as stupid, dirty, and even dangerous animals. The words "pig" and "hog" are uncomplimentary.

The fact is, pigs are among the most intelligent animals, and much prefer cleanliness to a "pigpen" environment. Mature boars can be dangerous critters, and sows with little piglets should be approached with caution. All pigs are slippery characters when it comes to running away and it's simply their nature to eat like pigs; to them, fat is beautiful. They make cute pets when small, but it is risky to let your emotions become involved, given a pig's ultimate destination.

Time required: 10 minutes a day, 30 extra minutes a week if kept inside.

Gestation period: 112 days.

Pig Glossary

Barrow—Castrated male   Piglet—Newborn
Boar—Adult male   Shoat—Young weaned pig
Drift—Herd or crowd of swine Sow—Adult female

Of all meat animals, pigs require the least time and work for the amount of meat produced. They are less susceptible to sickness than most other animals, and rapidly convert grain, garbage, and pasture into ham, roast pork, chops, sausage, bacon, and lard. Efficient butchers claim they can use everything from the animal but the squeal.

Our childhood memories of pigs on the farm are not the best. We hated everything about them, from castration to cleaning out the pens. But lots of people we know, even our new neighbors with metropolitan backgrounds, have a completely different view. They wouldn't think of not raising a couple of porkers each year, and some even do their own butchering and meat processing. One boy told us that, from the day his father brought home two little piglets, he and his brother began reserving their favorite cuts of meat.

Pigs need little space and don't demand elaborate surroundings. If they are warm, reasonably clean, and well fed, they will be blissfully content. They fit in well with a working schedule, needing care only night and morning, and make a good project for young people.

Before you buy your first pig, check to see if the local zoning regulations allow them. Pigs are not welcomed in every neighborhood. We know of a family that kept theirs in the cellar until the neighbors got wind of it and notified the authorities. Another local couple lived in a town without zoning, but they made the national newscasts when they raised their swine across the fence from their neighbor's swimming pool. The neighbor took them to court.

Getting Started

It is impractical to keep a sow and boar and raise your own piglets because of the labor and cost of grain involved. Instead, buy a couple of weaned piglets, four to six weeks old, in the spring. These piglets are called "feeder pigs," and weigh 35 to 40 pounds—about the right size to carry home in a burlap bag. Be sure they have been de-wormed, and males should already have been castrated. (If they have not, call your vet—it is not an easy job to do yourself.) The meat of boars has a strong, offensive taste.

Most people like to raise two or more pigs at a time rather than one alone, because they grow faster when they compete for food. If your family needs only one animal, you can sell the extra hog just before butchering time. Or, as we suggested with beef, you might join forces with a neighbor to raise a pair together.

Although there are many breeds of pigs, no one breed stands above the rest, and yours will probably be a combination of several. You may be able to locate farmers with pigs to sell through your local newspaper. Most litters are born in the spring, and this gives you a chance to get them well started before putting them outside for the summer.

Try to pick up yours as soon as they are old enough to leave their mother. That way you can get the pick of the litter—large, active piglets that are long and lean, rather than round and fat. If the weather is cool, be sure to keep them warm on the way home, and put them in a warm barn. If it is bitter cold, you may need to put a heat lamp overhead for a few days.

The Pig Pen

It will be better for the pigs, and save you lots of cleaning, if you move your pigs outdoors in spring. Choose a spot where they can eat grass and dig in the cool earth, and preferably at a distance away from your home, since the fragrance may be very permeating.

We have friends who keep their pigs in either of two pens. The pen of one year becomes the garden plot of the next. By annually rotating the two areas, they are always ensured of a well-tilled, weed-free, organically fertilized garden.

The fence around the pen must be "hog tight." Hogs use brute force to topple fences and knock out boards; and after they are three months old they become "rooters" and delight in burrowing beneath fences. A 3-foot fence of well-anchored woven wire should contain them. Just make sure the base is stapled to a strong board that extends into the ground all around the pen. Don't rely on an electric fence unless you are assured that the power will never go off. The smart pigs will soon notice the absence of electricity, and trying to catch a loose pig can really mess up your day. Pigs cannot be herded like cattle and geese. If you try to corral them, they'll squeal at the top of their lungs and invariably run in the wrong direction. If you jump in front of a charging pig, you'll be knocked flat. The best method is to let them quiet down and then lure them back to the pen with a bucket of feed.

Humans are not alone in their enjoyment of fresh pork chops, so if wolves or bears frequent your area, make your fence additionally

❖

strong and be sure it is high enough to keep these animals out. Or keep a guard dog on duty, to warn you in case of an attack.

The pen should contain a roofed shelter to protect your swine from hard rains and hot sun. Pigs have a high body temperature and become overheated easily, and white pigs can even become sunburned.

If the pigs are not large enough to butcher before cold weather, move them inside to finish their growth. Indoor pens should be kept as clean as possible, with bedding of sawdust, wood shavings, or straw. Shovel them out twice a week and add it to your compost pile. Plan on lots of bedding because you will need it. If they are given enough space, pigs will choose a spot to put their manure so that it will not contaminate the rest of their living area.

Pig Diet

Build a V-shaped trough and anchor it so that it cannot be tipped over easily. It should provide at least 1 foot of feeding space per pig. There is a definite pecking order at a trough, and the weaker pigs are easily shoved aside by the more aggressive, so if you are raising several, check to see that each pig gets enough. Provide them with all they can eat, but if they don't eat the food quickly, cut back because they are likely getting too much.

"Fattening up" is the crucial part of raising a pig. Two or three times a day feed young pigs a commercial pig starter formula that is high in protein and contains vitamins and minerals. When the pigs reach 40 to 50 pounds, gradually switch to a hog grower feed composed of grains such as corn, oats, barley, wheat, and soybeans. You can add your own supplements if you wish—clover or alfalfa, surplus garden vegetables, apples, and most table scraps—but never citrus fruit, coffee or tea grounds, or raw meat (especially pork, since it may carry dangerous disease). We used to feed our pigs only homegrown cornmeal in warm water, skim milk left after separating the cream out for butter, garbage, and vegetables. Without commercial pig food, pigs take longer to reach butchering size, but those who feed without commercial food say the quality of the meat is as good or better, and it is much more economical.

Keep plenty of water available for your pigs at all times, and provide extra in summer. The grain should be moistened, and many mix it with water or buttermilk to make a tasty pig "swill."

Diseases

When kept outdoors all summer, spring pigs usually stay disease-free, especially if their environment is kept clean and they are fed a balanced diet. Disease is more prevalent in the winter, so check frequently for signs of sickness, such as lack of appetite or diarrhea.

Butchering

By fall, after eating like pigs all summer, your animals should have changed into hogs weighing from 200 to 240 pounds. This is the most efficient time to convert them into pork. It is a waste of grain and labor to allow them to grow larger, because after reaching that size, much more grain is required to produce additional pounds, especially in cool weather. What's more, a heavy pig is difficult to handle.

Butchering a hog is more complicated than butchering most other animals. A lot of equipment is necessary, including a large tub filled with near-boiling water to soak the bristles so they can be easily scraped off. It is rather impractical to attempt to home-butcher only one or two pigs a year by yourself. A butcher shop will kill, dress, and cut up your porkers in a very short time, and may even wrap the meat, prepare the lard, hams, and salt pork, and grind the sausage. There is very little waste on a hog, and one usually dresses out at 75 percent of its live weight.

Chapter 32
COUNTING ON SHEEP

Sheep are a part of our heritage. They figure prominently in the Bible, our folklore, and our expressions. They were one of the first animals to be domesticated, and through their long dependence on man, they have lost all their natural fear, aggressiveness, and even their judgment. Consequently, they are totally defenseless against dogs and wild animals, and trustingly follow one another to their doom. "Lost" sheep and "poor little lambs who have gone astray" are symbols of despair in our language—and accurate descriptions of the creature. Horses, cattle, cats, dogs, and even rabbits can turn wild and look after themselves, but never sheep. If you choose to raise them, you should be aware of this dependence.

Sheep Glossary

Cosset—Bottle-fed lamb   Lamb—Young
Drove—Herd or crowd   Ram—Adult male
Ewe—Adult female

The image of a shepherd with a crook, tending his hillside flock day after day, is far removed from today's flock owner, who is likely to spend workdays at an office while the sheep are confined by an electric fence.

Raising a few sheep can be a most satisfying project on a country place. They need little care and equipment, and they are not as expensive to buy as dairy or beef cattle. They keep pastures mowed, provide fertilizer for the land, and convert the brush, weeds, and grass they browse into food and fiber. A cosset lamb makes a cute pet, and even grown sheep are friendly souls if they have been well treated. Because they are also gregarious animals, you should not keep only one; it will be lonely, and bleat most of the time.

You may choose to simply raise spring lambs for meat, or to get more involved by shearing, carding, and spinning your own wool, and tanning the hides for sheepskins and leathers.

Getting Started

Although much of New England was sheep country a century ago, they are rarer now. We know a number of people who raised them in recent years and then stopped. One reason was because the animals had to be kept inside for so much of the year, requiring extra care and feed. Another was their tendency to break loose and eat up the garden. One family, who loved their flock dearly, could not bear to have them killed by the coyotes that had become a problem in their area. Another told us that stray dogs killed a dozen sheep in a single night, without eating any of them; and once, a bear carried one away. A young couple said it was difficult to see their young lambs trucked off to the butcher, after they had grown attached to them. Another common complaint was that the local vets were familiar with cows and horses but not sheep, and could not help with the various ailments the animals developed.

Some of these problems can be overcome by putting up good fences and putting the sheep in at night. And a small flock is easier to care for than a large number. If you plan to keep sheep year-round, a flock of a half dozen is a good size to start with. Before you decide on a breed, decide why you are raising them. Will it be primarily for meat, wool, sheepskin rugs, breeding stock, to show at the county fair, or simply for dressing up your country acres and keeping the pasture brush and weeds under control? Then, talk with your extension agent and local sheep raisers about the best breeds for your needs and climate. Fine-stranded wool is produced in the warmer climates, such as Spain; the medium grades originate in the more temperate zones such as the British Isles; and the coarser grades in the cooler, damper climates.

Good, all-around choices for most areas are Cheviots, Columbias, Dorsets, Hampshires, Suffolks, Southdowns, and Shropshires. The last-named are primarily grown for meat, although they also produce good wool.

Having said all this, experts recommend that beginners buy crossbred ewes, since they are more vigorous than most purebreds and less expensive. Buy them, if possible, from a reputable breeder with a high-production flock, rather than at an auction where usually only culls are available.

The best time to buy sheep is in late fall, when the recently bred ewes come on the market. Buy two- or three-year-old ewes that have had lambs at least once, and if possible, have an experienced friend help you choose them. Sheep vary in personality, so choose those that appear docile rather than nervous or pushy. Examine their teeth, too, to help determine their age. Young lambs have eight milk teeth, only in their lower jaw. At one year they have two permanent teeth; at two years, four; at three years, six; and by age four they'll have all eight teeth.

Lambiculture

The usual mating season for most breeds of sheep lasts from early September through December; the ewes come into heat for a 1- to 3-day period, every 17 days. It is not practical to keep a ram in a small flock, so you'll have to import one or have the ewes artificially inseminated.

They give birth approximately five months after breeding—often, it seems, on the coldest night of late winter. You must be on hand for lambing in case anything goes wrong. Be sure the pens are draft-free, and if your barn is chilly, keep towels or blankets handy and install a heat bulb or two to keep the lambs warm. At birth, you should dip the lamb's navel cord into an iodine solution to prevent infection.

Birthing can be an exhausting time for people with a medium- or large-sized flock. Friends tell us that, during lambing season, the family checked the ewes every two hours around the clock. Ewes often have twins, and sometimes one of these is frail and needs special attention, since the mother may only notice one and ignore or step on and kill the other. If a lamb doesn't nurse on its own within a half hour, hold it near the mother's udder and squirt her colostrum milk directly into its mouth. You may also milk the mother and feed the kid from a bottle, but from that time on you will have a cosset to bottle feed, and it will follow you instead of its mother, yelling "Ma-a-a." This flattering nuisance is likely to continue for the duration of its lambhood.

Because rams are apt to be bad tempered and dangerous and the meat not as good, the male lambs should be castrated within two weeks of birth, unless you're raising them to sell for breeding purposes. All lambs should also be docked (have their tails cut off) so they will not collect manure, burdocks, and other things that soil the wool. Both operations can be performed by a vet, or you can do them with heavy rubber bands from a farm store.

At approximately two months, the lambs will begin to eat grass, and will be ready to go out on their own.

Sheep as a Summer Project

If you are raising a lamb strictly for meat, you won't need to provide winter shelter, or worry about breeding, birthing, and storing feed for winter. Friends of ours buy a lamb each spring from a breeder, keep it in a pasture all summer, and butcher it in the fall. They have a lush pasture and feed it no grain. Their daughter's small pony also grazes there, so their lamb doesn't get lonely.

Most sheep ranchers in our area keep one or more rams if they don't use artificial insemination. They either sell their spring lambs for others to raise as summer projects, or keep them for various periods to sell either as lamb or mutton. Some furnish spring lamb to religious groups for Passover or Easter ceremonies. A few of the small-scale sheep folks card, spin, and weave their own wool.

Shelter and Pasture

Although sheep need less shelter than goats and chickens, they should have protective quarters in areas where winter temperatures fall much below freezing, and they must have unfrozen water available at all times.

An old shed or barn should be fine. So should a simple three-sided building, since sheepskin coats do a good job of insulating them from nearly all kinds of weather. They must have dry, clean, warm quarters at lambing time, however, and also immediately after losing their coats to shearing in early spring. You will have to provide pens, hay racks, feeders, and a creep, which is a small feeder that will allow only the lambs to enter and eat.

The summer pasture should have a good water supply, and salt available at all times. The amount of pasture needed will depend on the quality of the feed. Five or six sheep can graze satisfactorily on one well-fertilized acre, but if it has poor growth and is filled with brush and weeds, you may have to provide two acres or more. Check with your extension service to see if there are local plants that may be poisonous to sheep, such as ragwort or lambkill.

Although they can grow to market weight on pasture grass, ewes are usually fed grain before lambing and while they are nursing their young. If you are raising sheep in a region with a short summer season, you'll need to supply plenty of winter hay and a great deal of additional labor to feed and clean out the animals.

❖

Although a herding dog may not be essential for a small flock, except possibly for protection against animals, don't miss an opportunity to visit a sheep show and watch the dog trials. Border Collies and certain other breeds have been bred and remarkably well trained to herd sheep in response to their master's whistles or calls.

Sheep-killing dogs, coyotes, and wolves may be the greatest threats to a flock. Many farmers in our area have given up raising sheep because of the damage done by these wild animals.

Since you're not likely to keep watch over your flock by night, sheep must be confined both for their own safety and to prevent the damage they are almost certain to do when they get loose. The fencing can be one of the major expenses for a first-time rancher. A long-time definition of a good fence in our area is "horse high and sheep tight." Sheep are notorious for finding the smallest opening and enlarging it until they can slip through. As soon as one gets out, the rest follow, and within minutes disgusted neighbors begin phoning.

Traditional sheep fences are of 6-foot-high woven wire, with barbed wire at top and bottom. High-powered electric fences, recently developed in New Zealand, are rapidly replacing these. They are more expensive than conventional electric fencing, but highly effective with sheep. They are easier to install than a regular wire sheep fence, too.

Disease is not usually a problem in a small herd if you start with sheep from a healthy flock, but it can appear at any time. Try to get a certificate of good health when you buy sheep. Proper care, good feed, and clean shelter all help to keep your animals in good condition. If you see a sheep limping, it may have foot rot, which you can treat by trimming the hoof and applying medication. It's a good idea to have remedies on hand for these problems and any others that your vet or farm store mentions as particularly troublesome.

Shearing

In spite of the marvels of synthetics, sheep's wool remains the most remarkable of all fibers. It absorbs moisture, and is durable, strong, and insulating.

Sheep should be sheared each spring before hot weather, whether you want the wool or not; otherwise the animal will be uncomfortable in the summer, and its coat will accumulate burrs and other irritating collectibles.

Even with electric clippers, shearing is a challenging job for an amateur. Professionals remove the entire coat in one piece and leave the animal smooth and neat. But amateurs can make quite a mess until they learn the skill. In sheep-raising areas, shearers travel from herd to herd, but if you are in an isolated region you may need to tackle the job yourself. Ask for help from an experienced shearer the first time, so neither you nor the sheep will be too ashamed of the results.

The price of wool is determined by the international wool market, which fluctuates considerably. Get in touch with the sheep association in your state to locate buyers or wool cooperatives in your vicinity. The association can also explain how to store wool until it is sold, and how to clean and spin it yourself if that is your plan. They may also sell shearing and wool-processing equipment.

Butchering

If you have carefully kept an impersonal attitude toward your sheep, you may be able to send Willie and Millie to the slaughterhouse without emotionally collapsing. The term "spring lamb" means any lamb under the age of five months, and is a delicacy much in demand. These lambs weigh approximately 100 pounds, but only 35 to 40 pounds of this weight is actually usable meat. It is usually not worthwhile to keep a lamb longer than five or six months, because it will not put on enough additional weight to pay for the extra feed.

Some areas are better customers for lamb and mutton than others, and you should investigate before becoming involved in the business.

A few butchers will take the sheepskin as part of the cost of butchering, or you can have it made into a rug or car blanket. Some country dwellers like to process the sheepskins themselves, but don't try this hobby unless you are willing to put up with a long, smelly job.

Chapter 33
HORSES

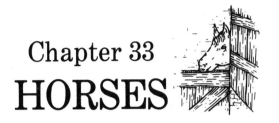

Many people have moved to the country in anticipation of a horse's companionship and rides along shaded, rural lanes. For them, horse ownership is apt to become a way of life, with frequent shows, trail rides, and other activities.

Horse Glossary

Colt—Young
Filly—Young female
Foal—Newborn
Foaling—Birthing
Gaits—Different walking and running styles
Gelding—Altered male
Herd—Crowd
Mare—Adult female
Stallion—Adult male
Tack—Gear and equipment

Horses are nice to have around a country place because, like sheep and cattle, they keep fields mowed and provide manure for soil conditioning. They are one of the more expensive country projects, however.

Horses are of two general types—draft horses, and riding or driving horses. Draft animals are heavy, utilitarian breeds that often work hard for their rations of hay and grain. Riding and driving horses are often referred to as pleasure animals and are kept mostly for fun and companionship, but they, too, are used for work by police officers, cowhands, professional hunters, and others. Some people keep horses specifically to race, fox hunt, or play polo, but the country horses we know are more likely to be ridden in Fourth of July parades and on country trails.

A family horse seldom serves as a serious mode of transportation, except in Amish country, although some people drive buggies for fun. Our neighbors, when their children were young, kept an old-fashioned carriage, and entertained us all with rides around the dirt roads.

Horses must be treated with a great deal of respect, for their sheer size if for no other reason, and if you do not know what you are doing, you may easily get hurt. Temperament varies greatly between breeds and also between individual horses. The quality of an animal's early care, health, and breeding may predispose it to be nervous or to bite, buck, or kick. If you are inexperienced, take lessons before you begin to ride, and always approach every horse with caution.

One part-time farmer we know likes horses but cannot afford his own, and he has developed a way to enjoy them for most of the year and make money at the same time. He boards several animals belonging to summer vacationers who use their mounts for a couple of months each summer. He and his family enjoy riding the animals for the rest of the year with no big investment in horseflesh. The owners are happy with the arrangement, too.

Horse Care

Horses require quite a bit of care. Before you buy one, be sure that you or someone in your family is willing to devote the necessary time to it. For one confined horse, expect to spend at least an hour a day feeding, watering, grooming, and cleaning the stalls. On top of this, time must be devoted to training, exercising, and simply keeping the horse company. A single horse, especially, needs companionship, and it is wrong to leave one alone for long periods.

Many people find they don't have the temperament to spend that much time with their charge. If you are at all uncertain about your willingness to make such a commitment, or wonder about the depth of your interest in a horse, it's a good idea to rent one for a few months before buying your own.

Shelter is necessary in any climate. Although they can survive lower temperatures than many other animals because of their insulating winter coats, horses can get chilled if cold rain soaks through their hair. In warm climates, a horse may be housed in a simple three-sided, roofed-over shed in a pasture; but where temperatures below zero are common, the animal should be kept in a barn for the winter months. A barn not only protects the animal against cold, snow, and wind, but also keeps its drinking water from freezing. Owners of extremely valuable animals often keep them in a barn every night all year for protection.

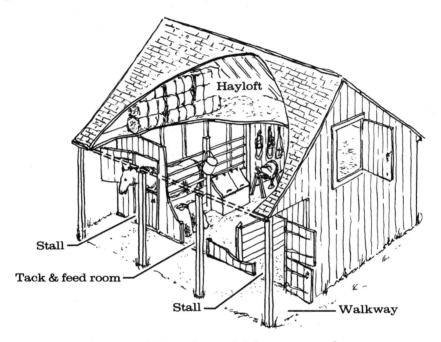

A two-stall horse barn with hay storage above.

If you do not already own a barn, build one adjacent to the pasture so that the horse has easy access. Plan on storage space for hay, grain, tools, and tack. Make sure grain is stored in a secure spot in case your horse breaks loose. Horses have died from overeating grain when given a chance. Your extension service can provide you with plans for

❖

building a barn, and you should visit a few horse stables for other ideas.

Although a horse can get by without a pasture if you feed and exercise it every day, this grazing animal is far happier with one. And it is much easier for you if you can turn the horse out to graze, too. Two acres per horse is usually enough if you have ordinary pasture, but you can get by with only one acre of particularly fine land. It should be well drained, with trees or an open shed for shade. The grass should be lush, and fairly free from large weeds. Timothy, combined with other grasses such as redtop and clover, would be excellent, but alfalfa is usually considered too rich for the horse's digestive system.

If possible, rotate pastures each month so the grass can grow back in one while the other is being grazed. Unlike cattle, horses have two sets of front teeth, and are able to graze the grass much closer to the ground, and in time this can damage an overused pasture. Resting it for a few weeks allows the grass to recover.

Horses can share a common pasture with other animals if there is feed enough for all, but check occasionally to see that the animals are getting along well and not annoying each other.

Fencing may be an expensive proposition. A post-and-rail fence is ideal; so is a high fence of woven wire. Double-strand electric fencing, with the top wire about 30 inches high, works well, too, and has the advantage of being easily moved if necessary. Never use barbed wire, because it can be dangerous. We once had a horse badly bloodied when another horse playfully squeezed her against a barbed wire fence.

Feed and Bedding

Although horses need a daily ration of grass or hay, they are also usually fed a special horse ration consisting of oats mixed with other grains, sometimes with molasses added. A horse's appetite varies considerably according to its size, temperament, and activity, and the label on the sack lists guidelines for the size of daily feed portions. When you get a new horse, check with the former owner about its accustomed ration, and do not change the feed abruptly. A gradual change is far easier on its digestive system. In the spring, introduce your horse to the pasture slowly by putting it out for longer periods each day.

Since horses are creatures of habit, feed them at regular intervals at least twice a day. Use a clean feed box, and place a block of mineralized salt close by. Although they like sugar and it makes a good reward, there is no indication that it is good for them, and it should be given sparingly.

Water should be available around the clock, and in the winter, if your barn is cold, you may need to add an electric water heater to the tub so it will not freeze. These heaters operate on a thermostat, are simple to install, and can be plugged into an ordinary electric outlet. They are available from farm stores and catalogs.

Confined horses need their stalls cleaned out at least once each day. They need a large amount of bedding; clean, fresh shavings or sawdust are best and should be provided each day. Store bedding inside the barn, both for convenience and to keep it dry.

Selecting a Horse

A horse may cost either a few dollars for a near over-the-hill model or many thousands. You might begin the search for a first horse at a riding school or stable, where good horses are sometimes available inexpensively at the end of summer. Breeders and private owners are also potentially good sources, but auctions usually are not. They are often the repository for problem animals, and you probably won't have the opportunity to check them out thoroughly before purchase. Decide in advance whether you want to ride Western or English style, and buy a horse that has been trained the way you prefer.

A horse shouldn't be chosen as impulsively as you might pick out a kitten. Once you decide on a price range, take someone knowledgeable along when you shop. If you are a new rider, don't consider a stallion, because stallions are unpredictable and difficult to manage. And beware of a young horse that hasn't been broken (trained). Until horses are four years old, they are considered adolescents and may act accordingly. So for your first horse, it is wise to invest in an older mare (adult female) or gelding (altered male).

A grade animal (one of mixed pedigree) is ideal for most riders, but if you decide to invest in a registered horse, choose a "cold-blooded" breed, one with a quiet disposition. These include Appaloosa, Quarter Horse, and Morgan. The term "hot-blooded" refers to the more spirited types, such as Arabian.

There is confusion about ponies. Although the term is sometimes incorrectly applied to any small horse, a true pony is one of several breeds that stay small all their lives, including the Hackney, Shetland, and Welsh. These animals are usually bought for children, and used for both riding and driving.

It takes knowledge and experience to train a horse to be a show animal, a racer, or a driving, herding, or riding animal. Check to see what kind of training your potential new horse has had, and inquire about its personality and behavior. Try it out yourself under the same conditions as you'll be using it. You and the horse should fit each other in physical size, and if possible, be a match in temperament, too. Before you take it home, get a certificate of health from the seller's veterinarian. If it is an expensive animal, have your own vet check it out, too.

Tack and Other Equipment

One father we know was in a mild state of shock recently when he realized that the expense of his daughter's horse went far beyond the initial price. By the time the tack room was fully outfitted, he had spent quite a bundle. Because she intended to show the animal, he couldn't very well buy at garage sales, and the halter, bridle, saddle, pad, blankets, medical supplies, and grooming equipment were only the beginning. His daughter chose an English saddle rather than a Western, and this cost nearly a thousand dollars, although he could easily have paid much more. Then there was the horse trailer to move her mount to shows. She needed riding outfits suitable for parade and dressage, and these couldn't be bought at the local K-Mart. He says he hasn't dared think about the on-going cost of hay, grain, and bedding, to say nothing of upcoming farrier and veterinarian bills.

If you are on a budget, check out the price of tack as carefully as you do the horse. We know many riders who don't own show horses, so they buy tack from somebody who has tired of horses, and ride in their blue jeans. They have no need of a trailer, and do most of their own vet work.

Health Care

Your veterinarian should give your horse annual preventative inoculations for tetanus and encephalitis, administer worm medication, and advise you about any special needs. Examine the animal frequently for injuries, and inspect its teeth, hooves, and hair for signs of poor health. Other problems you'll learn to watch for include breathing troubles, lameness, sores, parasites, and odd behavior such as chewing on wooden feed crib or stalls. A good book on horse ownership will help you to diagnose abnormalities. Keep your veterinarian's phone number handy, too.

Horses' teeth develop sharp edges which the vet should file periodically, but in spite of all the talk about the horse's mouth, its feet should be of the most concern. The hooves need to be picked out before and after riding, and a farrier (blacksmith) should trim the hooves and replace the iron horseshoes every six to eight weeks.

In our town years ago, the blacksmith shop with its roaring forge not only produced the horseshoes, but supplied most of the ironwork for the community. The shop was also the loafing place for all the elderly men on a winter day. Cards and checkers were played and gossip and reminiscences exchanged. Modern farriers specialize entirely in horses, and are as much experts on equine foot ailments as they are on ironwork.

Donkeys and Mules

Donkeys and mules are credited with being the work animals that built most of the nation before machinery became popular. They are still used for riding and as pack animals, because they can carry so much weight and are sure-footed in difficult terrain. Many of the animals in our region are bought for pets and some of our friends acquired theirs when they heard the animals were going to be shot because the western lands they inhabited were overpopulated and overgrazed.

Donkeys are friendly animals and make good companions for country children. They can be ridden or driven, eat less than horses, and are usually less expensive to buy and keep than either horses or ponies. Like goats, they have acquired a bad reputation with the unknowledgeable public. It is true that they are often noisy, stubborn, and sometimes mean. Their resale value may be low, too, when the time comes to get rid of them.

A mule is a cross between a horse and a donkey, and because of its big ears, is also often ridiculed and considered stupid and obstinate. Actually, few animals have proved as valuable over the years on farms, mines, ranches, construction sites, and in the military. Although their numbers have declined, they still do many jobs more effectively than either horses or machinery. In many parts of the country they are used for stringing telephone and power lines where machines cannot go easily, for cultivating crops on small farms, and for backpacking the equipment needed by hunters, fishermen, and prospectors.

In recent years, superior sporting horses have been artificially bred with high-grade donkeys, resulting in animals with exceptional qualities. These are proving popular as riding and driving animals, but since mules seldom reproduce, no stabilized breed has emerged or been named. The price of this modern creation has kept pace with the improvements, however, and can range up into the thousands of dollars.

Buying and caring for mules or donkeys is the same as for horses, and they suffer from the same ailments described for saddle horses. They can be as unpredictable as any other animal when startled, or when they are not feeling well, so the same cautions apply when dealing with them.

Draft Horses

After World War II it seemed likely that the draft horse would become a curiosity seen only in shows and at fairs. Now, however, draft horses are again much in evidence. Draft horse shows are common, and in addition to appearing prominently in parades, they are used to construct utility lines in the backcountry, skid timber, and much more. On small farms they haul maple sap; cut, rake, and haul hay; and plow just as in the past. Special equipment for them is once more being manufactured, too. Woodlot owners we know insist that their pulp and lumber be harvested with horses, because the large machines normally used damage young trees and make deep ruts.

Those who predicted the demise of the horse forgot that a large number of people love horses and would keep them even if tractors might be more efficient. The popularity of draft horses at shows, in parades, and at horse-pulling contests attests to this interest, and assures that the draft horse will remain a permanent part of our rural culture.

Draft horses are heavier, slower moving, and usually not as spirited as saddle horses. In most respects their needs are the same, however. They need hay, grain, water, salt, grooming, winter shelter, and they appreciate summer pasture. A work horse requires more feed than a saddle horse, the amount varying according to the size of the animal and the work it is doing. In summer, a good pasture may furnish sufficient feed if the horse is not working, but a balanced horse feed mixture should be added to the diet otherwise. If you change grain mixtures, do it gradually by mixing the two kinds for the first few days. As with saddle horses, the ideal pasture is one that is rotated frequently, occasionally mowed to get rid of the tall weeds, and spike-harrowed once a year to work the manure clods into the soil.

At the beginning of the century, most farmers had from two to six horses, and only a few wealthy people had cars. Now the reverse is true, and owning a pair of premium work horses can be an expensive project.

There are several leading breeds of draft horses. The Percheron (grey or black) and Belgian (chestnut colored) are well-known Continental breeds, and the Clydesdale, Suffolk, and Shire are British exports. Although some people keep thoroughbreds, most of the work horses sold in farm country are a mixture of two or more breeds.

The supply varies widely throughout the country, and in some sections it may take a great deal of persistence and thousands of dollars to locate and buy a matched pair of good draft horses. Some of the best buys are often found in the Midwest or in Canada, where work horses are common. Farm and horse magazines, such as the *Draft Horse Journal* (P.O. Box 670, Waverly, IA 50677), are good sources of ads for breeders, but occasionally good animals turn up at auctions or in the classifieds of country newspapers. Although there are many honest horse traders, as a novice you cannot count on getting a good deal, so take plenty of time and get help from an expert if possible.

Ask for the complete history of the horse you are considering, so you will know exactly what it has been trained to do, and hopefully, how it has been treated. You can get a veterinarian to determine its state of health, but you may have to determine its disposition yourself.

A draft horse needs a harness, collar, collar pad, and bridle—all of which should either already fit or be easily adjustable to fit comfortably. Inspect the leather goods regularly for weak parts, and keep them cleaned and oiled. Grooming and care are like that for saddle horses, as are health and safety precautions.

Chapter 34
MANAGING THE WOODLOT

Although the farm woodlot once tended to be the neglected stepchild of a country place, most landowners today realize that their forest land can be the most interesting part of their property. And if managed properly, it can be profitable as well.

Just what does a productive woodlot look like? It does not resemble a city park, where large, mature trees rise from a clean, barren forest floor. Such a forest lacks browse for deer and protective undergrowth for small animals and birds; and as the large trees die, there will be no younger ones to replace them. A healthy forest consists of trees of all ages and of several varieties, although one may predominate. As trees reach maturity, they are harvested, and younger ones are allowed to replace them. Large, untouched wilderness areas have their place in our world, but your own back forty is not likely to be one of them.

Beyond the environmental advantages of having a healthy woodland, you might also want each acre to be productive enough to help pay your taxes. On our land, for example, we convert woodlot trees into firewood and fenceposts for our own use. We harvest firs that have been pruned and sheared tightly for Christmas trees and greens, use the maples to make syrup, and compost leaves for fertilizer and mulch. We sell mature hardwoods for lumber, softwoods for pulpwood for making paper, and the cedars for railroad ties, fence rails, posts, and poles.

Managing Your Forest

A well-managed forest will be continuously productive. Rather than harvesting the trees once in your lifetime, you cut them selectively at frequent periods. Small trees are thinned when necessary, and undesirable species weeded out so they will not occupy valuable space and reproduce. If good varieties do not seed themselves sufficiently, seedlings are brought in and planted.

Get to know a good forester early in your woodland development. County foresters work with the extension service, and private foresters are available for hire in most areas. They can help you understand your various options for tree farming. If your woods have been well managed in the past, you may simply be advised to continue the present practices. However, if trees are overgrown or there is an abundance of young seedlings and weed trees, you probably have plenty of work ahead before your forest reaches its potential.

A good forester can mark the trees to be harvested and those to be weeded out, plan the location of the necessary roads, and oversee the harvesting to be certain it will not wreck your land. He or she will probably be able to recommend a contractor to work under his or her supervision, and write up a legal agreement between the two of you, as well as a contract with the mill that buys the timber.

Gradually, mistakes that have been made over the years will be corrected, and your forest coaxed into regular production. If the woods has been clear-cut each time it was harvested, the trees will all be about the same age. Over time, you can convert the forest into a grove containing trees of all ages, so that you can make a light cutting every eight or ten years. The woods will always remain a pleasant place for you and wildlife.

No single management plan can serve every woodlot. Maples grown for firewood are handled differently from those that are destined to become fine maple lumber. Still different is the management of a lot devoted to producing maple syrup. Explain to your forester what you would like to have happen on your land, and what sort of income you would like it to produce. If you and your forester can't agree on a course of action, don't hesitate to get a second opinion.

The first phase in working with a woodlot is to harvest the trees the forester identifies as saleable, and cut out any that are diseased,

❖

Fire scarred   Firewood candidate   Crooked   Forked   Wolf tree   Undesirable species

Rating the trees in your woodlot.

broken, or insect-riddled. These may be usable for firewood. In the second phase, weed out all the undesirable species. The "weed" trees are different in each region and what you cut out will depend on your long-range plans. Third, thin out the young trees. The amateur's rule of thumb is that a tree should never be any closer to another tree of approximately the same age than could be spanned by a hammock. You can exempt from this rule all small replacement trees and large trees that will soon be harvested. Don't thin young trees until they're nearly an inch in caliper, though; crowded conditions during their first years will help them grow straighter and taller, and discourage them from developing low-growing branches.

Your forester may also recommend cutting all the lower branches of trees not yet large enough for harvest, up to a height of 15 feet or more. This cutting makes it easier to walk through the woods, and also ensures one knot-free log in each tree, which may bring a higher price. On the other hand, low branches offer a better shelter for wildlife. Decide with your forester which course is most practical for your woodland.

Planting Trees

If you have some scrubby old pastureland growing up to weeds, you could put it to work growing black walnut (see Chapter 16), pine, spruce, oak, or birch for lumber, or a variety of hardwoods for firewood. A worn-out hayfield might make a good Christmas tree plantation or maple grove.

Your forester can help you decide what to plant and locate a source of small trees. Species that are already growing in the locality are less likely to be troubled by disease, insects, and climatic conditions than those brought in from areas with different soils and climatic conditions. But occasionally there are good reasons for introducing new ones; a fast-growing exotic variety may be a better choice than a slower-maturing native.

Look into the market for the trees you are considering. Some trees, such as maple, oak, spruce, pine, and birch, are always in demand because they are valued highly for a wide variety of uses, but the market for beech, larch, and hemlock varies. The white cedar that grows beautifully on the moist limestone soil in our area brought little money until several local factories began producing decorative fencing. What was once considered a weed tree is now in brisk demand.

Let's Make a Deal

Most phases of forestry require special equipment and skills, and if you have a lot of forestland, you may find it practical to have someone else manage your woodlot, maple syrup production, or Christmas tree operation. You may be able to rent your land for a certain period of years, sell the timber rights outright, or have the work done for you on commission.

Before you sign anything, get advice from your forester and an attorney, because later misunderstandings can arise if the terms of agreement are not clearly understood, and in print. You won't want to be involved with someone who might "accidentally" cut on a neighbor's property, disturb your water lines, or mess up your woods by the careless use of equipment. There are many shady characters in the forestry business, and some move from area to area quickly, leaving a trail of unfulfilled promises and bad checks behind them. Even some of the honest woodcutters may get careless. Like farmers, most have bought expensive equipment and must pay for it. In cutting corners

❖

they often damage small trees and leave compacted soil, deeply rutted roads, and piles of culled tree butts and stumps in their wake.

In our area, loggers with draft horses are doing a brisk business because forest owners are increasingly concerned about the damage heavy equipment could do to their property.

Timber of all sorts is sometimes sold "on the stump," meaning the amount is estimated, often by a forester, and a total price agreeable to both buyer and seller is paid in advance of the cutting. More often the timber is paid for only as it is cut and delivered to the mill where it is measured.

Homegrown Energy

If you live in the country you will probably burn wood occasionally, and it may be your primary heat source. There is nothing like a cozy wood heater to warm you when you first come in from the cold, damp outdoors, and it is wonderful to sit beside a roaring fireplace on a winter evening.

Our wood stove sits in a corner of our kitchen and burns round the clock for nearly nine months of the year. It not only heats the whole house with the help of fans in the doorways, but is used for cooking and providing a constant supply of hot water. In the fall we dry seeds and fruit; and in winter, we dry mittens and other outdoor clothes on nearby racks. We even boil small amounts of maple sap on it in the spring.

The hardwoods are best for heating. Softwood burns well in airtight stoves and furnaces, but it sparks too much for open fireplaces, and since it is lightweight, a large amount is required to get the same amount of heat that far less hardwood would supply. In theory, the same amount of heat is available from a pound of wood no matter what kind, but in actuality the condition and dryness of the wood and the efficiency of the heater all affect the volume of heat produced. Firewood should be air-dried for at least a year before it is burned.

The woods that produce the most heat per cord are American beech, apple, black locust, ironwood, shagbark hickory, and white oak. Next in efficiency are black cherry, black walnut, red oak, sugar maple, white ash, and white and yellow birch. Third in line are American elm, black and green ash, pitch pine, red and silver maple, sycamore, and tamarack (larch). Trees with low heat-producing qualities are the softwood species, aspen (poplar), balsam fir, basswood, butternut, hemlock, red and white spruce, red and white pine, and willow.

If you burn the softwoods, you'll need more storage space and your heater will have to be stoked more frequently. Some softwoods also produce an abundance of creosote, which may present a fire hazard in the chimney and stovepipe. Softwood has these advantages, however: it tends to grow quickly, is light to handle, and may dry faster than hardwoods. You can use softwoods when you need only a bit of quick heat in the morning, or burn them in combination with hardwoods.

If possible, continue to grow the kinds of trees that already are doing well on your lot, since each variety has a specific soil preference. Some trees, such as maple, need a rich, deep soil to thrive, and it is usually futile to try to grow them on thin, worn-out soil. Red maples prefer a moist soil, oaks do well only on acid land, and birches need soil with a trace of copper in it to grow at the fastest rate. If nothing of value for firewood is presently growing on your land, your forester may recommend other species for planting.

Certain species produce a constant supply of firewood without replanting, a truly renewable source of energy. When wild cherry, poplar, and willow are cut as young trees, they have the ability to resprout and grow a new tree from the stump. Sucker trees also sprout from their shallow, spreading roots. Another fast-growing firewood tree is alder, which often frequents damp areas along streams and replenishes itself readily. In places where black locust grows rapidly, it is a good choice for poor land because it is a legume and, like clover, supplies its own nitrogen.

Can your woodlot produce enough firewood for your needs? After a couple of years, you'll be able to estimate the annual number of trees burned each year, and since it takes 20 to 30 years to grow a medium-size hardwood tree, you can calculate the trees you will need to yield a perpetual supply.

For example, since we cut about 25 medium-sized maples each year, we need a woodlot of about 750 trees (25 × 30 years) to be sure of getting our annual supply. In fact, we need a somewhat larger woodlot because now and then we accidentally fell a tree the wrong way and break off a nice small one. Weather and animals take their toll, too.

MANAGING THE WOODLOT

❖

It is possible to grow 750 trees on an acre, but two to four acres is a more honest estimate, since not every space will have a tree in it and not every tree will grow at the same speed.

Each woodlot has different characteristics and requires different methods of management. When we started to manage our old maple grove as a woodlot, it contained some very large trees. We began by cutting most of them for lumber. Seedlings sprouted and grew rapidly in the newly opened areas. After these were about 12 feet tall and 1 inch in diameter, we thinned them to about 7 feet apart so they wouldn't be competing with each other for nutrients and space. We continue to thin them whenever they begin to crowd each other, and use the culled trees for firewood.

When cutting the larger trees, we clear-cut small patches of the woods entirely rather than cutting every other tree. Clearings of 100 to 150 feet in diameter allow the sun to reach the young sprouting seedlings, permitting them to grow quickly and eventually replace the trees we harvest.

The Cutting

Harvesting firewood is hard work, and it can be dangerous. The job has been made far easier by the chain saw, which must rank as one of the most practical inventions of modern times; but a chain saw needs a lot of respect. Many woodlot owners we know prefer to hire a skilled woodcutter for a couple of days to cut their woodpile, rather than risk their own limbs with an unfamiliar machine. We like to tackle the job ourselves, but for only a few hours at a time so that we do not get overly tired and careless. You have probably heard the saying, "There are two times when it is dangerous to use a chain saw. One, when you don't know how, and the other, when you think you do."

A weekend woodcutter won't need a heavy-duty saw of the size and quality required by lumberjacks, but yours should have the recommended safety devices such as kickback prevention. You will also need a light axe, a sledgehammer, a couple of wedges, a peavy to roll the logs, and a set of files and tools for the saw. It'll take a truck or small tractor to haul the wood from the lot to your home unless you hire someone else to do the job. If you are cutting large amounts of wood or are working with large, limby trees that are difficult to split by hand, you may want to buy or rent a power wood splitter.

Selling Firewood

Firewood is expensive, but the profits from selling it aren't as great as they might first appear. Wood must be handled many times—perhaps eight or ten—and so labor costs are high. The equipment must be more powerful and of better quality than for home use. And even the best chain saws and wood splitters depreciate rapidly and need considerable maintenance.

Most people want wood to be dry when they buy it. Since the drying process takes a year, you will need drying sheds. Customers also want it delivered, so you will need a truck with a rugged body and a guard over the rear window. You may also be expected to pile it for measuring after delivery.

Usually firewood is sold by the cord, a unit 8 feet long, 4 feet high, and 4 feet wide—or any other equivalent of 128 cubic feet. A running cord is 8 feet long, 4 feet high, and as wide as the wood is cut—2 feet wide for most fireplaces and furnaces, so two running cords (or runs, as they are commonly called) make a solid cord. Stove wood is often cut 16 inches in length, and at this length it takes three runs to make a cord.

Some of our enterprising acquaintances tie up bundles of hardwood or softwood kindling, sized to fit a car trunk. They market it at roadside stands and gift shops aimed at an urban clientele who use a fireplace only for special occasions and don't mind paying extra for the convenience.

Sugaring

Next to gardening, making maple syrup is our favorite country activity. Most of us who have grown up in maple sugar country look forward to sugaring as a ritual that hails the coming of spring. The sap starts running, the birds return, and the moist earth emerges, patch by patch, from the snow. The scent of sap boiling and the subsequent taste of warm maple syrup, like Proust's cakes, conjure up more than the flavor alone. " . . . (they) bear unfaltering, in the tiny and almost impalpable drop of their essence, the vast structure of recollection."

If your country homeplace is endowed with a sugarbush populated with the sweetest of all trees, the sugar maple (*Acer saccharum*), you may want to consider making maple syrup, too. Be sure your grove consists of sugar maples before you start, though. Norway, red, and silver maples also produce a sweet sap that can be boiled into a syrup, but it won't have the rich maple flavor of *Acer saccharum*.

You don't need a large lot or lots of equipment to get started. Only half a dozen large trees can yield enough sap to make several quarts of liquid ambrosia.

The sap runs best when late winter days begin to warm but night temperatures continue to plunge below freezing. (Why is this? One theory explains that rising temperatures cause carbon dioxide bubbles to form in the sap, and this pressure causes it to flow upward from the roots.) A large, healthy tree can produce from 10 to 25 gallons of sap during the season without damage. Depending on the sugar content of the sap, approximately 40 gallons must be boiled to make 1 gallon of syrup.

Sugaring is even more closely tied to the weather than other farm operations. Because the sap flow is contingent on nightly freezes and warm days during a few critical weeks each spring, an early warm spell will lower production.

If you tap more than 20 good-sized trees, you may be wise to consider a small sugar house with steam vents on the roof. Small-scale equipment is available for modest sugaring operations, and you may be able to find second-hand items. Since syrup needs to be boiled quickly for the best flavor and color, a large, shallow pan is better for evaporating the water from the sap than a smaller, deeper one. Regular evaporators do this best, but if you have a wide-topped heater, you can use it quite satisfactorily for small amounts of sap.

You'll need to store the sap. For a small operation, plastic garbage cans will suffice, but a large metal tank is essential if you have many trees. You'll need a hand drill, boring bit (7/16-inch), and spouts. Then there's the gathering system—either buckets, covers, and gathering pails, or a pipeline directly from the trees to a sugar house on a lower level. Necessary also are a hydrometer for testing syrup density, felt strainers, syrup containers, and fuel for the fire.

If you are making just a little syrup from a half-dozen trees, you will still need the spouts, bit, and drill, but you can simply collect in small pails or jars, and boil the syrup in a pan on your wood stove or kitchen range. Remember, though, that steam can damage wallpaper, furniture, and insulation. Families we know boil on small wood stoves in the greenhouse and workshop. Boiling outdoors in a large kettle over an open fire, early American style, looks romantic, but it is far from practical. Even a light breeze cools the sap, and slow boiling produces a dark-colored, strong-flavored syrup. Also, the open kettle collects a variety of insects, leaves, and windblown litter.

It is best to tap the trees on a warm day in late winter or early spring. If you have a choice of sugar maples, choose large limby ones, especially well-spaced, bushy shade trees and roadside trees growing in full sun. These will be far more productive than crowded, shaded trees, and the sap will be sweeter as well. A tree of 12 inches in diameter should have only a single tap; those measuring 15 to 20 inches in diameter can have two, and trees larger than 20 inches, three. To go beyond these recommendations may weaken trees for future production. Each year, drill tap holes in healthy wood at least 6 inches away from any holes, made in previous years, that have not healed completely.

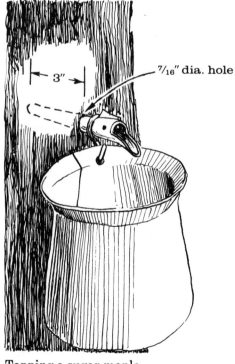

Tapping a sugar maple.

Maple trees vary greatly in the sweetness of their sap, depending both on the individual tree and the fertility of the soil. If you want to be scientific and save boiling time and fuel, buy a sap tester from a maple equipment firm (see Appendix), test all your trees, and then collect only the sap from the sweetest ones. If you make syrup on a larger scale, you can use the same test to find out which trees to leave in your orchard for syrup production and which ones to cut for fuel.

Tap on the south-facing, sunny side of the tree. Drill a $\frac{7}{16}$-inch hole about 3 inches into the wood, tilting it slightly upward. Then drive in a metal or plastic spout and hang a bucket.

Some sugarmakers place a tablet of paraformaldehyde or other chemical in the tap hole to prolong the sap flow by slowing the healing of cells in the cambium layers. But homeowners we know feel that the tablets hurt the tree by not allowing the hole to heal when the season is over, allowing rot and canker wounds to start. There is also the chance the chemical may not evaporate in the boiling, and end up in the syrup in concentrated form.

To make syrup and sugar with a light color and delicate flavor, gather the sap promptly after each run, keep it cool, and boil it quickly in small batches. The syrup is ready when it tests 32 on the hydrometer when boiling hot (36 when at room temperature) or whenever it reaches 7 degrees F. above the boiling point of water. (The boiling point is affected by elevation and the weather, so you must check it frequently if you use that method.) Because small amounts of syrup boil very quickly as they near the end of the cooking process, the syrup must be watched so that it doesn't scorch. Syrup that is too thick will crystallize, and it will not keep well if it is too thin. A gallon of properly concentrated syrup should weigh 11 pounds.

Even with the best of care, the last runs of sap are likely to produce dark, strong-flavored syrup, and some makers don't bother with it because it doesn't bring premium prices. It is suited for cooking, however, and in fact, some people prefer it for all uses. Our family always made the last run of sap into a dark, thin syrup for vinegar, and our neighbors fermented theirs into beer.

Syrup will keep for several years if sealed in cans or jars while near the boiling point and then stored in a freezer or cold root cellar. If mold forms, skim it off and boil the syrup for a few minutes; the mold will disappear and the good flavor will be restored.

You'll find plenty of uses for maple syrup beyond pancakes—flavoring desserts, ice cream, yogurt, and many other things. One of our elderly Vermont uncles always kept a bottle on the table, pouring it generously on cereal, mashed potatoes, macaroni, apple pie, and even in his coffee. Sugar-on-snow parties are a seasonal celebration in our area. The syrup is boiled until it reaches soft ball or candy stage. Then it is poured in thin strips over pans of hard packed snow, and eaten with a fork. The flavor is guaranteed to make you forget completely anything you have ever read about the evils of eating too much sugar. Sour pickles and raised doughnuts are traditional side dishes to the treat.

Maple production is not limited to syrup. If the syrup is boiled a bit longer and stirred vigorously, it becomes maple cream; if boiled even more, it becomes maple sugar. Sugar is packed in tins, or formed into fancy-shaped cakes that are wrapped and sold in gift boxes.

Commercial Sugaring

Because sap runs at a time of year that is relatively quiet for many home businesses, a sugaring operation can fit in well with dairy, vegetable, fruit farming, or a craft business geared to either the summer or winter vacation trade. On many farms, sugaring is still done as it was 50 years ago. Spouts are inserted in the trees, and buckets hung under them. The buckets of sap are dumped into a large tub on a sled or trailer, and horses or tractors draw it to the sugar house. There, a hot wood fire boils the sap, releasing volumes of steam into the spring air and leaving behind the syrup.

In a modern sugaring operation, plastic tubing runs from each spout to a main pipeline, which flows to a storage tank and then into a large oil-fired evaporating pan in the sugarhouse. In some systems, a vacuum pump is used to draw the sap from the trees. Although this method is efficient and labor-saving, many sugarmakers in our area have tried it, only to return to their former method. They point out that the plastic tubing is difficult to clean, pumping out sap is harmful to the trees, and oil heat makes little sense when they have all that free firewood available.

There are several reasons to make you think twice about going into sugaring on a large scale. It requires long, intense hours of labor over a short period, and the harvest is critically dependent on the weather. Since it is difficult to know when the sap will run, you may find it hard to hire help only when you need it, although you may have friends who are willing to help you for the experience and a few gallons of syrup. A second impediment to going commercial is the equipment, which is expensive and useful only during the short sugar season. This means you have to make a great deal of syrup each year to make the enterprise economically feasible. And you must be prepared for an occasional bad season, when there is little sap for your effort. We don't want to sound too pessimistic, though. In good years, the profits can be excellent.

You can sell your entire crop wholesale in large metal drums, cash your check, and be done with it. But you'll make the best profits from selling syrup retail, especially if you process it into gift confections, package it in neat containers, and sell it directly from a roadside stand or gift shop. Many New Englanders sell direct from their homes, with a simple Maple Syrup sign in the front yard. Some of our neighbors truck their products to a large city to sell, and others sell their entire crop by mail, through classified ads in magazines.

Chapter 35

CHRISTMAS TREES

Because we no longer raise animals and don't need the pasture, we have planted 24,000 Christmas trees on this poorer land. Christmas trees are an ideal way to put unused open acres to work. Since the trees will be harvested before they grow large, the land is kept somewhat open, and vistas are not obstructed. For small-scale growing, little investment and equipment are involved; and best of all, much of the necessary planting, weed control, feeding, shearing, and harvesting can be done in your spare time. It takes from six to ten years to grow most kinds of trees to saleable size, so the project can be viewed as an investment for a special luxury, a college education, or retirement income.

Not many years ago, only wild trees were cut and sold as Christmas trees, but the popularity of perfectly formed artificial trees meant that the sparse-looking wild trees became unmarketable. Growers began to cultivate trees especially for the holiday market, and each fall now, millions of tightly sheared, well-shaped, dark green beauties leave old farm fields for city homes.

Before you get into such a project, visit successful plantations in your area. You might also join the Christmas tree association in your state to learn more about cultural methods and potential markets. Your state extension forester can also supply information.

Each section of the country has its favorite Christmas tree. In the Northeast, where we live, millions of balsam firs are grown. They are also popular in Canada, Michigan, Wisconsin, and Minnesota. Further south, Scotch and white pines are in vogue. In the Appalachians, Fraser fir is a favorite tree, and in the West, the Douglas, noble, and concolor firs are first choices. Other favorites include white and blue spruce, cypress, cedar, juniper, and hemlock. You will probably concentrate on growing the trees that grow best where you live, and those that are envisioned as "Christmas trees" by the public.

Starting a Plantation

Christmas trees will grow on most any soil that is not wet—even on cool, north-facing slopes that discourage fruit trees and other crops.

On a small scale, trees can be planted easily with only a spade, which is the way we did it. Two people working together can set about 1,000 per day. Large acreages are planted by machine, and if you live in tree country you can probably hire people who have mechanical tree planters to do this for you.

Space the trees about 5 feet apart—more or less depending on whether you will harvest them at larger or smaller than the usual 6- to 7-foot size. This means from 1,000 to 1,300 trees can be grown per acre, with a harvest of from 700 to 1,000. Leave space for roads at convenient

❖

intervals, because you'll need to transport fertilizers and pest control materials, to remove the trees during harvest, and to allow access in case of fire.

To ensure an annual harvest, plant new trees every two or three years. Annual planting is not necessary because all the trees do not grow at the same rate, and all those planted at once won't need to be cut the same year. To decrease the time between harvests on the same acreage, growers often plant small trees between each large tree two years before cutting.

If you have the land but not enough time, you might make an arrangement with a grower who will manage your lot and sell the trees, paying you a percentage of the price he or she receives. Insist on a legal contract, rather than a gentlemen's agreement, and study it carefully before signing, since many things can befall the trees before they are harvested. Make sure that the trees will automatically revert to you if your contractor fails to keep up his or her end of the bargain.

Buying Stock

Buy local trees, if possible, because they will be acclimated to the climate. When northern growers plant trees or seed from warmer climates, the young trees often start to grow early in the spring, just as they would in their native habitat, making them susceptible to late spring frosts. Some states maintain nurseries and sell their trees at a low price to growers and woodlot owners. Your extension forester will be able to tell you if such trees are available, and how to order them. He may also recommend planting a special strain of Scotch pine, Colorado blue spruce, or balsam fir that has been grown from the seed of trees with outstanding color and a compact habit of growth.

You can buy either seedlings (trees that have been grown in a seed bed) or transplants. Tree catalogs describe them with a pair of numbers, such as 2-0, 2-1, or 2-2. The first number tells how many years the tree has spent in the seed bed, the second tells how many years it has spent in the transplant bed. Transplanted trees may not be any taller than seedlings but they have developed a strong set of roots, which helps them survive competition from grass and weeds in the field. Pines of seedling size (2-0 or 3-0) are often satisfactory, but spruce and fir trees will grow far faster and sturdier in the field if you use transplants.

If you are in no hurry, you can buy the less expensive seedlings, transplant them 4 inches apart into a well-prepared bed, and grow your own transplants. The 2-2 size, measuring 8 to 12 inches in height, is best for large commercial plantations, since the bigger 2-3 or 2-4 trees take longer to plant by hand, and often cannot be mechanically planted.

Because we live in evergreen country, we collect our own balsam seedlings from forests where lumber was cut six or seven years previously. We locate a spot where the ground is green with young trees from 5 to 15 inches tall, and pull them from the moist earth in early spring when they come out easily. We tie them in bundles of 50, and if they have a good root system, plant them directly in the field; or if they are smaller, we grow them in transplant beds for two years before setting them in rows in the field.

We like native seedlings because we can pull and plant them the same day; and we know they are acclimated to the soil and climate in our area.

Culture

For the first few years after planting, grass and weeds may steal nutrients from the trees, and also deform the lower branches by crowding them and blocking out sunlight. Large plantations rely on herbicides to kill competing growth, but organic growers prefer to mow and clip.

Most kinds of Christmas trees must be sheared every year or two if they are to develop a tight, symmetrical appearance, and shearing should begin when the tree is young. The process is best learned by watching an expert. Fast-growing trees such as pines need heavier shearing than the slower-growing firs and spruces. To get the best-shaped and tightest-growing trees, shear only the new growth during the growing season in early summer. Firs and spruces, but not pines, can be sheared at other times, as long as the resulting irregular growth, such as extra tops, is pruned off later.

Check the growth rate and color of your trees each year. If the trees are not a rich green color and growing well, they probably lack fertilizer, or need to be rescued from weed and grass growth. Although nitrogen is the most valuable nutrient, a balanced food should be applied in early spring for the best results. Overfeeding, especially with strong chemical fertilizers, encourages insects and diseases, so be prepared for extra troubles if you use them.

Many growers remove the lowest circle ("whorl") of branches from their trees a few years before harvest. This so-called basal pruning makes trees easier to cut, especially when there is snow on the ground; and it creates a good stem for easy handling.

Trees shouldn't be harvested until the needles have been "hardened" by cool weather. If you are growing Scotch pine, be aware that certain strains turn yellow late in the season, so they must be cut before this happens. Trees may be cut with a chain saw, axe, or hand saw. Some growers still tie them with twine before shipping, but they are more often pulled through a cone that quickly wraps each one in a plastic netting sleeve. This makes a neat package, and keeps the branches from being broken in transit, even if they freeze. (Frozen wood is very susceptible to breakage.)

Unless the season is rainy or snowy, the cut trees should be stored out of the wind and sun or covered with boughs to protect them against drying out, and they may even have to be sprinkled during the driest years. One year it stayed very warm, and we watered our piled-up trees on a hot sunny day with disastrous results. The water quickly evaporated, causing the needles to fall off. Now we sprinkle them in the cool of the evening.

Marketing

When you plant acres of trees, you are taking a chance that the demand will be good a decade down the road. The business has gone through feast and famine periods in the past, and growers tend to plant huge numbers of trees directly after a shortage develops.

Most large producers of greens and wreaths sell them to a wholesale buyer, who re-sells them to florists or others who decorate and retail them. If you market only a few trees or wreaths, you can usually sell them locally at a roadside stand, or at a lot in a nearby city. We have friends who pay for their vacation in Florida each December by taking along a truckload of wreaths, decorated with cones, dried flowers, and pods. They return to the snowy North with a beautiful tan in March. Others sell wreaths and trees by mail, advertising in city magazines and newspapers. Some contract to supply municipalities with trees, garlands, and wreaths for street decorations each year. Gas stations in our area often retail trees to create extra business during a slow period.

We sell all our trees to a wholesale buyer, and our wreaths go to a civic group in a nearby state. The members decorate and sell them as an annual money-making activity. Scouts, church groups, auxiliaries, and other clubs often appreciate this opportunity and remain regular customers for years. Some small producers we know always hang out a few decorated wreaths during the hunting season so deer hunters will buy one to take home to their wives, perhaps as a peace token for their long absence.

Many families like the fun of going to the country to select their own trees, and you may do well with a cut-your-own operation. Some northern growers allow prospective buyers to tag their trees in the fall and return before Christmas to cut the one they want, even though it may be covered with snow and otherwise hard to find. Other growers dig trees, put the rootballs into large tubs or plastic bags, and sell living Christmas trees to people who hate to waste a tree after using it for only a few days.

If you are a larger producer, you will probably need to ship your products to an urban market. Your extension service or state Christmas tree organization may be able to help you locate markets, but there are caveats to be observed before you become involved with a buyer. Buyers may operate in a different location each year, and many of us who grow trees have found that few industries have as many dishonest people in them as the Christmas tree business. Smooth-talking individuals buy trees, promising to pay for them later, and never come through; others pay with a bad check. We have even had buyers fold over bills in a pack in an attempt to make it look as if we were getting more cash than was actually there. To avoid trouble, get a deposit for the trees when you make the arrangements, and insist on cash or a certified check for the rest when the trees are picked up. After you shake to close the deal, count your fingers.

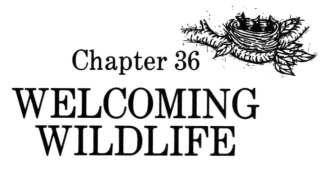

Chapter 36
WELCOMING WILDLIFE

Watching the wildlife is a favorite sport in the country, whether you are on an organized birdwalk or simply looking out the window. Sharing our recent sightings is a favorite topic of conversation at neighborhood get-togethers, and some of our friends keep a naturalist's log of their experiences.

The best way to encourage wildlife is to provide the foods and habitats they prefer. Grouse, for example, eat berries, crab apples, and beechnuts. Deer enjoy browsing hardwood shrubs, hemlock, yews, and arborvitae, and are especially attracted to apples. Each species of bird and animal prefers a particular type of homesite. Hawks and eagles nest on high cliffs and in tall trees, small songbirds choose open meadows and hedgerows, and water birds obviously need a pond or swamp. Beavers gravitate to slow-moving streams that they can dam up. Rabbits like to hide in thickets, squirrels live in holes in old trees, and foxes, coyotes, and wolves need protected areas where they can build dens.

A large piece of land can support a variety of wildlife in different habitats. On a smaller place, however, you must make decisions about which animals you want to attract and which you want to discourage.

If songbirds are your choice, you should not encourage wolves, foxes, and bobcats. A small area would probably not support deer, moose, or elk, but if you provide the proper food, they are likely to visit so that you can view them from your living room. A cedar swamp or grove of young hemlock will provide fall and winter feed, and deer lovers can plant a patch of winter rye.

Wildlife habitats: (1) an abandoned pasture overgrown with small trees, shrubs, and brambles; (2) a hedgerow; (3) a field planted to corn; (4) a neglected orchard; (5) a cut-over woodlot; (6) low shrubs and cattails along edge of pond.

WELCOMING WILDLIFE

259

❖

Plants to Attract Wildlife

a = Deer, elk, moose
b = Bear
c = Small animals
d = Songbirds
e = Game birds
f = Water birds

Arborvitae, hemlock, yew—a, c,
  d, e
Barberry—c, d, e
Beech—b, c, e
Berry bushes—a, b, d, e
Crab apples—a, b, c, d, e
Dogwood, native and wild—d, e
Grains—a, b, d, e, f
Grapes—b, c, d, e
Hazelnut—b, c, e
Juniper—d, e
Maple—a, c, d

Mountain ash—a, c, d, e
Oak—b, c, e
Pine and evergreens—c, d
Quince—a, c, d, e
Rugosa rose—a, c, d, e
Russian and autumn olive—d, e
Viburnum—d, e
Wild fruits (apples, cherry,
  pears, plums)—a, b, c, d, e
Yews—a, d

There are many shrubs and trees that you could plant to attract birds and animals (see box), or you may prefer only to encourage the natural plantings already on your property. Maintaining such plantings may mean that not everything will look neat and orderly. Many animal and bird species began to disappear after farmers cleaned out their hedgerows and began to grow large fields of only one crop.

Here is a quick description of several attractive homesites.

• Hollow trees and rotting logs provide forest homes for small animals and birds. Hedgerows, stone walls, rocky ledges, and thorny shrubs also make good places for animals to hide from larger predators.

• Cut-over woodlots that grow up to small trees, blueberry and raspberry bushes, and shrubs will attract rabbits, deer, bear, elk, and porcupines.

- Abandoned orchards, with their tree holes and fruit, make ideal homes and visiting places for birds, squirrels, deer, bear, and the mice that attract foxes, wolves, and hawks. Abandoned pastures offer berry-producing shrubs, wild fruit trees, roses, and evergreens as sources of food and shelter for a variety of animals.
- The caves formed under the roots of big tree stumps are ideal homesites for a variety of animals. The largest may even house hibernating bears.

In addition to encouraging natural areas, you can plant small patches of corn, oats, wheat, millet, or buckwheat to provide fall and winter feed for ducks, geese, wild turkeys, quail, or pheasants.

Biologists differ on the wisdom of feeding wildlife during the winter. Some encourage the practice when it prevents starvation in large populations. Others believe that twigs and small trees are the natural feed of deer, and that the animals cannot properly digest dried hay and grain; further, a dependence on people causes game animals to lose the natural fear that enables them to safely elude hunters and trappers.

If you feed birds or other animals in winter, do it consistently. People with the best of intentions sometimes provide food for the first part of winter, but then go south for a vacation. If there are no other feeders in the vicinity, it is unfair to leave wild creatures to shift for themselves.

Protecting Animals

A retired ornithologist friend of ours has established a tiny bird sanctuary in the midst of a small village by providing a variety of shrubs and trees and by feeding the birds throughout the winter. He has a long list not only of species that spend the winter or summer, but also of migrating birds that make brief stopovers enroute. Each year he records hundreds of bird species in his log, and we all call on him to identify unusual visitors.

Birds can be attracted on an impressive scale in a small area if cats and other predators are not a problem, but do not attempt to build an animal sanctuary unless you have a lot of land available. It is unfair to attract wildlife to your place if they will be in danger from a busy highway, hunters, or angry farmers on whose crops they are feeding.

If your land holdings are small, you may be able to work together with adjoining landowners to create a large area.

Backcountry farms that have been unworked for years may make excellent game preserves. They often contain woods with a variety of trees in various ages and conditions, pastures growing up to shrubs and small trees, old orchards, wild berry patches, brooks, swamps, and rocky ledges—all suitable for wildlife.

To help you choose and manage your refuge, work closely with your local fish and game warden. He or she can give advice on how to best manage the existing plant life and natural features, and may suggest building a pond or creating a swamp. A warden can also tell you how to post your sanctuary against hunting in a way that is least likely to offend other citizens, and how to patrol the land. You may also want to visit areas managed by such groups as the Nature Conservancy to get ideas.

Even after it is well established, you will need to keep your sanctuary maintained. Regular timber harvests will prevent the trees from growing so tall that they offer little food or protection for wildlife. Your warden can suggest how to remedy imbalances in the wildlife population if they should arise. Too many coyotes, foxes, and bobcats can eliminate the bird and rabbit population, and an over-supply of deer, beavers, or porcupines will soon wreck the food supply for themselves and other animals.

APPENDIX
SUPPLIES
AND PUBLICATIONS

Farm and Homestead Supplies

Bailey's
P.O. Box 550
Laytonville, CA 95454
Equipment for foresters and loggers

Gardener's Eden
P.O. Box 7307
San Francisco, CA 94120
Garden fixtures and tools

Gardener's Supply Co.
133 Elm St.
Winooski, VT 05301
Garden tools, frost protectors, and food-processing equipment

Green River Tools, Inc.
P.O. Box 1919
Brattleboro, VT 05301
Tools and cultivators

A. M. Leonard Inc.
P.O. Box 816
Piqua, OH 45356
Tools and supplies for foresters, landscapers, nurseries, greenhouses, and Christmas tree growers

Ben Meadows
P.O. Box 2781
Eugene, OR 97402
Tools for foresters, surveyors, and conservationists

Melinger's
2310 W. South Range
North Lima, OH 44452
Tools, natural pest controls, and seeds

Mist-O-Gation, Inc.
RD 2
Middletown, DE 19709
Mist propagation systems

Orchard Equipment and
Supply Co.
P.O. Box 146
Conway, MA 01341
Fruit grower's supplies and grafting needs

George W. Park Seed Co.
Greenwood, SC 29647
Greenhouse and nursery supplies—seeds, plants, seed starters

Safer Agro
13910 Lyons Valley
Jamul, CA 92035
Insecticidal soaps

Sandoz Inc.
Crop Protection Division
480 Camino Del Rio South
San Diego, CA 92108
Thuricide and other natural insect controls

Smith and Hawken
25 Corte Madera
Mill Valley, CA 94941
Imported tools and garden furniture

Timm Enterprises Ltd.
P.O. Box 157
Oakville, Ontario L6J 4Z5
Canada
Orchard supplies

Greenhouses

Four Seasons Greenhouses
910 Rt. 110
Farmingdale, NY 11735

Lord and Burnam
Melville, NY 11746

National Greenhouse Co.
P.O. Box 308
Carmel Valley, CA 93924

Maple Sugaring Equipment

Berliner Plastics
1973 Lake Ave.
Lake Luzerne, NY 12846

Leader Evaporator Co. Inc.
25 Stowell St.
St. Albans, VT 05478

Waterloo Evaporators
201 Western Ave.
Waterloo, Quebec J0E 2N0
Canada

Seeds and Nursery Companies

Beaverlodge Nursery Ltd.
P.O. Box 127
Beaverlodge, Alberta T0H 0C0
Canada
Hardy fruits and ornamentals

W. Atlee Burpee Co.
5395 Burpee Bldg.
Warminster, PA 18974
Seeds and supplies

C & O Nursery
P.O. Box 116
Wenatchee, WA 98801
Fruit trees

Carroll Gardens
P.O. Box 310
Westminster, MD 21157
Wild flowers, shrubs, and trees

Converse Nursery
Amherst, NH 03031
Antique apples

Cumberland Valley Nurseries, Inc.
P.O. Box 430
McMinnville, TN 37110
Peach, other fruit and nut trees

Digiorgi Co. Inc.
P.O. Box 413
Council Bluffs, IA 51502
Flower and vegetable seeds

Farmer Seed and Nursery Co.
Faribault, MN 55021
Seeds, fruit trees, and berry plants

Grimo Nut Nursery
RR 3
Niagra-on-the-Lake
Ontario L0S 1J0
Canada
Seedling and grafted nut trees, and persimmons

Grootendorst Nurseries
Lakeside, MI 49116
Dwarf rootstocks for grafting

Harris Seeds
P.O. Box 432
Gresham, OR 97030
Flower and herb seeds

Johnny's Selected Seeds
Albion, ME 04910
Seeds, particularly for short growing seasons

Lawyer Nursery
Rt. 2, P.O. Box 95
Plains, MT 59859
Hardy conservation plants, wildlife attracters, and ornamentals

Makielski Berry Farm
7130 Platt Rd.
Ypsilanti, MI 48197
Bush and bramble fruits, including black and purple raspberries, black currants

J. E. Miller Nurseries, Inc.
Canandaigua, NY 14424
New and old fruits, grapes, and berries

Musser Forests
P.O. Box 340
Indiana, PA 15701
Tree seedlings for nurseries, wildlife habitats, Christmas tree and forest planting

St. Lawrence Nurseries
Rt. 2
Potsdam, NY 13676
Edible landscape plants, nut trees, antique and modern fruits for northern growers

F. W. Schumacher Co.
36 Spring Hill Rd.
Sandwich, MA 02563
Forest tree and shrub seed

Southmeadow Fruit Gardens
Lakeside, MI 49116
Antique and modern fruits

Van Pines, Inc.
West Olive, MI 49460
Seedling trees for forest, Christmas tree, windbreak, and wildlife plantings

Vesey's Seeds, Ltd.
York, Prince Edward Island
C0A 1P0
Canada
Seeds for short growing seasons

White Flower Farm
Litchfield, CT 06759
Perennial plants and some shrubs

Wildlife Nurseries
P.O. Box 2724
Oshkosh, WI 54903
Seeds for wildlife, food, also bog plants

Magazines

American Bee Journal
Dadant and Sons, Inc.
51 S. 2d St.
Hamilton, IL 62341

American Tree Farmer
American Forest Council
1619 Massachusetts Ave., NW
Washington, DC 20036

Audubon
P.O. Box 2666
Boulder, CO 80322

Beef
The Webb Co.
1999 Shepard Rd.
St. Paul, MN 55116

Bio-Dynamic Farming and Gardening
P.O. Box 253
Wyoming, RI 02898

Blair and Ketchum's Country Journal
P.O. Box 870
Manchester Center, VT 05255

The Cattleman Magazine
Texas and Southwestern Cattle Raisers Assn.
1301 W. 7th St.
Ft. Worth, TX 76102

The Country Gentleman
1100 Waterway Blvd.
Indianapolis, IN 46202

Countryside
Rt. 1, Box 239
Waterloo, WI 53594

Dairy Goat Journal
P.O. Box 1808
Scottsdale, AZ 85252

Dairy Herd Management
Miller Publishing Co.
P.O. Box 67
Minneapolis, MN 55440

Draft Horse Journal
P.O. Box 670
Waverly, IA 50677

Duck, Goose and Swan
J. Todd Miles, Publisher
Greystone Farm
Millbury, MA 01527

Farm Journal
230 W. Washington Square
Philadelphia, PA 19105

Farm Money Management
P.O. Box 67
Minneapolis, MN 55440

Farmstead Magazine
P.O. Box 111
Freedom, ME 04941

Farm Wife News
P.O. Box 643
Milwaukee, WI 53201

The Furrow
John Deere Rd.
Moline, IL 61265

Harrowsmith (U.S. edition)
The Creamery
Charlotte, VT 05445

Harrowsmith (Canadian edition)
Camden House Publishing Ltd
7 Queen Victoria Rd.
Camden East, Ontario K0K 1J0
Canada

Hoard's Dairyman
Fort Atkinson, WI 53538

Horticulture
755 Boylston St.
Boston, MA 02116

Journal of Forestry
5400 Grosvenor La.
Bethesda, MD 20814

Mother Earth News
P.O. Box 70
Hendersonville, NC 28791

New England American
Agriculturist
P.O. Box 369
Ithaca, NY 14851

Rodale's Organic Gardening
Emmaus, PA 18049

Sheep! Magazine
Countryside Publications
Rt. 1, Box 239
Waterloo, WI 53594

Small Farmer's Journal (for
horse farmers)
3908 W. First
Eugene, OR 97402

Successful Farming
1716 Locust St.
Des Moines, IA 50336

INDEX

Entries referring to entire chapters are indicated in **boldface** type; entries referring to charts, tables, and illustrations are indicated in *italics*.

Chicory, 97
Christmas trees, 84, **252–57.** *See also*
   Evergreens
      cash-per-acre yield of, *83*
      climate affecting, 17
      culture of, 255–56
      marketing of, 256–57
      purchase of, 254–55
      soil for, 18, 61
      starting plantation of, 253–54
      types of, 253
Cider, 82
Climate
      affecting vegetable gardens, 100
      cold, coping with, 48–49
      for planting, 17
Cloning, 142
Clover, 18, 19, 61, 66
Cohosh, 55
Cold climates, coping with, 48–49
Communities, **41–49.** *See also* Social-
   izing
      acceptance in, 42-43, 44
      evaluation of, 12-14
Community organizations, 43–45
Composting, 62–63, 64, 65–66
Condiments, *76*, 86
Connecticut River, 42
Cooling, cost of, 4
Corms, 146
Corn, 40, 92, 93, 159–60
      planting recommendations for,
        98
      sweet
         cash-per-acre yield of, *83*
         time to harvest, 96
      time to sell, *76*
Costs
      of country living, 3-4
      of equipment, 4
      of food, 3

of insurance, 4
of utilities, 4, 14
Cows, 58, 161, 199–207. *See also* Beef
   cattle; Milk, production of; Steers
   dairy
         breeding and calving of,
           206–7
         diseases of, 205–6
         maintenance of, 202-4
         purchase of, 204
         renting of, 207
         types of, 204
      glossary of, *200*
Coyotes, 57, 258, 262
      attacking sheep, 226, 229
Crabapple trees, flowering, 134
Cranberries, 18, 107-8
Crops
      cash-per-acre yields of, *83*
      climate for growing, 17
      soil for, 17–19, *68*
Cucumbers, *83*, *98*
Currants, 105, 106-7

D

Daffodils, in landscaping, 135
Dairy products
      from cows, 200, 203, 204
      from goats, 208
      sale of, laws regarding, 205
Dandelions, 19, 91
Dawson, Adele, 132
Daylilies, in landscaping, 135
Deadly nightshade, 55
Deer, 56, 57, 258, 260, 261, 262
      destruction by, 58, 92, 124
Doctors, 15-16
Dogs, 59
      attacking sheep, 226, 229
      to herd sheep, 229
      for security, 46, 190, 223
Dogwood trees, in landscaping, 134

Donkeys, 237, 238
Ducks, 161, 163, 172–73, 261. *See also*
   Poultry
      breeds of, 177–78
      butchering of, 179
      glossary of, *173*
      in ponds, 173, 186
      raising of, 178–79

E

Eagles, 258
Earwigs, 57
East Coast, 130, 158
Edible plants, 55–56
Education, 13
Eggplants, 17, 94, *98*
Eggs
      production of, 167–70
      selling of, 172
Elderberries, 105, 107
Elderly persons, 30
Electricity, 14–15
      loss of, 49
      sources of, 31–33
Elk, 258, 260
Emergencies, 46–49
Endive, *98*
Energy, 31–33
Environmental laws, 15, 23
Equipment
      cost of, 4
      for maintaining orchards,
        122–24
      for nursery operation, 142
      for vegetable gardens, 92–93
Evergreens. *See also* Christmas trees
      in landscaping, 134–35

F

Farm and homestead supplies, 263
Farm animals, **160–64**

Farmland, various values of, *10*
Farms, small, number in U.S., *2*
Fences, for animals, 164
Ferns, in landscaping, 135
Fertilization, 18, 62–66, *91*
      of fruit trees, 121
Filberts, 129
Fire hazards, 20
Fireplaces, 30
Fire protection, 46–48
Firewood
      harvesting of, 246
      selling of, 247
      soil for, 18, 61
      trees for, 245
Fir trees, 20, 134
Fish, 72, 189–91. *See also specific fish*
Fishing, 59–60
Florida, 130
Flower gardens, 136–40
Flowering shrubs, 134
Flowers, 58, 62
      dried arrangements of, 139–40
      lifespans of, 137–38
      perennial, 138, 144–45
      selling of, 138-39
Food
      cost of, 4
      storage of, 27, 28
Forests
      evaluation of, 19–20
      management of, **240–52**
Forsythia, in landscaping, 134
Foxes, 57, 258, 261, 262
      destruction by, 56, 58
Frost, *16*, 17
Fruits
      bramble, 108–10
      bush, 105–8
      selling of, *76*, 82, 84, 125
      tree, climate affecting, 17
      vine, time to harvest, 96

Fruit trees. *See* Orchards
Fuel, for vehicles, 40

G

Geese, 58, 163, 172–77, 261. *See also*
Poultry
    glossary of, *173*
    in ponds, 186
    raising of, 175–77
    removing feathers from, 177
    for security, 46
    as weeders, 174–75
Generators, 49
Georgia, 130
Ginseng, soil for, 67
Goats, 161, 163, **207–12**
    breeding and birthing of, 211
    destruction by, 208, 209
    diseases of, 212
    glossary of, *208*
    maintenance of, 210–12
    for milk, 71, 208
    purchase of, 209
    types of, 209–10
Goldenrod, soil for, 19
Gooseberries, 105, 106–7
Government, local, 3, 13
Grains, 156–60. *See also specific grains*
Grapes, 16, **111–15**
Grass, tall, 19, 34
Greenhouses, 147–52, 264. *See also*
Horticulture; Plants
Groundsel, 91
Grouse, 258
Guano, 64

H

Handicapped persons, 30
Hawks, 258, 261

Hay, 153–56
    cash-per-acre yield of, *83*
    climate affecting, 17
    as fertilizer, 69, 70
    as fire hazard, 47
    harvesting of, 155–56
    soil for, 60
Hayfields, 64, 154
Health care, 15–16
Heating, 28–31
    cost of, 4
    firewood for, 244–45
Hedges, in landscaping, 135
Hellebore, 55
Hemlock trees, soil for, 19
Herbicides, 22
Herbs, 94, 97, 144
Hickories, 129
Holsteins, 204, 215
Home businesses. *See* Businesses, at
home
Home improvements, record-keep-
ing of, *26*
Homes, 25–28. *See also* Real estate
Honey, 82, 196–97, 199
Hornets, 57
Horseradish plants, 96, 97
Horses, 161, **231–39**
    draft, 238–39
    glossary of, *231*
    health care of, 236–37
    purchase of, 235
    raising of, 234–37
    types of, 231–32
Horticultural services, 146–47
Horticulture, 140–47. *See also* Green-
houses; Plants
Humus, 61–64
Hunting, 53, 59–60
Huxley, Anthony, 91
Hyacinths, 146
Hydrangea, in landscaping, 134

planting recommendations for, *99*

time to plant, 94

Pheasants, 261

Pick-your-own businesses, 82–84

Pigs, 64, 72, 163, **220–24**

Pine trees, 19, 20, 107

Plains, North Central, 158

Plants, 143–45, *260. See also* Greenhouses; Horticulture

Plums, 84

Plum trees, 118, 119

Poconos, 9

Poisonous plants, 55

Poisonous snakes, 57

Pollution, of water, 22

Ponds, **186–91**

Poplar trees, for firewood, 245

Porcupines, 58, 260, 262

Posting, of land, 53

Potatoes, 84, 93

planting recommendations for, *99*

soil for, 61, 67

time to sell, *76*

Potentilla, in landscaping, 134

Poultry, 161. *See also* Chickens;
Ducks; Geese

butchering of, 163, 171

glossary of, *165*

income from, 72

predators of, 169

Power, loss of, 49

Power take-off (PTO), 38, 39

Privacy, 5, 42, **50–53**, 86. *See also*
Socializing

Pruning, of fruit trees, 121

Publications, on country living,
266–67

Pumpkins, 84, 93, 96

cash-per-acre yield of, *83*

climate affecting, 17

planting recommendations for, *99*

time to plant, 94

Q

Quail, 261

R

Rabbits, 163, 258, 260, 262

butchering of, 185

destruction by, 58, 92, 124, 181

diseases of, 185

glossary of, *180*

meat from, 180–81

raising of, **180–85**

skins of, 181

types of, 181–82

Raccoons, destruction by, 58, 92

Radishes, 95, *99*

Radon, 11, 22

Raspberries, 58, 84

commercial potential of, 101

growing of, 108–10

yields of, 102

Rats, 58

Rattlesnakes, 11

Real estate, 10–11, 15. *See also*
Homes; Land

Recreation, income from, 7–8

Relocating, to country, 1–8

Rhododendrons, in landscaping, 134

Rhubarb, 96, 97

Rock gardens, in landscaping, 135

Rodents, 20, 58

Rose gardens, in landscaping, 135

Rotary tiller, 91, 92–93

S

Safety, 45–46

Schools, 13

Security, 45–46

Seedlings, 94–95

Seeds and nursery companies,
  264–66
Septic systems, 23–24, 89
Sewage systems, evaluation of, 22–24
Sheds, 28, 34, 48, 93
  evaluation of, 20, 21
  potting, 151
  refrigerated, 142
Sheep, 58, **224–30**
  butchering of, 230
  diseases of, 229
  glossary of, *225*
  predators of, 226, 229
  purchase of, 226–27
  raising of, 225–29
  shearing of, 229–30
Shrubs, in landscaping, 134–35
Silage, 156
Skunks, 57–58
Smoke detectors, 48
Snakes, 11, 57, 58
Socializing, 5, 13, 41–45. *See also*
  Communities; Privacy
Sod growing, 146
Soil
  acidity versus alkalinity of,
    18–19, 61, 67–69
  elimination of waste in, 23–24
  evaluation of, 17–19
  improvement of, **60–70**
  types of, 61
Soil Conservation Service, 61, 186,
  188
Soil maps, 18
Solar energy, 15, 33
Solar heating, 30–31
Southern U.S., 9
Spinach, *76, 99*
Spruce trees, 20, 134
Squash, 93
  climate affecting, 17
  planting recommendations for,
    99

time to harvest, 96
time to plant, 94
time to sell, *76*
Squirrels, 58, 258, 261
Steers, 72, 214, 216–18
Sterno, 49
Stout, Ruth, 69
Stoves, 30
Strawberries, 84
  climate affecting, 17, 104–5
  commercial potential of, 101
  growing of, 103–5
  soil for, 61, 67, 103
  time to plant, 103
  yields of, 102
Sucker trees, for firewood, 245
Sugaring, 247–52
Sun, as source of electricity, 33
Sycamore trees, in landscaping, 134

T
Taxes, 4, 13–14, 20
  for home businesses, 80, 81
  income exempt from, 73–74
Telephone systems, 14
Temperatures, 17
Theft, 45–46
Thuricide, 107
Tiller, rotary, 91, 92–93
Timber, 18, 61, 244
Tomatoes, 84, 93
  cash-per-acre yield of, *83*
  climate affecting, 16, 17
  grown in greenhouses, 149
  planting recommendations for,
    99
  time to plant, 94
Tools, for orchards, *123*
Tractors, 35–41, 93
  attachments for, 38
Transportation, **34–41**
Trapping, 59–60

Trees. *See also specific trees*
    affecting ponds, 189
    deciding which to plant, 243
    for firewood, 244
    fruit (*see also* Orchards)
        heights of, 117
        time to plant, 118
    location of, *16*
    for shade, in landscaping,
      134–35
    soil for, 19
Tree seedlings, 145
Trout, 189, 190
Trucks, 35
Tubers, 146
Tulips, 146
Turkeys, 261
Turnips, *76*, 95, 97, *99*

U
Utilities, 14–15

V
Vandalism, 46
Veal, production of, 218
Vegetable gardens, **90–100**
    development of, *91*
    equipment for, 92–93
    insects in, 96
    planting basics for, 95, *98–99*
    size of, 93
    in summer, 96
    in winter, 97
Vegetables, 62, 65
    green, climate affecting, 17
    planting guidelines for, *98–99*
    selling of, *76*
    soil for, 60
    time to harvest, 96
    time to plant, 94, 95
Vehicles, **34–41**

Vermont, 42, 84, 147, 158
    central, 82
    northern, 8, 70, 126, 132
    southern, 134
Violets, 19

W
Walnuts, 126, 127, 128, 130
Water, as electricity source, 33
Watermelon, *99*
Water pollution, 22
Water pumps, 47
Water supply, evaluation of, 22–23
Weasels, 58, 59
Weather, for planting, 17
Weeds, 34
    elimination of, 69, 70, 91–92
    in flower gardens, 137
    soil for, 19
West Coast, 128, 130, 146, 253
Weston (Vt.), 88
West Virginia, 9
Wheat, 82, 158
Wildlife, 56–59, **258–62**
    feeding of, 260–61
    habitats of, *259*, 260–61
    nuts attracting, 126
    plants attracting, *260*
    protection of, 261–62
Willow trees, 19, 245
Wind, as electricity source, 31–32
Windmills, 32, 33
Winemaking, 115
Wisconsin, 253
Wolves, 19, 56, 258, 261
    destruction by, 58, 222, 229
Wood, heat from, 28–30, 244
Woodchucks, 58–59, 92
Woods, evaluation of, 19–20
Work. *See* Occupations
Worms, 63, 69, 107, 183

INDEX

277

❖

Rodale Press, Inc., publishes RODALE'S ORGANIC GARDENING®,
the all-time favorite gardening magazine.
For information on how to order your subscription,
write to RODALE'S ORGANIC GARDENING®, Emmaus, PA 18049.

COUNTRY LIVING

❖